Python Programming Blueprints

Build nine projects by leveraging powerful frameworks such as Flask, Nameko, and Django

Daniel Furtado
Marcus Pennington

BIRMINGHAM - MUMBAI

Python Programming Blueprints

Copyright © 2018 Packt Publishing

Commissioning Editor: Merint Mathew
Acquisition Editor: Sandeep Mishra
Content Development Editor: Lawrence Veigas
Technical Editor: Mehul Singh
Copy Editor: Safis Editing
Project Coordinator: Prajakta Naik
Proofreader: Safis Editing
Indexer: Rekha Nair
Graphics: Jisha Chirayil
Production Coordinator: Arvindkumar Gupta

First published: February 2018

Production reference: 1260218

Published by Packt Publishing Ltd.
Livery Place
35 Livery Street
Birmingham
B3 2PB, UK.

ISBN 978-1-78646-816-1

www.packtpub.com

I dedicate this book to my family—my sister, Camila, my mother, Silvia, and my father, Simão, who have done everything in their power to help me achieve all my dreams. There are no words to express how grateful and lucky I feel for being their child.
To my lovely Maria, who every day gives me strength, encouragement, inspiration, and love. I wouldn't have made it without you. I love you! Also, to my loyal French bulldog friends, Edit and Ella.

– Daniel Furtado

My parents, Dawn and Robert, who over my lifetime have always pushed me to do my best. They instilled in me the ability to accomplish anything I put my mind to.
Fabrizio Romano for convincing me to contribute to this book. He is the greatest mentor an aspiring developer could ask for.
And finally, my partner, Emily, for always being there for me.

– Marcus Pennington

Contributors

About the authors

Daniel Furtado is a software developer with over 20 years of experience in different technologies such as Python, C, .NET, C#, and JavaScript. He started programming at the age of 13 on his ZX Spectrum.

He joined the Bioinformatics Laboratory of the Human Cancer Genome Project in Brazil, where he developed web applications and tools in Perl and Python to help researchers analyze data. He has never stopped developing in Python ever since.

Daniel has worked on various open source projects; the latest one is a PyTerrier web micro-framework.

Marcus Pennington started his journey into computer science at Highams Park Sixth Form College where he took a Cisco CCNA course.

He then went to the University of Hertfordshire, where he graduated with a degree in Computer Science with Artificial Intelligence. Since then, he has had the privilege of working with some of the best developers and learning the benefits and pitfalls of many of the software practices we use today.

He has a passion for writing clean, cohesive, and beautiful code.

I would like to acknowledge Tom Viner for giving my chapters a thorough review; his insights not only improved the quality of my chapters but also taught me a great deal.
Julio Trigo, an expert at using PostgreSQL with Python; his knowledge supplemented my own when creating the database dependency.
Edward Melly, a JavaScript and React craftsman, for reviewing the frontend code in my chapters.

About the reviewers

Tom Viner is a senior software developer living in London. He has over 10 years of experience in building web applications and has been using Python and Django for 8 years. He has special interests in open source software, web security, and Test-driven development.

Tom has given two conference talks, *Testing with two failure seeking missiles: fuzzing and property based testing* and *Exploring unit-testing, unittest v pytest: FIGHT!*

Tom works for Sohonet in central London and sometimes goes backpacking around the world.

I would like to thank Marcus Pennington for inviting me to review this book.

Radovan Kavický is the principal data scientist and president at GapData Institute based in Bratislava, Slovakia, harnessing the power of data and wisdom of economics for public good.

He has an academic background in macroeconomics and is a consultant and data scientist by profession.

Radovan is also an instructor at DataCamp and a founder of PyData Bratislava, R <- Slovakia & SK/CZ Tableau User Group (skczTUG).

Packt is searching for authors like you

If you're interested in becoming an author for Packt, please visit `authors.packtpub.com` and apply today. We have worked with thousands of developers and tech professionals, just like you, to help them share their insight with the global tech community. You can make a general application, apply for a specific hot topic that we are recruiting an author for, or submit your own idea.

`mapt.io`

Mapt is an online digital library that gives you full access to over 5,000 books and videos, as well as industry leading tools to help you plan your personal development and advance your career. For more information, please visit our website.

Why subscribe?

- Spend less time learning and more time coding with practical eBooks and Videos from over 4,000 industry professionals

- Improve your learning with Skill Plans built especially for you

- Get a free eBook or video every month

- Mapt is fully searchable

- Copy and paste, print, and bookmark content

PacktPub.com

Did you know that Packt offers eBook versions of every book published, with PDF and ePub files available? You can upgrade to the eBook version at `www.PacktPub.com` and as a print book customer, you are entitled to a discount on the eBook copy. Get in touch with us at `service@packtpub.com` for more details.

At `www.PacktPub.com`, you can also read a collection of free technical articles, sign up for a range of free newsletters, and receive exclusive discounts and offers on Packt books and eBooks.

Table of Contents

Preface

If you have been within the software development industry for the last 20 years, you most certainly have heard of a programming language named Python. Created by Guido van Rossum, Python first appeared in 1991 and has captured the hearts of many software developers across the globe ever since.

However, how is it that a language that is over 20 years old is still around and is gaining more and more popularity every day?

Well, the answer to this question is simple. Python is awesome for everything (or almost everything). Python is a general-purpose programming language, which means that you can create simple terminal applications, web applications, microservices, games, and also complex scientific applications. Even though it is possible to use Python for different purposes, Python is a language that is well known for being easy to learn, which is perfect for beginners as well as people with no computer science background.

Python is a *batteries included* programming language, which means that most of the time you will not need to make use of any external dependencies when developing your projects. Python's standard library is feature rich and most of the time contains everything you need to create your programs, and just in case you need something that is not in the standard library, the PyPI (Python Package Index) currently contains 117,652 packages.

The Python community is welcoming, helpful, diverse, and extremely passionate about the language, and everyone in the community is always happy to help each other.

If you still not convinced, the popular website StackOverflow published this year's statistics about the popularity of programming languages based on the number of questions the users add to the site, and Python is one of the top languages, only behind JavaScript, Java, C#, and PHP.

It is a perfect time to be a Python developer, so let's get started!

Who this book is for

This book is for software developers who are familiar with Python and want to gain hands-on experience with web and software development projects. Basic knowledge of Python programming is required.

What this book covers

Chapter 1, *Implementing the Weather Application*, guides you through developing a terminal application that shows the current weather for a specific region and a forecast for the next 5 days. This chapter will introduce you to the basic concepts of Python programming. You will learn how to parse command-line arguments to add more interactivity to programs, and you will finally see how to scrape data from websites using the popular Beautiful Soup framework.

Chapter 2, *Creating a Remote-Control Application with Spotify*, will teach you how to perform authentication with the Spotify API using OAuth. We will use the curses library to make the application more interesting and user-friendly.

Chapter 3, *Casting Votes on Twitter*, will teach you how to use the Tkinter library to create beautiful user interfaces using Python. We will use Reactive Extensions for Python to detect when a vote has been made in the backend, after which, we will publish the changes in the user interface.

Chapter 4, *Exchange Rates and the Currency Conversion Tool*, will enable you to implement a currency converter that will get foreign exchange rates in real time from different sources and use the data to perform currency conversion. We will develop an API that contains helper functions to perform the conversions. To start with, we will use opensource foreign exchange rates and a currency conversion API (http://fixer.io/).
The second part of the chapter will teach you how to create a command-line application makes use of our API to fetch data from the data sources and also get the currency conversion results with a few parameters.

Chapter 5, *Building a Web Messenger with Microservices*, will teach you how to use Nameko, a microservice framework for Python. You will also learn how to make dependency providers for external resources such as Redis. This chapter will also touch upon integration testing Nameko services and basic AJAX requests to an API.

Chapter 6, *Extending TempMessenger with a User Authentication Microservice*, will build upon your app from Chapter 5, *Building a Web Messenger with Microservices*. You will create a user authentication microservice that stores users in a Postgres database. Using Bcrypt, you will also learn how to store passwords in a database securely. This chapter also covers creating a Flask web interface and how to utilize cookies to store web session data. By the end of these chapters, you will be well equipped to create scalable and cohesive microservices.

Chapter 7, *Online Video Game Store with Django*, will enable you to create an online video game store. It will contain features such as browsing video games by category, performing searches using different criteria, viewing detailed information about each game, and finally adding games to a shopping cart and placing an order. Here, you will learn about Django 2.0, the administration UI, the Django data model, and much more.

Chapter 8, *Order Microservice*, will help you build a microservice that will be responsible for receiving orders from the web application that we developed in the previous chapter. The order microservice also provides other features such as the ability to update the status of orders and provide order information using different criteria.

Chapter 9, *Notification Serverless Application*, will teach you about Serverless functions architecture and how to build a notification service using Flask and deploy the final application to AWS Lambda using the great project Zappa. You will also learn how to integrate the web application that was developed in Chapter 7, *Online Video Game Store with Django*, and the order microservice developed in Chapter 8, *Order Microservice*, with the serverless notification application.

To get the most out of this book

In order to execute the code from this book on your local machine, you will need the following:

- An internet connection
- Virtualenv
- Python 3.6
- MongoDB 3.2.11
- pgAdmin (refer to the official documentation at http://url.marcuspen.com/pgadmin for installation instructions)
- Docker (refer to the official documentation at http://url.marcuspen.com/docker-install for installation instructions)

All other requirements will be installed as we progress through the chapters.
All instructions in this chapter are tailored toward macOS or Debian/Ubuntu systems; however, the authors have taken care to only use cross-platform dependencies.

Download the example code files

You can download the example code files for this book from your account at
`www.packtpub.com`. If you purchased this book elsewhere, you can visit
`www.packtpub.com/support` and register to have the files emailed directly to you.

You can download the code files by following these steps:

1. Log in or register at `www.packtpub.com`.
2. Select the **SUPPORT** tab.
3. Click on **Code Downloads & Errata**.
4. Enter the name of the book in the **Search** box and follow the onscreen instructions.

Once the file is downloaded, please make sure that you unzip or extract the folder using the latest version of:

- WinRAR/7-Zip for Windows
- Zipeg/iZip/UnRarX for Mac
- 7-Zip/PeaZip for Linux

The code bundle for the book is also hosted on GitHub at `https://github.com/PacktPublishing/Python-Programming-Blueprints`. We also have other code bundles from our rich catalog of books and videos available at `https://github.com/PacktPublishing/`. Check them out!

Conventions used

There are a number of text conventions used throughout this book.

`CodeInText`: Indicates code words in text, database table names, folder names, filenames, file extensions, pathnames, dummy URLs, user input, and Twitter handles. Here is an example: "This method will call the method `exec` of the `Runner` to execute the function that performs the requests to the Twitter API."

A block of code is set as follows:

```
def set_header(self):
    title = Label(self,
                  text='Voting for hasthags',
                  font=("Helvetica", 24),
                  height=4)
    title.pack()
```

When we wish to draw your attention to a particular part of a code block, the relevant lines or items are set in bold:

```
def start_app(args):
    root = Tk()

    app = Application(hashtags=args.hashtags, master=root)
    app.master.title("Twitter votes")
    app.master.geometry("400x700+100+100")
    app.mainloop()
```

Any command-line input or output is written as follows:

```
python app.py --hashtags debian ubuntu arch
```

Bold: Indicates a new term, an important word, or words that you see onscreen. For example, words in menus or dialog boxes appear in the text like this. Here is an example: "It says, **Logged as** with your username, and right after it there is a logout link. Give it a go, and click on the link **Log off**"

Warnings or important notes appear like this.

Tips and tricks appear like this.

Get in touch

Feedback from our readers is always welcome.

General feedback: Email feedback@packtpub.com and mention the book title in the subject of your message. If you have questions about any aspect of this book, please email us at questions@packtpub.com.

Errata: Although we have taken every care to ensure the accuracy of our content, mistakes do happen. If you have found a mistake in this book, we would be grateful if you would report this to us. Please visit www.packtpub.com/submit-errata, selecting your book, clicking on the Errata Submission Form link, and entering the details.

Piracy: If you come across any illegal copies of our works in any form on the Internet, we would be grateful if you would provide us with the location address or website name. Please contact us at copyright@packtpub.com with a link to the material.

If you are interested in becoming an author: If there is a topic that you have expertise in and you are interested in either writing or contributing to a book, please visit authors.packtpub.com.

Reviews

Please leave a review. Once you have read and used this book, why not leave a review on the site that you purchased it from? Potential readers can then see and use your unbiased opinion to make purchase decisions, we at Packt can understand what you think about our products, and our authors can see your feedback on their book. Thank you!

For more information about Packt, please visit packtpub.com.

1
Implementing the Weather Application

The first application in this book is going to be a web scraping application that will scrape weather forecast information from `https://weather.com` and present it in a terminal. We will add some options that can be passed as arguments to the application, such as:

- The temperature unit (Celsius or Fahrenheit)
- The area where you can get the weather forecast
- Output options where the user of our application can choose between the current forecast, a five-day forecast, a ten-day forecast, and the weekend
- Ways to complement the output with extra information such as wind and humidity

Apart from the aforementioned arguments, this application will be designed to be extendable, which means that we can create parsers for different websites to get a weather forecast, and these parsers will be available as argument options.

In this chapter, you will learn how to:

- Use object-oriented programming concepts in Python applications
- Scrape data from websites using the `BeautifulSoup` package
- Receive command line arguments
- Utilize the `inspect` module
- Load Python modules dynamically
- Use Python comprehensions
- Use `Selenium` to request a webpage and inspect its DOM elements

Before we get started, it is important to say that when developing web scraping applications, you should keep in mind that these types of applications are susceptible to changes. If the developers of the site that you are getting data from change a CSS class name, or the structure of the HTML DOM, the application will stop working. Also, if the URL of the site we are getting the data from changes, the application will not be able to send requests.

Setting up the environment

Before we get right into writing our first example, we need to set up an environment to work and install any dependencies that the project may have. Luckily, Python has a really nice tooling system to work with virtual environments.

Virtual environments in Python are a broad subject, and beyond the scope of this book. However, if you are not familiar with virtual environments, it will suffice to know that a virtual environment is a contained Python environment that is isolated from your global Python installation. This isolation allows developers to easily work with different versions of Python, install packages within the environment, and manage project dependencies without interfering with Python's global installation.

Python's installation comes with a module called `venv`, which you can use to create virtual environments; the syntax is fairly straightforward. The application that we are going to create is called `weatherterm` (weather terminal), so we can create a virtual environment with the same name to make it simple.

To create a new virtual environment, open a terminal and run the following command:

```
$ python3 -m venv weatherterm
```

If everything goes well, you should see a directory called `weatherterm` in the directory you are currently at. Now that we have the virtual environment, we just need to activate it with the following command:

```
$ . weatherterm/bin/activate
```

I recommend installing and using `virtualenvwrapper`, which is an extension of the `virtualenv` tool. This makes it very simple to manage, create, and delete virtual environments as well as quickly switch between them. If you wish to investigate this further, visit: `https://virtualenvwrapper.readthedocs.io/en/latest/#`.

Now, we need to create a directory where we are going to create our application. Don't create this directory in the same directory where you created the virtual environment; instead, create a projects directory and create the directory for the application in there. I would recommend you name it with the same name as the virtual environment for simplicity.

I am setting the environment and running all the examples in a machine with Debian 9.2 installed, and at the time of writing, I am running the latest Python version (3.6.2). If you are a Mac user, it shouldn't be so different; however, if you are on Windows, the steps can be slightly different, but it is not hard to find information on how to set up virtual environments on it. A Python 3 installation works nicely on Windows nowadays.

Go into the project's directory that you just created and create a file named `requirements.txt` with the following content:

```
beautifulsoup4==4.6.0
selenium==3.6.0
```

These are all the dependencies that we need for this project:

- `BeautifulSoup`: This is a package for parsing HTML and XML files. We will be using it to parse the HTML that we fetch from weather sites and to get the weather data we need on the terminal. It is very simple to use and it has a great documentation available online at: `http://beautiful-soup-4.readthedocs.io/en/latest/`.
- `Selenium`: This is a well-known set of tools for testing. There are many applications, but it is mostly used for the automated testing of web applications.

To install the required packages in our virtual environment, you can run the following command:

```
pip install -r requirements.txt
```

It is always a good idea to make use of version-control tools like GIT or Mercurial. It is very helpful to control changes, check history, rollback changes, and more. If you are not familiar with any of these tools, there are plenty of tutorials on the internet. You can get started by checking the documentation for GIT at: `https://git-scm.com/book/en/v1/Getting-Started`.

One last tool that we need to install is PhantomJS; you can download it from: `http://phantomjs.org/download.html`

After downloading it, extract the contents inside the `weatherterm` directory and rename the folder to `phantomjs`.

With our virtual environment set up and PhantomJS installed, we are ready to start coding!

Core functionality

Let's start by creating a directory for your module. Inside of the project's root directory, create a subdirectory called `weatherterm`. The subdirectory `weatherterm` is where our module will live. The module directory needs two subdirectories - `core` and `parsers`. The project's directory structure should look like this:

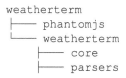

```
weatherterm
├── phantomjs
└── weatherterm
        ├── core
        ├── parsers
```

Loading parsers dynamically

This application is intended to be flexible and allow developers to create different parsers for different weather websites. We are going to create a parser loader that will dynamically discover files inside of the `parsers` directory, load them, and make them available to be used by the application without requiring changes to any other parts of the code. Here are the rules that our loader will require when implementing new parsers:

- Create a file with a class implementing the methods for fetching the current weather forecast as well as five-day, ten-day, and weekend weather forecasts
- The file name has to end with `parser`, for example, `weather_com_parser.py`
- The file name can't start with double underscores

With that said, let's go ahead and create the parser loader. Create a file named
parser_loader.py inside of the weatherterm/core directory and add the following
content:

```python
import os
import re
import inspect


def _get_parser_list(dirname):
    files = [f.replace('.py', '')
                for f in os.listdir(dirname)
                if not f.startswith('__')]

    return files


def _import_parsers(parserfiles):

    m = re.compile('.+parser$', re.I)

    _modules = __import__('weatherterm.parsers',
                          globals(),
                          locals(),
                          parserfiles,
                          0)

    _parsers = [(k, v) for k, v in inspect.getmembers(_modules)
                    if inspect.ismodule(v) and m.match(k)]

    _classes = dict()

    for k, v in _parsers:
        _classes.update({k: v for k, v in inspect.getmembers(v)
                            if inspect.isclass(v) and m.match(k)})

    return _classes


def load(dirname):
    parserfiles = _get_parser_list(dirname)
    return _import_parsers(parserfiles)
```

First, the `_get_parser_list` function is executed and returns a list of all files located in `weatherterm/parsers`; it will filter the files based on the rules of the parser described previously. After returning a list of files, it is time to import the module. This is done by the `_import_parsers` function, which first imports the `weatherterm.parsers` module and makes use of the inspect package in the standard library to find the parser classes within the module.

The `inspect.getmembers` function returns a list of tuples where the first item is a key representing a property in the module, and the second item is the value, which can be of any type. In our scenario, we are interested in a property with a key ending with `parser` and with the value of type class.

Assuming that we already have a parser in place in the `weatherterm/parsers` directory, the value returned by the `inspect.getmembers(_modules)` will look something like this:

```
[('WeatherComParser',
  <class
'weatherterm.parsers.weather_com_parser.WeatherComParser'>),
  ...]
```

 `inspect.getmembers(_module)` returns many more items, but they have been omitted since it is not relevant to show all of them at this point.

Lastly, we loop through the items in the module and extract the parser classes, returning a dictionary containing the name of the class and the class object that will be later used to create instances of the parser.

Creating the application's model

Let's start creating the model that will represent all the information that our application will scrape from the weather website. The first item we are going to add is an enumeration to represent each option of the weather forecast we will provide to the users of our application. Create a file named `forecast_type.py` in the directory `weatherterm/core` with the following contents:

```
from enum import Enum, unique


@unique
class ForecastType(Enum):
```

```
TODAY = 'today'
FIVEDAYS = '5day'
TENDAYS = '10day'
WEEKEND = 'weekend'
```

Enumerations have been in Python's standard library since version 3.4 and they can be created using the syntax for creating classes. Just create a class inheriting from `enum.Enum` containing a set of unique properties set to constant values. Here, we have values for the four types of forecast that the application will provide, and where values such as `ForecastType.TODAY`, `ForecastType.WEEKEND`, and so on can be accessed.

Note that we are assigning constant values that are different from the property item of the enumeration, the reason being that later these values will be used to build the URL to make requests to the weather website.

The application needs one more enumeration to represent the temperature units that the user will be able to choose from in the command line. This enumeration will contain Celsius and Fahrenheit items.

First, let's include a base enumeration. Create a file called `base_enum.py` in the `weatherterm/core` directory with the following contents:

```python
from enum import Enum


class BaseEnum(Enum):
    def _generate_next_value_(name, start, count, last_value):
        return name
```

`BaseEnum` is a very simple class inheriting from `Enum` . The only thing we want to do here is override the method `_generate_next_value_` so that every enumeration that inherits from `BaseEnum` and has properties with the value set to `auto()`   will automatically get the same value as the property name.

Now, we can create an enumeration for the temperature units. Create a file called `unit.py` in the `weatherterm/core` directory with the following content:

```
from enum import auto, unique

from .base_enum import BaseEnum


@unique
class Unit(BaseEnum):
    CELSIUS = auto()
    FAHRENHEIT = auto()
```

This class inherits from the `BaseEnum` that we just created, and every property is set to `auto()`, meaning the value for every item in the enumeration will be set automatically for us. Since the `Unit` class inherits from `BaseEnum`, every time the `auto()` is called, the `_generate_next_value_` method on `BaseEnum` will be invoked and will return the name of the property itself.

Before we try this out, let's create a file called `__init__.py` in the `weatherterm/core` directory and import the enumeration that we just created, like so:

```
from .unit import Unit
```

If we load this class in the Python REPL and check the values, the following will occur:

```
Python 3.6.2 (default, Sep 11 2017, 22:31:28)
[GCC 6.3.0 20170516] on linux
Type "help", "copyright", "credits" or "license" for more information.
>>> from weatherterm.core import Unit
>>> [value for key, value in Unit.__members__.items()]
[<Unit.CELSIUS: 'CELSIUS'>, <Unit.FAHRENHEIT: 'FAHRENHEIT'>]
```

Another item that we also want to add to the core module of our application is a class to represent the weather forecast data that the parser returns. Let's go ahead and create a file named `forecast.py` in the `weatherterm/core` directory with the following contents:

```
from datetime import date

from .forecast_type import ForecastType


class Forecast:
    def __init__(
            self,
            current_temp,
```

```
              humidity,
              wind,
              high_temp=None,
              low_temp=None,
              description='',
              forecast_date=None,
              forecast_type=ForecastType.TODAY):
        self._current_temp = current_temp
        self._high_temp = high_temp
        self._low_temp = low_temp
        self._humidity = humidity
        self._wind = wind
        self._description = description
        self._forecast_type = forecast_type

        if forecast_date is None:
            self.forecast_date = date.today()
        else:
            self._forecast_date = forecast_date

    @property
    def forecast_date(self):
        return self._forecast_date

    @forecast_date.setter
    def forecast_date(self, forecast_date):
        self._forecast_date = forecast_date.strftime("%a %b %d")

    @property
    def current_temp(self):
        return self._current_temp

    @property
    def humidity(self):
        return self._humidity

    @property
    def wind(self):
        return self._wind

    @property
    def description(self):
        return self._description

    def __str__(self):
        temperature = None
        offset = ' ' * 4
```

```
if self._forecast_type == ForecastType.TODAY:
    temperature = (f'{offset}{self._current_temp}\xb0\n'
                   f'{offset}High {self._high_temp}\xb0 / '
                   f'Low {self._low_temp}\xb0 ')
else:
    temperature = (f'{offset}High {self._high_temp}\xb0 / '
                   f'Low {self._low_temp}\xb0 ')

return(f'>> {self.forecast_date}\n'
       f'{temperature}'
       f'({self._description})\n'
       f'{offset}Wind: '
       f'{self._wind} / Humidity: {self._humidity}\n')
```

In the Forecast class, we will define properties for all the data we are going to parse:

current_temp	**Represents the current temperature. It will only be available when getting today's weather forecast.**
humidity	The humidity percentage for the day.
wind	Information about today's current wind levels.
high_temp	The highest temperature for the day.
low_temp	The lowest temperature for the day.
description	A description of the weather conditions, for example, *Partly Cloudy*.
forecast_date	Forecast date; if not supplied, it will be set to the current date.
forecast_type	Any value in the enumeration ForecastType (TODAY, FIVEDAYS, TENDAYS, or WEEKEND).

We can also implement two methods called forecast_date with the decorators @property and @forecast_date.setter . The @property decorator will turn the method into a getter for the _forecast_date property of the Forecast class, and the @forecast_date.setter will turn the method into a setter. The setter was defined here because, every time we need to set the date in an instance of Forecast, we need to make sure that it will be formatted accordingly. In the setter, we call the strftime method, passing the format codes %a (weekday abbreviated name), %b (monthly abbreviated name), and %d (day of the month).

The format codes %a and %b will use the locale configured in the machine that the code is running on.

Lastly, we override the __str__ method to allow us to format the output the way we would like when using the print, format, and str functions.

By default, the temperature unit used by weather.com is Fahrenheit, and we want to give the users of our application the option to use Celsius instead. So, let's go ahead and create one more file in the weatherterm/core directory called unit_converter.py with the following content:

```python
from .unit import Unit


class UnitConverter:
    def __init__(self, parser_default_unit, dest_unit=None):
        self._parser_default_unit = parser_default_unit
        self.dest_unit = dest_unit

        self._convert_functions = {
            Unit.CELSIUS: self._to_celsius,
            Unit.FAHRENHEIT: self._to_fahrenheit,
        }

    @property
    def dest_unit(self):
        return self._dest_unit

    @dest_unit.setter
    def dest_unit(self, dest_unit):
        self._dest_unit = dest_unit

    def convert(self, temp):

        try:
            temperature = float(temp)
        except ValueError:
            return 0

        if (self.dest_unit == self._parser_default_unit or
                self.dest_unit is None):
            return self._format_results(temperature)

        func = self._convert_functions[self.dest_unit]
```

```
        result = func(temperature)

        return self._format_results(result)

    def _format_results(self, value):
        return int(value) if value.is_integer() else f'{value:.1f}'

    def _to_celsius(self, fahrenheit_temp):
        result = (fahrenheit_temp - 32) * 5/9
        return result

    def _to_fahrenheit(self, celsius_temp):
        result = (celsius_temp * 9/5) + 32
        return result
```

This is the class that is going to make the temperature conversions from Celsius to Fahrenheit and vice versa. The initializer of this class gets two arguments; the default unit used by the parser and the destination unit. In the initializer, we will define a dictionary containing the functions that will be used for temperature unit conversion.

The convert method only gets one argument, the temperature. Here, the temperature is a string, so the first thing we need to do is try converting it to a float value; if it fails, it will return a zero value right away.

You can also verify whether the destination unit is the same as the parser's default unit or not. In that case, we don't need to continue and perform any conversion; we simply format the value and return it.

If we need to perform a conversion, we can look up the _convert_functions dictionary to find the conversion function that we need to run. If we find the function we are looking for, we invoke it and return the formatted value.

The code snippet below shows the _format_results method, which is a utility method that will format the temperature value for us:

```
        return int(value) if value.is_integer() else f'{value:.1f}'
```

The _format_results method checks if the number is an integer; the value.is_integer() will return True if the number is, for example, 10.0. If True, we will use the int function to convert the value to 10; otherwise, the value is returned as a fixed-point number with a precision of 1. The default precision in Python is 6. Lastly, there are two utility methods that perform the temperature conversions, _to_celsius and _to_fahrenheit.

Now, we only need to edit the __init__.py file in the `weatherterm/core` directory and include the following import statements:

```
from .base_enum import BaseEnum
from .unit_converter import UnitConverter
from .forecast_type import ForecastType
from .forecast import Forecast
```

Fetching data from the weather website

We are going to add a class named `Request` that will be responsible for getting the data from the weather website. Let's add a file named `request.py` in the `weatherterm/core` directory with the following content:

```
import os
from selenium import webdriver


class Request:
    def __init__(self, base_url):
        self._phantomjs_path = os.path.join(os.curdir,
'phantomjs/bin/phantomjs')
        self._base_url = base_url
        self._driver = webdriver.PhantomJS(self._phantomjs_path)

    def fetch_data(self, forecast, area):
        url = self._base_url.format(forecast=forecast, area=area)
        self._driver.get(url)

        if self._driver.title == '404 Not Found':
            error_message = ('Could not find the area that you '
                             'searching for')
            raise Exception(error_message)

        return self._driver.page_source
```

This class is very simple; the initializer defines the base URL and creates a PhantomJS driver, using the path where PhantomJS is installed. The `fetch_data` method formats the URL, adding the forecast option and the area. After that, the `webdriver` performs a request and returns the page source. If the title of the markup returned is `404 Not Found`, it will raise an exception. Unfortunately, `Selenium` doesn't provide a proper way of getting the HTTP Status code; this would have been much better than comparing strings.

You may notice that I prefix some of the class properties with an underscore sign. I usually do that to show that the underlying property is private and shouldn't be set outside the class. In Python, there is no need to do that because there's no way to set private or public properties; however, I like it because I can clearly show my intent.

Now, we can import it in the __init__.py file in the `weatherterm/core` directory:

```
from .request import Request
```

Now we have a parser loader to load any parser that we drop into the directory `weatherterm/parsers`, we have a class representing the forecast model, and an enumeration `ForecastType` so we can specify which type of forecast we are parsing. The enumeration represents temperature units and utility functions to convert temperatures from `Fahrenheit` to `Celsius` and `Celsius` to `Fahrenheit`. So now, we should be ready to create the application's entry point to receive all the arguments passed by the user, run the parser, and present the data on the terminal.

Getting the user's input with ArgumentParser

Before we run our application for the first time, we need to add the application's entry point. The entry point is the first code that will be run when our application is executed.

We want to give the users of our application the best user experience possible, so the first features that we need to add are the ability to receive and parse command line arguments, perform argument validation, set arguments when needed, and, last but not least, show an organized and informative help system so the users can see which arguments can be used and how to use the application.

Sounds like tedious work, right?

Luckily, Python has batteries included and the standard library contains a great module that allows us to implement this in a very simple way; the module is called `argparse`.

Another feature that would be good to have is for our application to be easy to distribute to our users. One approach is to create a __main__.py file in the `weatherterm` module directory, and you can run the module as a regular script. Python will automatically run the __main__.py file, like so:

```
$ python -m weatherterm
```

Another option is to zip the entire application's directory and execute the Python passing the name of the ZIP file instead. This is an easy, fast, and simple way to distribute our Python programs.

There are many other ways of distributing your programs, but they are beyond the scope of this book; I just wanted to give you some examples of the usage of the __main__.py file.

With that said, let's create a __main__.py file inside of the weatherterm directory with the following content:

```python
import sys
from argparse import ArgumentParser

from weatherterm.core import parser_loader
from weatherterm.core import ForecastType
from weatherterm.core import Unit


def _validate_forecast_args(args):
    if args.forecast_option is None:
        err_msg = ('One of these arguments must be used: '
                   '-td/--today, -5d/--fivedays, -10d/--tendays, -
                   w/--weekend')
        print(f'{argparser.prog}: error: {err_msg}',
        file=sys.stderr)
        sys.exit()

parsers = parser_loader.load('./weatherterm/parsers')

argparser = ArgumentParser(
    prog='weatherterm',
    description='Weather info from weather.com on your terminal')

required = argparser.add_argument_group('required arguments')

required.add_argument('-p', '--parser',
                      choices=parsers.keys(),
                      required=True,
                      dest='parser',
                      help=('Specify which parser is going to be
                       used to '
                            'scrape weather information.'))

unit_values = [name.title() for name, value in
Unit.__members__.items()]

argparser.add_argument('-u', '--unit',
```

```
                                   choices=unit_values,
                                   required=False,
                                   dest='unit',
                                   help=('Specify the unit that will be used to
                                   display '
                                          'the temperatures.'))

        required.add_argument('-a', '--areacode',
                                   required=True,
                                   dest='area_code',
                                   help=('The code area to get the weather
                                   broadcast from. '
                                          'It can be obtained at
                                             https://weather.com'))

        argparser.add_argument('-v', '--version',
                                   action='version',
                                   version='%(prog)s 1.0')

        argparser.add_argument('-td', '--today',
                                   dest='forecast_option',
                                   action='store_const',
                                   const=ForecastType.TODAY,
                                   help='Show the weather forecast for the
                                   current day')

        args = argparser.parse_args()

        _validate_forecast_args(args)

        cls = parsers[args.parser]

        parser = cls()
        results = parser.run(args)

        for result in results:
            print(results)
```

The weather forecast options (today, five days, ten days, and weekend forecast) that our application will accept will not be required; however, at least one option must be provided in the command line, so we create a simple function called `_validate_forecast_args` to perform this validation for us. This function will show a help message and exit the application.

First, we get all the parsers available in the `weatherterm/parsers` directory. The list of parsers will be used as valid values for the parser argument.

It is the `ArgumentParser` object that does the job of defining the parameters, parsing the values, and showing help, so we create an instance of `ArgumentParser` and also create an argument group for the required parameters. This will make the help output look much nicer and organized.

In order to make the parameters and the help output more organized, we are going to create a group within the `ArgumentParser` object. This group will contain all the required arguments that our application needs. This way, the users of our application can easily see which parameters are required and the ones that are not required.

We achieve this with the following statement:

```
required = argparser.add_argument_group('required arguments')
```

After creating the argument group for the required arguments, we get a list of all members of the enumeration `Unit` and use the `title()` function to make only the first letter a capital letter.

Now, we can start adding the arguments that our application will be able to receive on the command line. Most argument definitions use the same set of keyword arguments, so I will not be covering all of them.

The first argument that we will create is `--parser` or `-p`:

```
required.add_argument('-p', '--parser',
                        choices=parsers.keys(),
                        required=True,
                        dest='parser',
                        help=('Specify which parser is going to be
                            used to '
                                'scrape weather information.'))
```

Let's break down every parameter of the `add_argument` used when creating the parser flag:

- The first two parameters are the flags. In this case, the user passes a value to this argument using either `-p` or `--parser` in the command line, for example, `--parser WeatherComParser`.
- The `choices` parameter specifies a list of valid values for that argument that we are creating. Here, we are using `parsers.keys()`, which will return a list of parser names. The advantage of this implementation is that if we add a new parser, it will be automatically added to this list, and no changes will be required in this file.

- The `required` parameter, as the name says, specifies if the argument will be required or not.
- The `dest` parameter specifies the name of the attribute to be added to the resulting object of the parser argument. The object returned by `parser_args()` will contain an attribute called `parser` with the value that we passed to this argument in the command line.
- Finally, the `help` parameter is the argument's help text, shown when using the `-h` or `--help` flag.

Moving on to the `--today` argument:

```
argparser.add_argument('-td', '--today',
                       dest='forecast_option',
                       action='store_const',
                       const=ForecastType.TODAY,
                       help='Show the weather forecast for the
                       current day')
```

Here we have two keyword arguments that we haven't seen before, `action` and `const`.

Actions can be bound to the arguments that we create and they can perform many things. The `argparse` module contains a great set of actions, but if you need to do something specific, you can create your own action that will meet your needs. Most actions defined in the `argparse` module are actions to store values in the parse result's object attributes.

In the previous code snippet, we use the `store_const` action, which will store a constant value to an attribute in the object returned by `parse_args()`.

We also used the keyword argument `const`, which specifies the constant default value when the flag is used in the command line.

Remember that I mentioned that it is possible to create custom actions? The argument unit is a great use case for a custom action. The `choices` argument is just a list of strings, so we use this comprehension to get the list of names of every item in the `Unit` enumeration, as follows:

```
unit_values = [name.title() for name, value in
Unit.__members__.items()]

required.add_argument('-u', '--unit',
                      choices=unit_values,
                      required=False,
                      dest='unit',
                      help=('Specify the unit that will be used to
```

```
                              display '
                                   'the temperatures.'))
```

The object returned by `parse_args()` will contain an attribute called unit with a string value (`Celsius` or `Fahrenheit`), but this is not exactly what we want. Wouldn't it be nice to have the value as an enumeration item instead? We can change this behavior by creating a custom action.

First, add a new file named `set_unit_action.py` in the `weatherterm/core` directory with the following contents:

```python
from argparse import Action

from weatherterm.core import Unit


class SetUnitAction(Action):

    def __call__(self, parser, namespace, values,
      option_string=None):
        unit = Unit[values.upper()]
        setattr(namespace, self.dest, unit)
```

This action class is very simple; it just inherits from `argparse.Action` and overrides the __call__ method, which will be called when the argument value is parsed. This is going to be set to the destination attribute.

The `parser` parameter will be an instance of `ArgumentParser`. The namespace is an instance of `argparser.Namespace` and it is just a simple class containing all the attributes defined in the `ArgumentParser` object. If you inspect this parameter with the debugger, you will see something similar to this:

```
Namespace(area_code=None, fields=None, forecast_option=None,
parser=None, unit=None)
```

The `values` parameter is the value that the user has passed on the command line; in our case, it can be either Celsius or Fahrenheit. Lastly, the `option_string` parameter is the flag defined for the argument. For the unit argument, the value of `option_string` will be –u.

Fortunately, enumerations in Python allow us to access their members and attributes using item access:

```
Unit[values.upper()]
```

Verifying this in Python REPL, we have:

```
>>> from weatherterm.core import Unit
>>> Unit['CELSIUS']
<Unit.CELSIUS: 'CELSIUS'>
>>> Unit['FAHRENHEIT']
<Unit.FAHRENHEIT: 'FAHRENHEIT'>
```

After getting the correct enumeration member, we set the value of the property specified by `self.dest` in the namespace object. That is much cleaner and we don't need to deal with magic strings.

With the custom action in place, we need to add the import statement in the `__init__.py` file in the `weatherterm/core` directory:

```
from .set_unit_action import SetUnitAction
```

Just include the line above at the end of the file. Then, we need to import it into the `__main__.py` file, like so:

```
from weatherterm.core import SetUnitAction
```

And we are going to add the `action` keyword argument in the definition of the unit argument and set it to `SetUnitAction`, like so:

```
required.add_argument('-u', '--unit',
                      choices=unit_values,
                      required=False,
                      action=SetUnitAction,
                      dest='unit',
                      help=('Specify the unit that will be used to
                        display '
                            'the temperatures.'))
```

So, when the user of our application uses the flag –u for Celsius, the value of the attribute unit in the object returned by the `parse_args()` function will be:

```
<Unit.CELSIUS: 'CELSIUS'>
```

The rest of the code is very straightforward; we invoke the `parse_args` function to parse the arguments and set the result in the `args` variable. Then, we use the value of `args.parser` (the name of the selected parser) and access that item in the parser's dictionary. Remember that the value is the class type, so we create an instance of the parser, and lastly, invoke the method run, which will kick off website scraping.

Creating the parser

In order to run our code for the first time, we need to create a parser. We can quickly create a parser to run our code and check whether the values are being parsed properly.

Let's go ahead and create a file called `weather_com_parser.py` in the `weatherterm/parsers` directory. To make it simple, we are going to create just the necessary methods, and the only thing we are going to do when the methods are invoked is to raise a `NotImplementedError`:

```python
from weatherterm.core import ForecastType


class WeatherComParser:

    def __init__(self):
        self._forecast = {
            ForecastType.TODAY: self._today_forecast,
            ForecastType.FIVEDAYS:
self._five_and_ten_days_forecast,
            ForecastType.TENDAYS: self._five_and_ten_days_forecast,
            ForecastType.WEEKEND: self._weekend_forecast,
            }

    def _today_forecast(self, args):
        raise NotImplementedError()

    def _five_and_ten_days_forecast(self, args):
        raise NotImplementedError()

    def _weekend_forecast(self, args):
        raise NotImplementedError()

    def run(self, args):
        self._forecast_type = args.forecast_option
        forecast_function = self._forecast[args.forecast_option]
        return forecast_function(args)
```

In the initializer, we create a dictionary where the key is a member of the `ForecasType` enumeration, and the value is the method bound to any of these options. Our application will be able to present today's, a five-day, ten-day, and the weekend forecast, so we implement all four methods.

The `run` method only does two things; it looks up the function that needs to be executed using the `forecast_option` that we passed as an argument in the command line, and executes the function returning its value.

Now, the application is finally ready to be executed for the first time if you run the command in the command line:

```
$ python -m weatherterm --help
```

You should see the application's help options:

```
usage: weatherterm [-h] -p {WeatherComParser} [-u {Celsius,Fahrenheit}] -a
AREA_CODE [-v] [-td] [-5d] [-10d] [-w]

Weather info from weather.com on your terminal

optional arguments:
  -h, --help show this help message and exit
  -u {Celsius,Fahrenheit}, --unit {Celsius,Fahrenheit}
                        Specify the unit that will be used to display
                        the temperatures.
  -v, --version show program's version number and exit
  -td, --today Show the weather forecast for the current day
require arguments:
  -p {WeatherComParser}, --parser {WeatherComParser}
                        Specify which parser is going to be used to scrape
                        weather information.
  -a AREA_CODE, --areacode AREA_CODE
                        The code area to get the weather broadcast from. It
                        can be obtained at https://weather.com
```

As you can see, the `ArgumentParse` module already provides out-of-the-box output for help. There are ways you can customize the output how you want to, but I find the default layout really good.

Notice that the `-p` argument already gave you the option to choose the `WeatherComParser`. It wasn't necessary to hardcode it anywhere because the parser loader did all the work for us. The `-u` (`--unit`) flag also contains the items of the enumeration `Unit`. If someday you want to extend this application and add new units, the only thing you need to do here is to add the new item to the enumeration, and it will be automatically picked up and included as an option for the `-u` flag.

Now, if you run the application again and this time pass some parameters:

```
$ python -m weatherterm -u Celsius -a SWXX2372:1:SW -p WeatherComParser -td
```

You will get an exception similar to this:

```
daniel@musashi: ~/Projects/github-repos/weatherterm                               _  □  ×
~/Projects/github-repos/weatherterm $ python -m weatherterm -u Celsius -a SWXX2372:1:SW -p WeatherComParser -td
Traceback (most recent call last):
  File "/home/daniel/Installs/Python3.6/lib/python3.6/runpy.py", line 193, in _run_module_as_main
    "__main__", mod_spec)
  File "/home/daniel/Installs/Python3.6/lib/python3.6/runpy.py", line 85, in _run_code
    exec(code, run_globals)
  File "/home/daniel/Projects/github-repos/weatherterm/weatherterm/__main__.py", line 91, in <module>
    results = parser.run(args)
  File "/home/daniel/Projects/github-repos/weatherterm/weatherterm/parsers/weather_com_parser.py", line 217, in run
    return forecast_function(args)
  File "/home/daniel/Projects/github-repos/weatherterm/weatherterm/parsers/weather_com_parser.py", line 207, in _today
_forecast
    raise NotImplementedError()
NotImplementedError
~/Projects/github-repos/weatherterm $ ▮
```

Don't worry -- this is exactly what we wanted! If you follow the stack trace, you can see that everything is working as intended. When we run our code, we call the `run` method on the selected parser from the `__main__.py` file, then we select the method associated with the forecast option, in this case, `_today_forecast`, and finally store the result in the `forecast_function` variable.

When the function stored in the `forecast_function` variable was executed, the `NotImplementedError` exception was raised. So far so good; the code is working perfectly and now we can start adding the implementation for each of these methods.

Getting today's weather forecast

The core functionality is in place and the entry point of the application with the argument parser will give the users of our application a much better experience. Now, it is finally the time we all have been waiting for, the time to start implementing the parser. We will start implementing the method to get today's weather forecast.

Since I am in Sweden, I will use the area code `SWXX2372:1:SW` (Stockholm, Sweden); however, you can use any area code you want. To get the area code of your choice, go to `https://weather.com` and search for the area you want. After selecting the area, the weather forecast for the current day will be displayed. Note that the URL changes, for example, when searching Stockholm, Sweden, the URL changes to:

`https://weather.com/weather/today/l/SWXX2372:1:SW`

For São Paulo, Brazil it will be:

`https://weather.com/weather/today/l/BRXX0232:1:BR`

Note that there is only one part of the URL that changes, and this is the area code that we want to pass as an argument to our application.

Adding helper methods

To start with, we need to import some packages:

```
import re

from weatherterm.core import Forecast
from weatherterm.core import Request
from weatherterm.core import Unit
from weatherterm.core import UnitConverter
```

And in the initializer, we are going to add the following code:

```
self._base_url = 'http://weather.com/weather/{forecast}/l/{area}'
self._request = Request(self._base_url)

self._temp_regex = re.compile('([0-9]+)\D{,2}([0-9]+)')
self._only_digits_regex = re.compile('[0-9]+')

self._unit_converter = UnitConverter(Unit.FAHRENHEIT)
```

In the initializer, we define the URL template we are going to use to perform requests to the weather website; then, we create a `Request` object. This is the object that will perform the requests for us.

Regular expressions are only used when parsing today's weather forecast temperatures.

We also define a `UnitConverter` object and set the default unit to `Fahrenheit`.

Now, we are ready to start adding two methods that will be responsible for actually searching for HTML elements within a certain class and return its contents. The first method is called _get_data:

```
def _get_data(self, container, search_items):
    scraped_data = {}

    for key, value in search_items.items():
        result = container.find(value, class_=key)
        data = None if result is None else result.get_text()
        if data is not None:
            scraped_data[key] = data

    return scraped_data
```

The idea of this method is to search items within a container that matches some criteria. The `container` is just a DOM element in the HTML and the `search_items` is a dictionary where the key is a CSS class and the value is the type of the HTML element. It can be a DIV, SPAN, or anything that you wish to get the value from.

It starts looping through `search_items.items()` and uses the find method to find the element within the container. If the item is found, we use `get_text` to extract the text of the DOM element and add it to a dictionary that will be returned when there are no more items to search.

The second method that we will implement is the _parser method. This will make use of the _get_data that we just implemented:

```
def _parse(self, container, criteria):
    results = [self._get_data(item, criteria)
                    for item in container.children]

    return [result for result in results if result]
```

Here, we also get a `container` and `criteria` like the _get_data method. The container is a DOM element and the criterion is a dictionary of nodes that we want to find. The first comprehension gets all the container's children elements and passes them to the _get_data method.

The results will be a list of dictionaries with all the items that have been found, and we will only return the dictionaries that are not empty.

There are only two more helper methods we need to implement in order to get today's weather forecast in place. Let's implement a method called _clear_str_number:

```
def _clear_str_number(self, str_number):
    result = self._only_digits_regex.match(str_number)
    return '--' if result is None else result.group()
```

This method will use a regular expression to make sure that only digits are returned.

And the last method that needs to be implemented is the _get_additional_info method:

```
def _get_additional_info(self, content):
    data = tuple(item.td.span.get_text()
                 for item in content.table.tbody.children)
    return data[:2]
```

This method loops through the table rows, getting the text of every cell. This comprehension will return lots of information about the weather, but we are only interested in the first 2, the wind and the humidity.

Implementing today's weather forecast

It's time to start adding the implementation of the _today_forecast method, but first, we need to import BeautifulSoup. At the top of the file, add the following import statement:

```
from bs4 import BeautifulSoup
```

Now, we can start adding the _today_forecast method:

```
def _today_forecast(self, args):
    criteria = {
        'today_nowcard-temp': 'div',
        'today_nowcard-phrase': 'div',
        'today_nowcard-hilo': 'div',
        }

    content = self._request.fetch_data(args.forecast_option.value,
                                       args.area_code)

    bs = BeautifulSoup(content, 'html.parser')

    container = bs.find('section', class_='today_nowcard-
container')

    weather_conditions = self._parse(container, criteria)
```

```
if len(weather_conditions) < 1:
    raise Exception('Could not parse weather foreecast for
    today.')

weatherinfo = weather_conditions[0]

temp_regex = re.compile(('H\s+(\d+|\-{,2}).+'
                         'L\s+(\d+|\-{,2})'))
temp_info = temp_regex.search(weatherinfo['today_nowcard-
hilo'])
high_temp, low_temp = temp_info.groups()

side = container.find('div', class_='today_nowcard-sidecar')
humidity, wind = self._get_additional_info(side)

curr_temp = self._clear_str_number(weatherinfo['today_nowcard-
temp'])

self._unit_converter.dest_unit = args.unit

td_forecast = Forecast(self._unit_converter.convert(curr_temp),
                       humidity,
                       wind,
                       high_temp=self._unit_converter.convert(
                           high_temp),
                       low_temp=self._unit_converter.convert(
                           low_temp),
                       description=weatherinfo['today_nowcard-
                        phrase'])

return [td_forecast]
```

That is the function that will be called when the `-td` or `--today` flag is used on the command line. Let's break down this code so that we can easily understand what it does. Understanding this method is important because these methods parse data from other weather forecast options (five days, ten days, and weekend) that are very similar to this one.

The method's signature is quite simple; it only gets `args`, which is the `Argument` object that is created in the `__main__` method. The first thing we do in this method is to create a `criteria` dictionary with all the DOM elements that we want to find in the markup:

```
criteria = {
    'today_nowcard-temp': 'div',
    'today_nowcard-phrase': 'div',
    'today_nowcard-hilo': 'div',
}
```

As mentioned before, the key to the `criteria` dictionary is the name of the DOM element's CSS class, and the value is the type of the HTML element:

- The `today_nowcard-temp` class is a CSS class of the DOM element containing the current temperature
- The `today_nowcard-phrase` class is a CSS class of the DOM element containing weather conditions text (Cloudy, Sunny, and so on)
- The `today_nowcard-hilo` class is the CSS class of the DOM element containing the highest and lowest temperature

Next, we are going to fetch, create, and use `BeautifulSoup` to parse the DOM:

```
content = self._request.fetch_data(args.forecast_option.value,
                                    args.area_code)

bs = BeautifulSoup(content, 'html.parser')

container = bs.find('section', class_='today_nowcard-container')

weather_conditions = self._parse(container, criteria)

if len(weather_conditions) < 1:
    raise Exception('Could not parse weather forecast for today.')

weatherinfo = weather_conditions[0]
```

First, we make use of the `fetch_data` method of the `Request` class that we created on the core module and pass two arguments; the first is the forecast option and the second argument is the area code that we passed on the command line.
After fetching the data, we create a `BeautifulSoup` object passing the `content` and a `parser`. Since we are getting back HTML, we use `html.parser`.

Now is the time to start looking for the HTML elements that we are interested in. Remember, we need to find an element that will be a container, and the `_parser` function will search through the children elements and try to find items that we defined in the dictionary criteria. For today's weather forecast, the element that contains all the data we need is a `section` element with the `today_nowcard-container` CSS class.

`BeautifulSoup` contains the `find` method, which we can use to find elements in the HTML DOM with specific criteria. Note that the keyword argument is called `class_` and not `class` because `class` is a reserved word in Python.

Now that we have the container element, we can pass it to the `_parse` method, which will return a list. We perform a check if the result list contains at least one element and raise an exception if it is empty. If it is not empty, we just get the first element and assign it to the `weatherinfo` variable. The `weatherinfo` variable now contains a dictionary with all the items that we were looking for.

The next step is split the highest and lowest temperature:

```
temp_regex = re.compile(('H\s+(\d+|\-{,2}).+'
                         'L\s+(\d+|\-{,2})'))
temp_info = temp_regex.search(weatherinfo['today_nowcard-hilo'])
high_temp, low_temp = temp_info.groups()
```

We want to parse the text that has been extracted from the DOM element with the `today_nowcard-hilo` CSS class, and the text should look something like H 50 L 60, H -- L 60, and so on. An easy and simple way of extracting the text we want is to use a regular expression:

```
H\s+(\d+|\-{,2}).L\s+(\d+|\-{,2})
```

We can break this regular expression into two parts. First, we want to get the highest temperature—`H\s+(\d+|\-{,2})`; this means that it will match an H followed by some spaces, and then it will group a value that matches either numbers or a maximum of two dash symbols. After that, it will match any character. Lastly, comes the second part that basically does the same; however, it starts matching an L.

After executing the search method, it gets regular expression groups that have been returned calling the `groups()` function, which in this case will return two groups, one for the highest temperature and the second for the lowest.

Other information that we want to provide to our users is information about wind and humidity. The container element that contains this information has a CSS class called `today_nowcard-sidecar`:

```
side = container.find('div', class_='today_nowcard-sidecar')
wind, humidity = self._get_additional_info(side)
```

We just find the container and pass it into the `_get_additional_info` method that will loop through the children elements of the container, extracting the text and finally returning the results for us.

Finally, the last part of this method:

```
curr_temp = self._clear_str_number(weatherinfo['today_nowcard-
temp'])

self._unit_converter.dest_unit = args.unit

td_forecast = Forecast(self._unit_converter.convert(curr_temp),
                       humidity,
                       wind,
                       high_temp=self._unit_converter.convert(
                           high_temp),
                       low_temp=self._unit_converter.convert(
                           low_temp),
                       description=weatherinfo['today_nowcard-
                        phrase'])

return [td_forecast]
```

Since the current temperature contains a special character (degree sign) that we don't want to have at this point, we use the `_clr_str_number` method to pass the `today_nowcard-temp` item of the `weatherinfo` dictionary.

Now that we have all the information we need, we construct the `Forecast` object and return it. Note that we are returning an array here; this is because all other options that we are going to implement (five-day, ten-day, and weekend forecasts) will return a list, so to make it consistent; also to facilitate when we will have to display this information on the terminal, we are also returning a list.

Another thing to note is that we are making use of the convert method of our `UnitConverter` to convert all the temperatures to the unit selected in the command line.

When running the command again:

```
$ python -m weatherterm -u Fahrenheit -a SWXX2372:1:SW -p WeatherComParser
-td
```

You should see an output similar to this:

```
(weatherterm-vYQW3SBX) weatherterm ) python -m weatherterm -u Fahrenheit -a SWXX2372:1:SW -p WeatherComParser -td
>> Sat Feb 10
    26°
   High 35° / Low 25° (Mostly Cloudy)
   Wind: E 2 mph  / Humidity: 100%
```

Congratulations! You have implemented your first web scraping application. Next up, let's add the other forecast options.

Getting five- and ten-day weather forecasts

The site that we are currently scraping the weather forecast from (`weather.com`) also provides the weather forecast for
five and ten days, so in this section, we are going to implement methods to parse these forecast options as well.

The markup of the pages that present data for five and ten days are very similar; they have the same DOM structure and share the same CSS classes, which makes it easier for us to implement just one method that will work for both options. Let's go ahead and add a new method to the `wheater_com_parser.py` file with the following contents:

```python
def _parse_list_forecast(self, content, args):
    criteria = {
        'date-time': 'span',
        'day-detail': 'span',
        'description': 'td',
        'temp': 'td',
        'wind': 'td',
        'humidity': 'td',
    }

    bs = BeautifulSoup(content, 'html.parser')

    forecast_data = bs.find('table', class_='twc-table')
    container = forecast_data.tbody

    return self._parse(container, criteria)
```

As I mentioned before, the DOM for the five- and ten-day weather forecasts is very similar, so we create the `_parse_list_forecast` method, which can be used for both options. First, we define the criteria:

- The `date-time` is a `span` element and contains a string representing the day of the week
- The `day-detail` is a `span` element and contains a string with the date, for example, `SEP 29`
- The `description` is a `TD` element and contains the weather conditions, for example, `Cloudy`

- `temp` is a `TD` element and contains temperature information such as high and low temperature
- `wind` is a `TD` element and contains wind information
- `humidity` is a `TD` element and contains humidity information

Now that we have the criteria, we create a `BeatufulSoup` object, passing the content and the `html.parser`. All the data that we would like to get is on the table with a CSS class named `twc-table`. We find the table and define the `tbody` element as a container. Finally, we run the `_parse` method, passing the `container` and the `criteria` that we defined. The return of this function will look something like this:

```
[{'date-time': 'Today',
  'day-detail': 'SEP 28',
  'description': 'Partly Cloudy',
  'humidity': '78%',
  'temp': '60°50°',
  'wind': 'ESE 10 mph '},
 {'date-time': 'Fri',
  'day-detail': 'SEP 29',
  'description': 'Partly Cloudy',
  'humidity': '79%',
  'temp': '57°48°',
  'wind': 'ESE 10 mph '},
 {'date-time': 'Sat',
  'day-detail': 'SEP 30',
  'description': 'Partly Cloudy',
  'humidity': '77%',
  'temp': '57°49°',
  'wind': 'SE 10 mph '},
 {'date-time': 'Sun',
  'day-detail': 'OCT 1',
  'description': 'Cloudy',
  'humidity': '74%',
  'temp': '55°51°',
  'wind': 'SE 14 mph '},
 {'date-time': 'Mon',
  'day-detail': 'OCT 2',
  'description': 'Rain',
  'humidity': '87%',
  'temp': '55°48°',
  'wind': 'SSE 18 mph '}]
```

Another method that we need to create is a method that will prepare the data for us, for example, parsing and converting temperature values and creating a `Forecast` object. Add a new method called _prepare_data with the following content:

```
def _prepare_data(self, results, args):
    forecast_result = []

    self._unit_converter.dest_unit = args.unit

    for item in results:
        match = self._temp_regex.search(item['temp'])
        if match is not None:
            high_temp, low_temp = match.groups()

        try:
            dateinfo = item['weather-cell']
            date_time, day_detail = dateinfo[:3], dateinfo[3:]
            item['date-time'] = date_time
            item['day-detail'] = day_detail
        except KeyError:
            pass

        day_forecast = Forecast(
            self._unit_converter.convert(item['temp']),
            item['humidity'],
            item['wind'],
            high_temp=self._unit_converter.convert(high_temp),
            low_temp=self._unit_converter.convert(low_temp),
            description=item['description'].strip(),
            forecast_date=f'{item["date-time"]} {item["day-
              detail"]}',
            forecast_type=self._forecast_type)
        forecast_result.append(day_forecast)

    return forecast_result
```

This method is quite simple. First, loop through the results and apply the regex that we created to split the high and low temperatures stored in `item['temp']`. If there's a match, it will get the groups and assign the value to `high_temp` and `low_temp`.

After that, we create a `Forecast` object and append it to a list that will be returned later on.

Lastly, we add the method that will be invoked when the $-5d$ or $-10d$ flag is used. Create another method called _five_and_ten_days_forecast with the following contents:

```
def _five_and_ten_days_forecast(self, args):
    content = self._request.fetch_data(args.forecast_option.value,
    args.area_code)
    results = self._parse_list_forecast(content, args)
    return self._prepare_data(results)
```

This method only fetches the contents of the page passing the forecast_option value and the area code, so it will be possible to build the URL to perform the request. When the data is returned, we pass it down to the _parse_list_forecast, which will return a list of Forecast objects (one for each day); finally, we prepare the data to be returned using the _prepare_data method.

Before we run the command, we need to enable this option in the command line tool that we implemented; go over to the __main__.py file, and, just after the definition of the $-td$ flag, add the following code:

```
argparser.add_argument('-5d', '--fivedays',
                       dest='forecast_option',
                       action='store_const',
                       const=ForecastType.FIVEDAYS,
                       help='Shows the weather forecast for the
next
                       5 days')
```

Now, run the application again, but this time using the $-5d$ or $--fivedays$ flag:

```
$ python -m weatherterm -u Fahrenheit -a SWXX2372:1:SW -p WeatherComParser
-5d
```

It will produce the following output:

```
>> [Today SEP 28]
   High 60° / Low 50° (Partly Cloudy)
   Wind: ESE 10 mph / Humidity: 78%

>> [Fri SEP 29]
   High 57° / Low 48° (Partly Cloudy)
   Wind: ESE 10 mph / Humidity: 79%

>> [Sat SEP 30]
   High 57° / Low 49° (Partly Cloudy)
   Wind: SE 10 mph / Humidity: 77%
```

```
>> [Sun OCT 1]
   High 55° / Low 51° (Cloudy)
   Wind: SE 14 mph / Humidity: 74%

>> [Mon OCT 2]
   High 55° / Low 48° (Rain)
   Wind: SSE 18 mph / Humidity: 87%
```

To wrap this section up, let's include the option to get the weather forecast for the next ten days as well, in the __main__.py file, just below the -5d flag definition. Add the following code:

```
argparser.add_argument('-10d', '--tendays',
                       dest='forecast_option',
                       action='store_const',
                       const=ForecastType.TENDAYS,
                       help='Shows the weather forecast for the
next
                       10 days')
```

If you run the same command as we used to get the five-day forecast but replace the -5d flag with -10d, like so:

```
$ python -m weatherterm -u Fahrenheit -a SWXX2372:1:SW -p WeatherComParser
-10d
```

You should see the ten-day weather forecast output:

```
>> [Today SEP 28]
   High 60° / Low 50° (Partly Cloudy)
   Wind: ESE 10 mph / Humidity: 78%

>> [Fri SEP 29]
   High 57° / Low 48° (Partly Cloudy)
   Wind: ESE 10 mph / Humidity: 79%

>> [Sat SEP 30]
   High 57° / Low 49° (Partly Cloudy)
   Wind: SE 10 mph / Humidity: 77%

>> [Sun OCT 1]
   High 55° / Low 51° (Cloudy)
   Wind: SE 14 mph / Humidity: 74%

>> [Mon OCT 2]
   High 55° / Low 48° (Rain)
   Wind: SSE 18 mph / Humidity: 87%
```

```
>> [Tue OCT 3]
     High 56° / Low 46° (AM Clouds/PM Sun)
     Wind: S 10 mph / Humidity: 84%

>> [Wed OCT 4]
     High 58° / Low 47° (Partly Cloudy)
     Wind: SE 9 mph / Humidity: 80%

>> [Thu OCT 5]
     High 57° / Low 46° (Showers)
     Wind: SSW 8 mph / Humidity: 81%

>> [Fri OCT 6]
     High 57° / Low 46° (Partly Cloudy)
     Wind: SW 8 mph / Humidity: 76%

>> [Sat OCT 7]
     High 56° / Low 44° (Mostly Sunny)
     Wind: W 7 mph / Humidity: 80%

>> [Sun OCT 8]
     High 56° / Low 44° (Partly Cloudy)
     Wind: NNE 7 mph / Humidity: 78%

>> [Mon OCT 9]
     High 56° / Low 43° (AM Showers)
     Wind: SSW 9 mph / Humidity: 79%

>> [Tue OCT 10]
     High 55° / Low 44° (AM Showers)
     Wind: W 8 mph / Humidity: 79%

>> [Wed OCT 11]
     High 55° / Low 42° (AM Showers)
     Wind: SE 7 mph / Humidity: 79%

>> [Thu OCT 12]
     High 53° / Low 43° (AM Showers)
     Wind: NNW 8 mph / Humidity: 87%
```

As you can see, the weather was not so great here in Sweden while I was writing this book.

Getting the weekend weather forecast

The last weather forecast option that we are going to implement in our application is the option to get the weather forecast for the upcoming weekend. This implementation is a bit different from the others because the data returned by the weekend's weather is slightly different from today's, five, and ten days weather forecast.

The DOM structure is different and some CSS class names are different as well. If you remember the previous methods that we implemented, we always use the _parser method, which gives us arguments such as the container DOM and a dictionary with the search criteria. The return value of that method is also a dictionary where the key is the class name of the DOM that we were searching and the value is the text within that DOM element.

Since the CSS class names of the weekend page are different, we need to implement some code to get that array of results and rename all the keys so the _prepare_data function can use scraped results properly.

With that said, let's go ahead and create a new file in the weatherterm/core directory called mapper.py with the following contents:

```python
class Mapper:

    def __init__(self):
        self._mapping = {}

    def _add(self, source, dest):
        self._mapping[source] = dest

    def remap_key(self, source, dest):
        self._add(source, dest)

    def remap(self, itemslist):
        return [self._exec(item) for item in itemslist]

    def _exec(self, src_dict):
        dest = dict()

        if not src_dict:
            raise AttributeError('The source dictionary cannot be
            empty or None')

        for key, value in src_dict.items():
            try:
                new_key = self._mapping[key]
```

```
                    dest[new_key] = value
             except KeyError:
                    dest[key] = value
        return dest
```

The `Mapper` class gets a list with dictionaries and renames specific keys that we would like to rename. The important methods here are `remap_key` and `remap`. The `remap_key` gets two arguments, `source` and `dest`. `source` is the key that we wish to rename and `dest` is the new name for that key. The `remap_key` method will add it to an internal dictionary called `_mapping`, which will be used later on to look up the new key name.

The `remap` method simply gets a list containing the dictionaries and, for every item on that list, it calls the `_exec` method that first creates a brand new dictionary, then checks whether the dictionary is empty. In that case, it raises an `AttributeError`.

If the dictionary has keys, we loop through its items, search for whether the current item's key has a new name in the mapping dictionary. If the new key name is found, will to create a new item with the new key name; otherwise, we just keep the old name. After the loop, the list is returned with all the dictionaries containing the keys with a new name.

Now, we just need to add it to the __init__.py file in the `weatherterm/core` directory:

```
from .mapper import Mapper
```

And, in the `weather_com_parser.py` file in `weatherterm/parsers`, we need to import the `Mapper`:

```
from weatherterm.core import Mapper
```

With the mapper in place, we can go ahead and create the `_weekend_forecast` method in the `weather_com_parser.py` file, like so:

```
def _weekend_forecast(self, args):
    criteria = {
        'weather-cell': 'header',
        'temp': 'p',
        'weather-phrase': 'h3',
        'wind-conditions': 'p',
        'humidity': 'p',
    }

    mapper = Mapper()
    mapper.remap_key('wind-conditions', 'wind')
    mapper.remap_key('weather-phrase', 'description')
```

```
content = self._request.fetch_data(args.forecast_option.value,
                                   args.area_code)

bs = BeautifulSoup(content, 'html.parser')

forecast_data = bs.find('article', class_='ls-mod')
container = forecast_data.div.div

partial_results = self._parse(container, criteria)
results = mapper.remap(partial_results)

return self._prepare_data(results, args)
```

The method starts off by defining the criteria in exactly the same way as the other methods; however, the DOM structure is slightly different and some of the CSS names are also different:

- `weather-cell`: Contains the forecast date: `FriSEP 29`
- `temp`: Contains the temperature (high and low): `57°F48°F`
- `weather-phrase`: Contains the weather conditions: `Cloudy`
- `wind-conditions`: Wind information
- `humidity`: The humidity percentage

As you can see, to make it play nicely with the `_prepare_data` method, we will need to rename some keys in the dictionaries in the result set—`wind-conditions` should be `wind` and `weather-phrase` should be the `description`.

Luckily, we have introduced the `Mapper` class to help us out:

```
mapper = Mapper()
mapper.remap_key('wind-conditions', 'wind')
mapper.remap_key('weather-phrase', 'description')
```

We create a `Mapper` object and say, remap `wind-conditions` to `wind` and `weather-phrase` to `description`:

```
content = self._request.fetch_data(args.forecast_option.value,
                                   args.area_code)

bs = BeautifulSoup(content, 'html.parser')

forecast_data = bs.find('article', class_='ls-mod')
container = forecast_data.div.div

partial_results = self._parse(container, criteria)
```

We fetch all the data, create a `BeautifulSoup` object using the `html.parser`, and find the container element that contains the children elements that we are interested in. For the weekend forecast, we are interested in getting the `article` element with a CSS class called `ls-mod` and within that `article` we go down to the first child element, which is a DIV, and gets its first child element, which is also a DIV element.

The HTML should look something like this:

```
<article class='ls-mod'>
  <div>
    <div>
      <!-- this DIV will be our container element -->
    </div>
  </div>
</article>
```

That's the reason we first find the article, assign it to `forecast_data`, and then use `forecast_data.div.div` so we get the DIV element we want.

After defining the container, we pass it to the `_parse` method together with the container element; when we get the results back, we simply need to run the `remap` method of the `Mapper` instance, which will normalize the data for us before we call `_prepare_data`.

Now, the last detail before we run the application and get the weather forecast for the weekend is that we need to include the `--w` and `--weekend` flag to the `ArgumentParser`. Open the `__main__.py` file in the `weatherterm` directory and, just below the `--tenday` flag, add the following code:

```
argparser.add_argument('-w', '--weekend',
                       dest='forecast_option',
                       action='store_const',
                       const=ForecastType.WEEKEND,
                       help=('Shows the weather forecast for the
                             next or '
                             'current weekend'))
```

Great! Now, run the application using the -w or --weekend flag:

```
>> [Fri SEP 29]
   High 13.9° / Low 8.9° (Partly Cloudy)
   Wind: ESE 10 mph / Humidity: 79%

>> [Sat SEP 30]
   High 13.9° / Low 9.4° (Partly Cloudy)
   Wind: SE 10 mph / Humidity: 77%

>> [Sun OCT 1]
   High 12.8° / Low 10.6° (Cloudy)
   Wind: SE 14 mph / Humidity: 74%
```

Note that this time, I used the -u flag to choose Celsius. All the temperatures in the output are represented in Celsius instead of Fahrenheit.

Summary

In this chapter, you learned the basics of object-oriented programming in Python; we covered how to create classes, use inheritance, and use the @property decorators to create getter and setters.

We covered how to use the inspect module to get more information about modules, classes, and functions. Last but not least, we made use of the powerful package Beautifulsoup to parse HTML and Selenium to make requests to the weather website.

We also learned how to implement command line tools using the argparse module from Python's standard library, which allows us to provide tools that are easier to use and with very helpful documentation.

Next up, we are going to develop a small wrapper around the Spotify Rest API and use it to create a remote control terminal.

2
Creating a Remote-Control Application with Spotify

Spotify is a music streaming service that was developed in Stockholm, Sweden. The first version was released back in 2008 and today it doesn't only provide music, but video and podcasts as well. Growing rapidly from a startup in Sweden to the biggest music service in the world, Spotify has apps running on video game consoles and mobile phones, and has integration with many social networks.
The company really has changed how we consume music and has also enabled not only well-known artists but small indie artists to share their music with the world.

Luckily, Spotify is also a great platform for developers and provides a really nice and well-documented REST API where it's possible to make searches by artists, albums, song names, and also create and share playlists.

For the second application in this book, we are going to develop a terminal application where we can:

- Search artists
- Search albums
- Search tracks
- Play music

Apart from all these features, we are going to implement functions so we can control the Spotify application through the terminal.

First, we are going to go through the process of creating a new application on Spotify; then, it will be time to develop a small framework that will wrap some parts of Spotify's REST API. We are also going to work on implementing different types of authentication supported by Spotify, in order to consume its REST API.

When all these core functionalities are in place, we are going to develop a terminal user interface using the `curses` package that is distributed with Python.

In this chapter, you will learn:

- How to create a `Spotify` app
- How to use `OAuth`
- Object-oriented programming concepts
- Using the popular package `Requests` to consume REST APIs
- How to design terminal user interfaces using curses

I don't know about you, but I really feel like writing code and listening to some good music, so let's get right into it!

Setting up the environment

Let's go ahead and configure our development environment. The first thing we need to do is create a new virtual environment, so we can work and install the packages that we need without interfering with the global Python installation.

Our application will be called `musicterminal`, so we can create a virtual environment with the same name.

To create a new virtual environment, run the following command:

```
$ python3 -m venv musicterminal
```

Make sure that you are using Python 3.6 or later, otherwise the applications in this book may not work properly.

And to activate the virtual environment, you can run the following command:

```
$ . musicterminal/bin/activate
```

Perfect! Now that we have our virtual environment set up, we can create the project's directory structure. It should have the following structure:

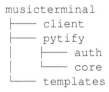

```
musicterminal
├── client
├── pytify
│   ├── auth
│   └── core
└── templates
```

Like the application in the first chapter, we create a project directory (called `musicterminal` here) and a sub-directory also named `pytify`, which will contain the framework wrapping Spotify's REST API.

Inside the framework directory, we split `auth` into two modules which will contain implementations for two authentication flows supported by Spotify—authorization code and client credentials. Finally, the `core` module will contain all the methods to fetch data from the REST API.

The client directory will contain all the scripts related to the client application that we are going to build.

Finally, the `templates` directory will contain some HTML files that will be used when we build a small Flask application to perform Spotify authentication.

Now, let's create a `requirements.txt` file inside the `musicterminal` directory with the following content:

```
requests==2.18.4
PyYAML==3.12
```

To install the dependencies, just run the following command:

```
$ pip install -r requirements.txt
```

```
daniel@musashi: ~/musicterminal                                    _ □ ✕
(musicterminal) musicterminal ❯ pip install -r requirements.txt
Collecting requests==2.18.4 (from -r requirements.txt (line 1))
  Using cached requests-2.18.4-py2.py3-none-any.whl
Collecting PyYAML==3.12 (from -r requirements.txt (line 2))
Collecting urllib3<1.23,>=1.21.1 (from requests==2.18.4->-r requirements.txt (line 1))
  Using cached urllib3-1.22-py2.py3-none-any.whl
Collecting certifi>=2017.4.17 (from requests==2.18.4->-r requirements.txt (line 1))
  Using cached certifi-2018.1.18-py2.py3-none-any.whl
Collecting chardet<3.1.0,>=3.0.2 (from requests==2.18.4->-r requirements.txt (line 1))
  Using cached chardet-3.0.4-py2.py3-none-any.whl
Collecting idna<2.7,>=2.5 (from requests==2.18.4->-r requirements.txt (line 1))
  Using cached idna-2.6-py2.py3-none-any.whl
Installing collected packages: urllib3, certifi, chardet, idna, requests, PyYAML
Successfully installed PyYAML-3.12 certifi-2018.1.18 chardet-3.0.4 idna-2.6 requests-2.18.4 urllib3-1.22
(musicterminal) musicterminal ❯
```

As you can see in the output, other packages have been installed in our virtual environment. The reason for this is that the packages that our project requires also require other packages, so they will also be installed.

Requests were created by Kenneth Reitz `https://www.kennethreitz.org/`, and it is one of the most used and beloved packages in the Python ecosystem. It is used by large companies such as Microsoft, Google, Mozilla, Spotify, Twitter, and Sony, just to name a few, and it is Pythonic and really straight-forward to use.

> Check out other projects from Kenneth, especially the `pipenv` project, which is an awesome Python packaging tool.
>
> Another module that we are going to use is curses. The curses module is simply a wrapper over the curses C functions and it is relatively simpler to use than programming in C. If you worked with the curses C library before, the curses module in Python should be familiar and easy to learn.
>
> One thing to note is that Python includes the curses module on Linux and Mac; however, it is not included by default on Windows. If you are running Windows, the curses documentation at `https://docs.python.org/3/howto/curses.html` recommends the UniCurses package developed by Fredrik Lundh.

Just one more thing before we start coding. You can run into problems when trying to import curses; the most common cause is that the `libncurses` are not installed in your system. Make sure that you have `libncurses` and `libncurses-dev` installed on your system before installing Python.

If you are using Linux, you will most likely find `libncurses` on the package repository of our preferred distribution. In Debian/Ubuntu, you can install it with the following command:

```
$ sudo apt-get install libncurses5 libncurses5-dev
```

Great! Now, we are all set to start implementing our application.

Creating a Spotify app

The first thing we need to do is create a Spotify app; after that, we are going to get access keys so we can authenticate and consume the REST API.

Head over to `https://beta.developer.spotify.com/dashboard/` and further down on the page you can find the Login button, and if you don't have an account, you can create a new one:

Create & manage your Spotify apps.

Meet your dashboard. Log in to create new apps and manage your Spotify credentials. Just connect Spotify Developer to your Spotify account.

LOG IN   Don't have an account? Sign up for a free Spotify account here.

 At the time of writing, Spotify started changing its developer's site and was currently in beta, so the address to log in and some screenshots may be different.

If you don't have a Spotify account, you will have to create one first. You should be able to create applications if you sign up for the free account, but I would recommend signing up for the premium account because it is a great service with a great music catalog.

When you log in to the Spotify developer website, you will see a page similar to the following:

At the moment, we don't have any application created (unless you have already created one), so go ahead and click on the **CREATE AN APP** button. A dialog screen to create the application will be displayed:

Here, we have three required fields: the application's name, description, and also some checkboxes where you will have to tell Spotify what you're building. The name should be `pytify` and in the description, you can put anything you want, but let's add something like `Application for controlling the Spotify client from the terminal`. The type of application we are building will be a website.

When you are done, click on the **NEXT** button at the bottom of the dialog screen.

The second step in the application's creation process is to inform Spotify whether you are creating a commercial integration. For the purposes of this book, we are going to select **NO**; however, if you are going to create an application that will monetize, you should definitely select **YES**.

In the next step, the following dialog will be displayed:

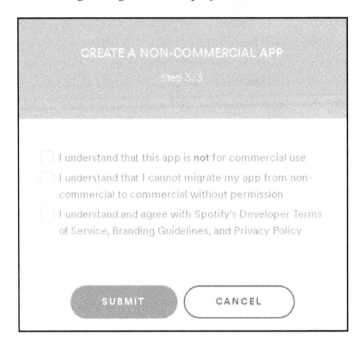

If you agree with all the conditions, just select all the checkboxes and click the **SUBMIT** button.

If the application has been created successfully, you will be redirected to the application's page, which is shown as follows:

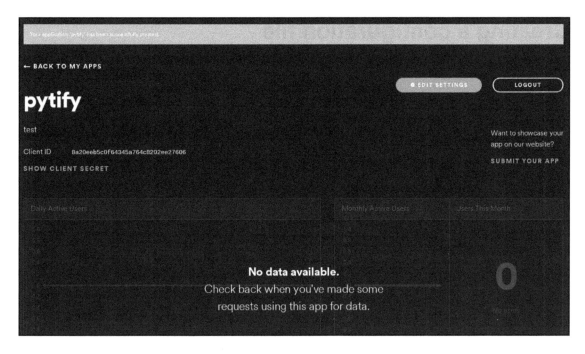

Click on the **SHOW CLIENT SECRET** link and copy the values of the Client ID and the Client Secret. We are going to need these keys to consume Spotify's REST API.

The application's configuration

To make the application more flexible and easy to configure, we are going to create a configuration file. This way, we don't need to hardcode the URL and access keys; also, if we need to change these settings, changes in the source code will not be required.
We are going to create a config file in the YAML format to store information that will be used by our application to authenticate, make requests to the Spotify RESP API endpoints, and so on.

Creating a configuration file

Let's go ahead and create a file called `config.yaml` in the `musicterminal` directory with the following contents:

```
client_id: '<your client ID>'
client_secret: '<your client secret>'
access_token_url: 'https://accounts.spotify.com/api/token'
auth_url: 'http://accounts.spotify.com/authorize'
api_version: 'v1'
api_url: 'https://api.spotify.com'
auth_method: 'AUTHORIZATION_CODE'
```

`client_id` and `client_secret` are the keys that were created for us when we created the Spotify application. These keys will be used to get an access token that we will have to acquire every time we need to send a new request to Spotify's REST API. Just replace the `<your client ID>` and `<your client secret>` with your own keys.

> Keep in mind that these keys have to be kept in a safe place. Don't share the keys with anyone and if you are having your project on sites like GitHub, make sure that you are not committing this configuration file with your secret keys. What I usually do is add the config file to my `.gitignore` file so it won't be source-controlled; otherwise, you can always commit the file as I did by presenting it with placeholders instead of the actual keys. That way, it will be easy to remember where you need to add the keys.

After the `client_id` and `client_secret` keys, we have the `access_token_url`. This is the URL to the API endpoint that we have to perform requests on in order to get the access token.

`auth_url` is the endpoint of Spotify's Account Service; we will use it when we need to acquire or refresh an authorization token.

The `api_version`, as the name says, specifies Spotify's REST API version. This is appended to the URL when performing requests.

Lastly, we have the `api_url`, which is the base URL for Spotify's REST API endpoints.

Implementing a configuration file reader

Before implementing the reader, we are going to add an enumeration to represent both kinds of authentication flow that Spotify provides us with. Let's go ahead and create a file called `auth_method.py` in the `musicterminal/pytify/auth` directory with the following content:

```
from enum import Enum, auto


class AuthMethod(Enum):
    CLIENT_CREDENTIALS = auto()
    AUTHORIZATION_CODE = auto()
```

This will define an enumeration with the `CLIENT_CREDENTIALS` and `AUTHORIZATION_CODE` properties. Now. we can use these values in the configuration file. Another thing we need to do is create a file called `__init__.py` in the `musicterminal/pytify/auth` directory and import the enumeration that we just created:

```
from .auth_method import AuthMethod
```

Now, we can continue and create the functions that will read the configuration for us. Create a file called `config.py` in the `musicterminal/pytify/core` directory, and let's start by adding some import statements:

```
import os
import yaml
from collections import namedtuple

from pytify.auth import AuthMethod
```

First, we import the `os` module so we can have access to functions that will help us in building the path where the YAML configuration file is located. We also import the `yaml` package to read the configuration file and, last but not least, we are importing `namedtuple` from the collections module. We will go into more detail about what `namedtuple` does later.

The last thing we import is the `AuthMethod` enumeration that we just created in the `pytify.auth` module.

Now, we need a model representing the configuration file, so we create a named tuple called `Config`, such as:

```
Config = namedtuple('Config', ['client_id',
                                'client_secret',
                                'access_token_url',
                                'auth_url',
                                'api_version',
                                'api_url',
                                'base_url',
                                'auth_method', ])
```

The `namedtuple` is not a new feature in Python and has been around since version 2.6. `namedtuple`'s are tuple-like objects with a name and with fields accessible by attribute lookup. It is possible to create `namedtuple` in two different ways; let's start Python REPL and try it out:

```
>>> from collections import namedtuple
>>> User = namedtuple('User', ['firstname', 'lastname', 'email'])
>>> u = User('Daniel','Furtado', 'myemail@test.com')
User(firstname='Daniel', lastname='Furtado', email='myemail@test.com')
>>>
```

This construct gets two arguments; the first argument is the name of the `namedtuple`, and the second is an array of `str` elements representing every field in the `namedtuple`. It is also possible to specify the fields of the `namedtuple` by passing a string with every field name separated by a space, such as:

```
>>> from collections import namedtuple
>>> User = namedtuple('User', 'firstname lastname email')
>>> u = User('Daniel', 'Furtado', 'myemail@test.com')
>>> print(u)
User(firstname='Daniel', lastname='Furtado', email='myemail@test.com')
```

The `namedtuple` constructor also has two keyword-arguments:

`Verbose`, which, when set to `True`, displays the definition of the class that defines the `namedtuple` on the terminal. Behind the scenes, `namedtuple`'s are classes and the `verbose` keyword argument lets us have a sneak peek at how the `namedtuple` class is constructed. Let's see this in practice on the REPL:

```
>>> from collections import namedtuple
>>> User = namedtuple('User', 'firstname lastname email',
verbose=True)
from builtins import property as _property, tuple as _tuple
from operator import itemgetter as _itemgetter
```

```
from collections import OrderedDict

class User(tuple):
    'User(firstname, lastname, email)'

    __slots__ = ()

    _fields = ('firstname', 'lastname', 'email')

    def __new__(_cls, firstname, lastname, email):
        'Create new instance of User(firstname, lastname, email)'
        return _tuple.__new__(_cls, (firstname, lastname, email))

    @classmethod
    def _make(cls, iterable, new=tuple.__new__, len=len):
        'Make a new User object from a sequence or iterable'
        result = new(cls, iterable)
        if len(result) != 3:
            raise TypeError('Expected 3 arguments, got %d' %
            len(result))
        return result

    def _replace(_self, **kwds):
        'Return a new User object replacing specified fields with
         new values'
        result = _self._make(map(kwds.pop, ('firstname',
'lastname',
                        'email'), _self))
        if kwds:
            raise ValueError('Got unexpected field names: %r' %
                            list(kwds))
        return result

    def __repr__(self):
        'Return a nicely formatted representation string'
        return self.__class__.__name__ + '(firstname=%r,
                                    lastname=%r, email=%r)'
        % self

    def _asdict(self):
        'Return a new OrderedDict which maps field names to their
         values.'
        return OrderedDict(zip(self._fields, self))

    def __getnewargs__(self):
        'Return self as a plain tuple. Used by copy and pickle.'
        return tuple(self)
```

```
firstname = _property(_itemgetter(0), doc='Alias for field
                        number 0')

lastname = _property(_itemgetter(1), doc='Alias for field
number
                                1')

email = _property(_itemgetter(2), doc='Alias for field number
                    2')
```

The other keyword argument is `rename`, which will rename every property in the `namedtuple` that has an incorrect naming, for example:

```
>>> from collections import namedtuple
>>> User = namedtuple('User', 'firstname lastname email 23445',
rename=True)
>>> User._fields
('firstname', 'lastname', 'email', '_3')
```

As you can see, the field `23445` has been automatically renamed to `_3`, which is the field position.

To access the `namedtuple` fields, you can use the same syntax when accessing properties in a class, using the `namedtuple` —User as shown in the preceding example. If we would like to access the `lastname` property, we can just write `u.lastname`.

Now that we have the `namedtuple` representing our configuration file, it is time to add the function that will perform the work of loading the YAML file and returning the `namedtuple`—Config. In the same file, let's implement the `read_config` function as follows:

```
def read_config():
    current_dir = os.path.abspath(os.curdir)
    file_path = os.path.join(current_dir, 'config.yaml')

    try:
        with open(file_path, mode='r', encoding='UTF-8') as file:
            config = yaml.load(file)

            config['base_url'] =
            f'{config["api_url"]}/{config["api_version"]}'

            auth_method = config['auth_method']
            config['auth_method'] =
            AuthMethod.__members__.get(auth_method)
```

```
        return Config(**config)

except IOError as e:
    print(""" Error: couldn''t file the configuration file
    `config.yaml`
    'on your current directory.

    Default format is:',

    client_id: 'your_client_id'
    client_secret: 'you_client_secret'
    access_token_url: 'https://accounts.spotify.com/api/token'
    auth_url: 'http://accounts.spotify.com/authorize'
    api_version: 'v1'
    api_url: 'http//api.spotify.com'
    auth_method: 'authentication method'

    * auth_method can be CLIENT_CREDENTIALS or
      AUTHORIZATION_CODE""")
    raise
```

The `read_config` function starts off by using the `os.path.abspath` function to get the absolute path of the current directory, and assigns it to the `current_dir` variable. Then, we join the path stored on the `current_dir` variable with the name of the file, in this case, the YAML configuration file.

inside the `try` statement, we try to open the file as read-only and set the encoding to UTF-8. In the event this fails, it will print a help message to the user saying that it couldn't open the file and will show help describing how the YAML configuration file is structured.

If the configuration file can be read successfully, we call the load function in the `yaml` module to load and parse the file, and assign the results to the `config` variable. We also include an extra item in the config called `base_url`, which is just a helper value that contains the concatenated values of `api_url` and `api_version`.

The value of the `base_url` will look something like this: `https://api.spotify.com/v1`.

Lastly, we create an instance of `Config`. Note how we spread the values in the constructor; this is possible because the `namedtuple`—`Config`, has the same fields as the object returned by `yaml.load()`. This would be exactly the same as doing this:

```
        return Config(
            client_id=config['client_id'],
            client_secret=config['client_secret'],
```

```
access_token_url=config['access_token_url'],
auth_url=config['auth_url'],
api_version=config['api_version'],
api_url=config['api_url'],
base_url=config['base_url'],
auth_method=config['auth_method'])
```

The final touch here is to create a __init__.py file in the pytify/core directory and import the read_config function that we just created:

```
from .config import read_config
```

Authenticating with Spotify's web API

Now that we have the code to load the configuration file for us, we are going to start coding the authentication part of our framework. Spotify currently supports three kinds of authentication: authorization code, client credentials, and implicitly grant. We are going to implement authorization code and client credentials in this chapter, and we will start by implementing the client credentials flow, which is the easiest to start with.

The client credentials flow has some disadvantages over the authorization code flow because the flow does not include authorization and cannot access the user's private data as well as control playback. We will implement and use this flow for now, but we will change to authorization code when we start implementing the terminal player.

First, we are going to create a file called authorization.py in the musicterminal/pytify/auth directory with the following contents:

```
from collections import namedtuple


Authorization = namedtuple('Authorization', [
    'access_token',
    'token_type',
    'expires_in',
    'scope',
    'refresh_token',
])
```

This is going to be the authentication model and it will contain the data we get after requesting an access token. In the following list, you can see a description of every property:

- `access_token`: The token that has to be sent together with every request to the Web API
- `token_type`: The type of the token, which is usually `Bearer`
- `expires_in`: The `access_token` expiration time, which is 3600 seconds (1 hour)
- `scope`: The scope is basically the permissions that Spotify's user granted to our application
- `refresh_token`: The token that can be used to refresh the `access_token` after the expiration

The last touch is to create a `__init__.py` file in the `musicterminal/pytify/auth` directory and import the `Authorization`, which is a `namedtuple`:

```
from .authorization import Authorization
```

Implementing the client credentials flow

The client credential flow is quite simple. Let's break down all the steps until we get the `access_token`:

1. Our application will request the access token from the Spotify accounts service; remember that in our configuration file, we have the `api_access_token`. That's the URL we need to send the request to get hold of an access token. There are three things that we will need to send the request, the client id, the client secret, and the grant type, which in this case is `client_credentials`.
2. The Spotify account service will validate that request, check if the keys match with the keys of the app that we register to the developer's site, and return an access token.
3. Now, our application has to use this access token in order to consume data from the REST APIs.
4. The Spotify REST API will return the data we requested.

Before we start implementing the functions that will make the authentication and get the access token, we can add a custom exception that we will throw if we get a bad request (HTTP `400`) from the Spotify account service.

Let's create a file named `exceptions.py` in the `musicterminal/pytify/core` directory with the following contents:

```
class BadRequestError(Exception):
    pass
```

This class doesn't do much; we simply inherit from `Exception`. We could have just thrown a generic exception, but it is a good practice to create your own custom exceptions with good names and descriptions when developing frameworks and libraries that other developers will make use of.

So, instead of throwing an exception like this:

```
raise Exception('some message')
```

We can be more explicit and throw a `BadRequestError`, like so:

```
raise BadRequestError('some message')
```

Now, developers using this code can handle this kind of exception properly in their code.

Open the `__init__.py` file in the `musicterminal/pytify/core` directory and add the following import statement:

```
from .exceptions import BadRequestError
```

Perfect! Now, it is time to add a new file called `auth.py` in the `musicterminal/pytify/auth` directory, and the first thing we are going to add to this file is a few imports:

```
import requests
import base64
import json

from .authorization import Authorization
from pytify.core import BadRequestError
```

 I usually put all the imports from standard library modules first and function imports in files from my applications last. It is not a requirement, but it is just something I think makes the code cleaner and more organized. This way, I can easily see which are standard library items and which aren't.

Now, we can start adding the functions that will send the request the to the Spotify account service and return the access token. The first function that we are going to add is called get_auth_key:

```
def get_auth_key(client_id, client_secret):
    byte_keys = bytes(f'{client_id}:{client_secret}', 'utf-8')
    encoded_key = base64.b64encode(byte_keys)
    return encoded_key.decode('utf-8')
```

The client credential flow requires us to send the client_id and the client_secret, which has to be base 64-encoded. First, we convert the string with the client_id:client_secret format to bytes. After that, we encode it using base 64 and then decode it, returning the string representation of that encoded data so we can send it with the request payload.

The other function that we are going to implement in the same file is called _client_credentials:

```
def _client_credentials(conf):

    auth_key = get_auth_key(conf.client_id, conf.client_secret)

    headers = {'Authorization': f'Basic {auth_key}', }

    options = {
        'grant_type': 'client_credentials',
        'json': True,
    }

    response = requests.post(
        'https://accounts.spotify.com/api/token',
        headers=headers,
        data=options
    )

    content = json.loads(response.content.decode('utf-8'))

    if response.status_code == 400:
        error_description = content.get('error_description','')
        raise BadRequestError(error_description)
    access_token = content.get('access_token', None)
    token_type = content.get('token_type', None)
    expires_in = content.get('expires_in', None)
    scope = content.get('scope', None)
    return Authorization(access_token, token_type, expires_in,
    scope, None)
```

This function gets an argument as the configuration and uses the `get_auth_key` function to pass the `client_id` and the `client_secret` to build a base 64-encoded `auth_key`. This will be sent to Spotify's accounts service to request an `access_token`.

Now, it is time to prepare the request. First, we set the `Authorization` in the request header, and the value will be the `Basic` string followed by the `auth_key`. The payload for this request will be `grant_type`, which in this case is `client_credentials`, and `json` will be set to `True`, which tells the API that we want the response in JSON format.

We use the requests package to make the request to Spotify's account service, passing the headers and the data that we configured.

When we get a response, we first decode and load the JSON data into the variable content.

If the HTTP status code is `400` `(BAD_REQUEST)` we raise a `BadRequestError`; otherwise, we get the values for `access_token`, `token_type`, `expires_in`, and `scope`, and finally create an `Authorization` tuple and return it.

 Note that we are setting `None` to the last parameter when creating an `Authentication, namedtuple`. The reason for this is that Spotify's account service doesn't return a `refresh_token` when the type of authentication is `CLIENT_CREDENTIALS`.

All the functions that we have created so far are meant to be private, so the last function that we are going to add is the `authenticate` function. This is the function that developers will invoke to start the authentication process:

```
def authenticate(conf):
    return _client_credentials(conf)
```

This function is pretty straightforward; the function gets an argument as an instance of the `Config, namedtuple`, which will contain all the data that has been read from the configuration file. We then pass the configuration to the `_client_credentials` function, which will obtain the `access_token` using the client credentials flow.

Let's open the `__init__.py` file in the `musicterminal/pytify/auth` directory and import the `authenticate` and `get_auth_key` functions:

```
from .auth import authenticate
from .auth import get_auth_key
```

Nice! Let's try this out in the Python REPL:

```
Python 3.6.2 (default, Oct 15 2017, 01:15:28)
[GCC 6.3.0 20170516] on linux
Type "help", "copyright", "credits" or "license" for more information.
>>> from pytify.core import read_config
>>> from pytify.auth import authenticate
>>> config = read_config()
>>> auth = authenticate(config)
>>> auth
Authorization(access_token='BQDM_DC2HcP9kq5iszgDwhgDvq7zm1TzvzXXyJQwFD7trl0
Q48DqoZirCMrMHn2uUml2YnKdHOszAviSFGtE6w', token_type='Bearer',
expires_in=3600, scope=None, refresh_token=None)
>>>
```

Exactly what we expected! The next step is to start creating the functions that will consume Spotify's REST API.

Implementing the authorization code flow

In this section, we are going to implement the authorization code flow, which we will be using in the client. We need to use this authentication flow because we need to acquire special access rights from the user using our application to execute certain actions. For instance, our application will have to be able to send a request to Spotify's Web API to play a certain track on the user's active device. In order to do that, we need to request `user-modify-playback-state`.

Here are the steps involved in the authorization code flow:

1. Our application will request authorization to access data, redirecting the user to a login page on Spotify's web page. There, the user can see all the access rights that the application requires.
2. If the user approves it, the Spotify account service will send a request to the callback URI, sending a code and the state.
3. When we get hold of the code, we send a new request passing the `client_id`, `client_secret`, `grant_type`, and `code` to acquire the `access_token`. This time, it will be different from the client credentials flow; we are going to get `scope` and a `refresh_token`
4. Now, we can normally send requests to the Web API and if the access token has expired, we can do another request to refresh the access token and continue performing requests.

With that said, open the `auth.py` file in the `musicterminal/pytify/auth` directory and let's add a few more functions. First, we are going to add a function called `_refresh_access_token`; you can add this function after the `get_auth_key` function:

```python
def _refresh_access_token(auth_key, refresh_token):

    headers = {'Authorization': f'Basic {auth_key}', }

    options = {
        'refresh_token': refresh_token,
        'grant_type': 'refresh_token',
        }

    response = requests.post(
        'https://accounts.spotify.com/api/token',
        headers=headers,
        data=options
    )

    content = json.loads(response.content.decode('utf-8'))

    if not response.ok:
        error_description = content.get('error_description', None)
        raise BadRequestError(error_description)

    access_token = content.get('access_token', None)
    token_type = content.get('token_type', None)
    scope = content.get('scope', None)
    expires_in = content.get('expires_in', None)

    return Authorization(access_token, token_type, expires_in,
    scope, None)
```

It basically does the same thing as the function handling the client credentials flow, but this time we send the `refresh_token` and the `grant_type`. We get the data from the response's object and create an `Authorization`, `namedtuple`.

The next function that we are going to implement will make use of the `os` module of the standard library, so before we start with the implementation, we need to add the following import statement at the top of the `auth.py` file:

```python
import os
```

Now, we can go ahead and add a function called _authorization_code. You can add this function after the get_auth_key function with the following contents:

```
def _authorization_code(conf):

    current_dir = os.path.abspath(os.curdir)
    file_path = os.path.join(current_dir, '.pytify')

    auth_key = get_auth_key(conf.client_id, conf.client_secret)

    try:
        with open(file_path, mode='r', encoding='UTF-8') as file:
            refresh_token = file.readline()
            if refresh_token:
                return _refresh_access_token(auth_key,
                    refresh_token)

    except IOError:
        raise IOError(('It seems you have not authorize the
                        application '
                       'yet. The file .pytify was not found.'))
```

Here, we try opening a file called .pytify in the musicterminal directory. This file will contain the refresh_token that we are going to use to refresh the access_token every time we open our application.

After getting the refresh_token from the file, we pass it to the _refresh_access_token function, together with the auth_key. If for some reason we are unable to open the file or the file does not exist in the musicterminal directory, an exception will be raised.

The last modification we need to do now is in the authenticate function in the same file. We are going to add support for both authentication methods; it should look like this:

```
def authenticate(conf):
    if conf.auth_method == AuthMethod.CLIENT_CREDENTIALS:
        return _client_credentials(conf)

    return _authorization_code(conf)
```

Now, we will start different authentication methods depending on what we have specified in the configuration file.

Since the authentication function has a reference to AuthMethod, we need to import it:

```
from .auth_method import AuthMethod
```

Before we try this type of authentication out, we need to create a small web app that will authorize our application for us. We are going to work on that in the next section.

Authorizing our application with authorization code flow

In order to make our Spotify terminal client work properly, we need special access rights to manipulate the user's playback. We do that by using the authorization code and we need to specifically request for the `user-modify-playback-state` access right.

There are a few more access rights which would be a good idea to add from the beginning if you intend to add more functionalities to this application; for example, if you want to be able to manipulate a user's private and public playlists, you may want to add the `playlist-modify-private` and `playlist-modify-public` scope.

You might also want to display a list of artists that the user follows on the client application, so you need to include `user-follow-read` to the scope as well.

It will suffice to request `user-modify-playback-state` access rights for the functionalities that we are going to implement in the client application.

The idea is to authorize our application using the authorization code flow. We are going to create a simple web application using the framework Flask that will define two routes. The / root will just render a simple page with a link that will redirect us to the Spotify authentication page.

The second root will be `/callback`, which is the endpoint that Spotify will call after the users of our application give authorization for our application to access their Spotify data.

Let's see how this is implemented, but first, we need to install Flask. Open a terminal and type the following command:

```
pip install flask
```

After you have installed it you can even include it in the `requirements.txt` file such as:

```
$ pip freeze | grep Flask >> requirements.txt
```

The command `pip freeze` will print all the installed packages in the requirements format. The output will return more items because it will also contain all the dependencies of the packages that we already installed, which is why we grep `Flask` and append it to the `requirements.txt` file.

Next time you are going to set up a virtual environment to work on this project you can just run:

```
pip install -r requirements.txt
```

Great! Now, we can start creating the web application. Create a file called spotify_auth.py.

First, we add all necessary imports:

```
from urllib.parse import urlencode

import requests
import json

from flask import Flask
from flask import render_template
from flask import request

from pytify.core import read_config
from pytify.core import BadRequestError
from pytify.auth import Authorization
from pytify.auth import get_auth_key
```

We are going to use the urlencode function in the urllib.parse module to encode the parameters that are going to be appended to the authorize URL. We are also going to use the requests to send a request to get the access_token after the user authorizes our app and use the json package to parse the response.
Then, we will import Flask-related things, so we can create a Flask application, render_template, so we can return a rendered HTML template to the user, and finally the request, so we can access the data sent back to us by Spotify's authorization service.

We will also import some functions that we included in the core and auth submodules of the pytify module: the read_config to load and read the YAML config file and the _authorization_code_request. The latter will be explained in more detail in a short while.

We will create a Flask app and the root route:

```
app = Flask(__name__)


@app.route("/")
def home():
```

```
config = read_config()

params = {
    'client_id': config.client_id,
    'response_type': 'code',
    'redirect_uri': 'http://localhost:3000/callback',
    'scope': 'user-read-private user-modify-playback-state',
}

enc_params = urlencode(params)
url = f'{config.auth_url}?{enc_params}'

return render_template('index.html', link=url)
```

Great! Starting from the top, we read the configuration file so we can get our `client_id` and also the URL for Spotify's authorization service. We build the parameters dictionary with the `client_id`; the response type for the authorization code flow needs to be set to `code`; the `redirect_uri` is the callback URI which Spotify's authorization service will use to send us the authorization code back. And finally, since we are going to send instructions to the REST API to play a track in the user's active device, the application needs to have `user-modify-playback-state` permissions.

Now, we encode all the parameters and build the URL.

The return value will be a rendered HTML. Here, we will use the `render_template` function, passing a template as a first argument. By default, Flask will search this template in a directory called `templates`. The second argument to this function is the model. We are passing a property named `link` and setting the value of the variable URL. This way, we can render the link in the HTML template such as: `{{link}}`.

Next, we are going to add a function to acquire the `access_token` and the `refresh_token` for us after we get the authorization code back from Spotify's account service. Create a function called `_authorization_code_request` with the following content:

```
def _authorization_code_request(auth_code):
    config = read_config()

    auth_key = get_auth_key(config.client_id, config.client_secret)

    headers = {'Authorization': f'Basic {auth_key}', }

    options = {
        'code': auth_code,
        'redirect_uri': 'http://localhost:3000/callback',
```

```
        'grant_type': 'authorization_code',
        'json': True
    }

    response = requests.post(
        config.access_token_url,
        headers=headers,
        data=options
    )

    content = json.loads(response.content.decode('utf-8'))

    if response.status_code == 400:
        error_description = content.get('error_description', '')
        raise BadRequestError(error_description)

    access_token = content.get('access_token', None)
    token_type = content.get('token_type', None)
    expires_in = content.get('expires_in', None)
    scope = content.get('scope', None)
    refresh_token = content.get('refresh_token', None)
    return Authorization(access_token, token_type, expires_in,
    scope, refresh_token)
```

This function is pretty much the same as the _refresh_access_token function that we previously implemented in the auth.py file. The only thing to note here is that in the options, we are passing the authorization code, and the grant_type is set to authorization_code:

```
@app.route('/callback')
def callback():
    config = read_config()
    code = request.args.get('code', '')
    response = _authorization_code_request(config, code)

    file = open('.pytify', mode='w', encoding='utf-8')
    file.write(response.refresh_token)
    file.close()

    return 'All set! You can close the browser window and stop the
    server.'
```

Here, we define the route that will be called by Spotify's authorization service to send back the authorization code.

We start off by reading the configuration, parsing the code from the request data, and calling the _authorization_code_request, passing the code we have just obtained.

This function will send another request using this code, and it will acquire an access token that we can use to send requests, along with a refresh token that will be stored in a file called .pytify in the musicterminal directory.

The access token that we obtain to make the requests to the Spotify REST API is valid for 3,600 seconds, or 1 hour, which means that within one hour, we can use the same access token to make requests. After that, we need to refresh the access token. We can do that by using the refresh token that is stored in the .pytify file.

Lastly, we send a message to the browser with a success message.

Now, to finish our Flask application, we need to add the following code:

```
if __name__ == '__main__':
    app.run(host='localhost', port=3000)
```

This tells Flask to run the server on the localhost and use port 3000.

The home function of our Flash application will, as a response, return a templated HTML file called index.html. We haven't created that file yet, so let's go ahead and create a folder called musicterminal/templates and inside the newly created directory, add a file called index.html with the following contents:

```
<html>
    <head>
    </head>
    <body>
        <a href={{link}}> Click here to authorize </a>
    </body>
</html>
```

There's not much to explain here, but note that we are referencing the link property that we passed to the render_template function in the home function of the Flask application. We are setting the href attribute of that anchor element to the value of the link.

Great! There is only more thing before we try this out and see if everything is working properly. We need to change the settings of our Spotify app; more specifically, we need to configure the callback function for the application, so we can receive the authorization code.

With that said, head to the https://beta.developer.spotify.com/dashboard/ website and log in with your credentials. The dashboard will show the pytify app that we created at the beginning of this chapter. Click on the app name and then click on the **EDIT SETTINGS** button on the top right of the page.

Scroll down until you find **Redirect URIs**, and in the text field, enter http://localhost:3000/callback and click on the ADD button. Your configuration should look as follows:

Great! Scroll down to the bottom of the dialog and click the **SAVE** button.

Now, we need to run the Flask application that we just created. On the terminal, in the projects root folder, type the following command:

```
python spotify_auth.py
```

You should see an output similar to this:

```
* Running on http://localhost:3000/ (Press CTRL+C to quit)
```

Open the browser of your choice and go to `http://localhost:3000`; you will see a simple page with the link that we created:

Click on the link and you will be sent to Spotify's authorization service page.

A dialog will be displayed asking to connect the `Pytify` app to our account. Once you authorize it, you will be redirected back to `http://localhost:3000/callback`. If everything goes well, you should see the **All set! You can close the browser window and stop the server** message on the page.

Now, just close the browser, and you can stop the Flask application.

Note that we now have a file named `.pytify` in the `musicterminal` directory. If you look at the contents, you will have an encrypted key similar to this one:

```
AQB2jJxziOvuj1VW_DOBeJh-
uYWUYaR03nWEJncKdRsgZC6ql2vaUsVpo21afco09yM4tjwgt6Kkb_XnVC50CR0SdjW
rrbMnr01zdemN0vVVHmrcr_6iMxCQSk-JM5yTjg4
```

Now, we are ready to start coding the player.

Next up, we are going to add some functions that will perform requests to Spotify's Web API to search for artists, get a list of an artist's albums and a list of tracks in an album, and play the selected track.

Querying Spotify's web API

So far, we have only prepared the terrain and now things start to get a bit more interesting. In this section, we are going to create the basic functions to send requests to Spotify's Web API; more specifically, we want to be able to search for an artist, get an artist's list of albums, get a list of tracks in that album, and finally we want to send a request to actually play a given track in Spotify's client that is currently active. It can be the browser, a mobile phone, Spotify's client, or even video game consoles. So, let's dive right into it!

To start off, we are going to create a file called `request_type.py` in the `musicterminal/pytify/core` directory with the following contents:

```python
from enum import Enum, auto


class RequestType(Enum):
    GET = auto()
    PUT = auto()
```

We have gone through enumerations before, so we won't be going into so much detail. It suffices to say that we create an enumeration with GET and PUT properties. This will be used to notify the function that performs the requests for us that we want to do a GET request or a PUT request.

Then, we can create another file named request.py in the same musicterminal/pytify/core directory, and we start by adding a few import statements and defining a function called execute_request:

```python
import requests
import json

from .exceptions import BadRequestError
from .config import read_config
from .request_type import RequestType


def execute_request(
        url_template,
        auth,
        params,
        request_type=RequestType.GET,
        payload=()):
```

This function gets a few arguments:

- url_template: This is the template that will be used to build the URL to perform the request; it will use another argument called params to build the URL
- auth: Is the Authorization object
- params: It is a dict containing all the parameters that will be placed into the URL that we are going to perform the request on
- request: This is the request type; it can be GET or PUT
- payload: This is the data that may be sent together with the request

As we continue to implement the same function, we can add:

```python
conf = read_config()

params['base_url'] = conf.base_url

url = url_template.format(**params)

headers = {
    'Authorization': f'Bearer {auth.access_token}'
```

```
    }
```

We read the configuration and add the base URL to the params so it is replaced in the `url_template` string. We add `Authorization` in the request headers, together with the authentication access token:

```
if request_type is RequestType.GET:
    response = requests.get(url, headers=headers)
else:
    response = requests.put(url, headers=headers,
data=json.dumps(payload))

    if not response.text:
        return response.text

result = json.loads(response.text)
```

Here, we check if the request type is `GET`. If so, we execute the `get` function from requests; otherwise, we execute the `put` function. The function calls are very similar; the only thing that differs here is the data argument. If the response returned is empty, we just return the empty string; otherwise, we parse the JSON data into the `result` variable:

```
if not response.ok:
    error = result['error']
    raise BadRequestError(
        f'{error["message"]} (HTTP {error["status"]})')

return result
```

After parsing the JSON result, we test whether the status of the request is not 200 (OK); in that case, we raise a `BadRequestError`. If it is a successful response, we return the results.

We also need some functions to help us prepare the parameters that we are going to pass to the Web API endpoints. Let's go ahead and create a file called `parameter.py` in the `musicterminal/pytify/core` folder with the following contents:

```
from urllib.parse import urlencode


def validate_params(params, required=None):

    if required is None:
        return

    partial = {x: x in params.keys() for x in required}
    not_supplied = [x for x in partial.keys() if not partial[x]]
```

```
        if not_supplied:
            msg = f'The parameter(s) `{", ".join(not_supplied)}` are
            required'
            raise AttributeError(msg)


    def prepare_params(params, required=None):

        if params is None and required is not None:
            msg = f'The parameter(s) `{", ".join(required)}` are
            required'
            raise ValueErrorAttributeError(msg)
        elif params is None and required is None:
            return ''
        else:
            validate_params(params, required)

        query = urlencode(
            '&'.join([f'{key}={value}' for key, value in
            params.items()])
        )

        return f'?{query}'
```

We have two functions here, `prepare_params` and `validate_params`. The `validate_params` function is used to identify whether there are parameters that are required for a certain operation, but they haven't been supplied. The `prepare_params` function first calls `validate_params` to make sure that all the parameters have been supplied and to also join all the parameters together so they can be easily appended to the URL query string.

Now, let's add an enumeration with the types of searches that can be performed. Create a file called `search_type.py` in the `musicterminal/pytify/core` directory with the following contents:

```
    from enum import Enum


    class SearchType(Enum):
        ARTIST = 1
        ALBUM = 2
        PLAYLIST = 3
        TRACK = 4
```

This is just a simple enumeration with the four search options.

Now, we are ready to create the function to perform the search. Create a file called search.py in the musicterminal/pytify/core directory:

```python
import requests
import json
from urllib.parse import urlencode

from .search_type import SearchType
from pytify.core import read_config


def _search(criteria, auth, search_type):

    conf = read_config()

    if not criteria:
        raise AttributeError('Parameter `criteria` is required.')

    q_type = search_type.name.lower()
    url = urlencode(f'{conf.base_url}/search?q={criteria}&type=
    {q_type}')

    headers = {'Authorization': f'Bearer {auth.access_token}'}
    response = requests.get(url, headers=headers)

    return json.loads(response.text)


def search_artist(criteria, auth):
    return _search(criteria, auth, SearchType.ARTIST)


def search_album(criteria, auth):
    return _search(criteria, auth, SearchType.ALBUM)


def search_playlist(criteria, auth):
    return _search(criteria, auth, SearchType.PLAYLIST)


def search_track(criteria, auth):
    return _search(criteria, auth, SearchType.TRACK)
```

We start by explaining the `_search` function. This function gets three criteria parameters (what we want to search for), the `Authorization` object, and lastly the search type, which is a value in the enumeration that we just created.

The function is quite simple; we start by validating the parameters, then we build the URL to make the request, we set the `Authorization` head using our access token, and lastly, we perform the request and return the parsed response.

The other functions `search_artist`, `search_album`, `search_playlist`, and `search_track` simply get the same arguments, the criteria and the `Authorization` object, and pass it to the `_search` function, but they pass different search types.

Now that we can search for an artist, we have to get a list of albums. Add a file called `artist.py` in the `musicterminal/pytify/core` directory with the following contents:

```
from .parameter import prepare_params
from .request import execute_request


def get_artist_albums(artist_id, auth, params=None):

    if artist_id is None or artist_id is "":
        raise AttributeError(
            'Parameter `artist_id` cannot be `None` or empty.')

    url_template = '{base_url}/{area}/{artistid}/{postfix}{query}'
    url_params = {
        'query': prepare_params(params),
        'area': 'artists',
        'artistid': artist_id,
        'postfix': 'albums',
        }

    return execute_request(url_template, auth, url_params)
```

So, given an `artist_id`, we just define the URL template and parameters that we want to make the request and run the `execute_request` function which will take care of building the URL, getting and parsing the results for us.

Now, we want to get a list of the tracks for a given album. Add a file called `album.py` in the `musicterminal/pytify/core` directory with the following contents:

```python
from .parameters import prepare_params
from .request import execute_request


def get_album_tracks(album_id, auth, params=None):

    if album_id is None or album_id is '':
        raise AttributeError(
            'Parameter `album_id` cannot be `None` or empty.')

    url_template = '{base_url}/{area}/{albumid}/{postfix}{query}'
    url_params = {
        'query': prepare_params(params),
        'area': 'albums',
        'albumid': album_id,
        'postfix': 'tracks',
        }

    return execute_request(url_template, auth, url_params)
```

The `get_album_tracks` function is very similar to the `get_artist_albums` function that we just implemented.

Finally, we want to be able to send an instruction to Spotify's Web API, telling it to play a track that we selected. Add a file called `player.py` in the `musicterminal/pytify/core` directory, and add the following contents:

```python
from .parameter import prepare_params
from .request import execute_request

from .request_type import RequestType


def play(track_uri, auth, params=None):

    if track_uri is None or track_uri is '':
        raise AttributeError(
            'Parameter `track_uri` cannot be `None` or empty.')

    url_template = '{base_url}/{area}/{postfix}'
    url_params = {
        'query': prepare_params(params),
        'area': 'me',
        'postfix': 'player/play',
```

```
        }

    payload = {
        'uris': [track_uri],
        'offset': {'uri': track_uri}
    }

    return execute_request(url_template,
                           auth,
                           url_params,
                           request_type=RequestType.PUT,
                           payload=payload)
```

This function is also very similar to the previous ones (`get_artist_albums` and `get_album_tracks`), except that it defines a payload. A payload is a dictionary containing two items: `uris`, which is a list of tracks that should be added to the playback queue, and `offset`, which contains another dictionary with the URIs of tracks that should be played first. Since we are interested in only playing one song at a time, `uris` and `offset` will contain the same `track_uri`.

The final touch here is to import the new function that we implemented. In the __init__.py file at the `musicterminal/pytify/core` directory, add the following code:

```
    from .search_type import SearchType

    from .search import search_album
    from .search import search_artist
    from .search import search_playlist
    from .search import search_track

    from .artist import get_artist_albums
    from .album import get_album_tracks
    from .player import play
```

Let's try the function to search artists in the python REPL to check whether everything is working properly:

```
Python 3.6.2 (default, Dec 22 2017, 15:38:46)
[GCC 6.3.0 20170516] on linux
Type "help", "copyright", "credits" or "license" for more information.
>>> from pytify.core import search_artist
>>> from pytify.core import read_config
>>> from pytify.auth import authenticate
>>> from pprint import pprint as pp
>>>
>>> config = read_config()
```

```
>>> auth = authenticate(config)
>>> results = search_artist('hot water music', auth)
>>> pp(results)
{'artists': {'href':
'https://api.spotify.com/v1/search?query=hot+water+music&type=artist&market
=SE&offset=0&limit=20',
               'items': [{'external_urls': {'spotify':
'https://open.spotify.com/artist/4dmaYARGTCpChLhHBdr3ff'},
                       'followers': {'href': None, 'total': 56497},
                       'genres': ['alternative emo',
                                  'emo',
                                  'emo punk',
```

The rest of the output has been omitted because it was too long, but now we can see that everything is working just as expected.

Now, we are ready to start building the terminal player.

Creating the player

Now that we have everything we need to authenticate and consume the Spotify Rest API, we are going to create a small terminal client where we can search for an artist, browse his/her albums, and select a track to play in the Spotify client. Note that to use the client, we will have to issue an access token from a premium account and the authentication flow we need to use here is the AUTHENTICATION_CODE.

We will also need to require from the user of our application the user-modify-playback-state scope, which will allow us to control playback. With that said, let's get right into it!

First, we need to create a new directory to keep all the client's related files in it, so go ahead and create a directory named musicterminal/client.

Our client will only have three views. In the first view, we are going to get the user input and search for an artist. When the artist search is complete, we are going to switch to the second view, where a list of albums for the selected artist will be presented. In this view, the user will be able to select an album on the list using the keyboard's *Up* and *Down* arrow keys and select an album by hitting the *Enter* key.

Lastly, when an album is selected, we are going to switch to the third and final view on our application, where the user will see a list of tracks for the selected album. Like the previous view, the user will also be able to select a track using the keyboard's *Up* and *Down* arrow key; hitting *Enter* will send a request to the Spotify API to play the selected track on the user's available devices.

One approach is to use `curses.panel`. Panels are a kind of window and they are very flexible, allowing us to stack, hide and show, and switch panels, go back to the top of the stack of panels, and so on, which is perfect for our purposes.

So, let's create a file inside the `musicterminal/client` directory called `panel.py` with the following contents:

```python
import curses
import curses.panel
from uuid import uuid1


class Panel:

    def __init__(self, title, dimensions):
        height, width, y, x = dimensions

        self._win = curses.newwin(height, width, y, x)
        self._win.box()
        self._panel = curses.panel.new_panel(self._win)
        self.title = title
        self._id = uuid1()

        self._set_title()

        self.hide()
```

All we do here is import the modules and functions we need and create a class called `Panel`. We are also importing the `uuid` module so we can create a GUID for every new panel.

The Panel's initializer gets two arguments: `title`, which is the title of the window, and `dimensions`. The `dimensions` argument is a tuple and follows the curses convention. It is composed of `height`, `width`, and the positions `y` and `x`, where the panel should start to be drawn.

We unpack the values of the `dimensions` tuple so it is easier to work with and then we use the `newwin` function to create a new window; it will have the same dimensions that we passed in the class initializer. Next, we call the box function to draw lines on the four sides of the terminal.

Now that we have the window created, it is time to create the panel for the window that we just created, calling `curses.panel.new_panel` and passing the window. We also set the window title and create a GUID.

Lastly, we set the state of the panel to hidden. Continuing working on this class, let's add a new method called `hide`:

```
def hide(self):
    self._panel.hide()
```

This method is quite simple; the only thing that it does is call the `hide` method in our panel.

The other method that we call in the initializer is `_set_title`; let's create it now:

```
def _set_title(self):
    formatted_title = f' {self._title} '
    self._win.addstr(0, 2, formatted_title, curses.A_REVERSE)
```

In `_set_title`, we format the title by adding some extra padding on both sides of the title string, and then we call the `addstr` method of the window to print the title in row zero, column two, and we use the constant A_REVERSE, which will invert the colors of the string, like this:

We have a method to hide the panel; now, we need a method to show the panel. Let's add the `show` method:

```
def show(self):
    self._win.clear()
    self._win.box()
    self._set_title()
    curses.curs_set(0)
    self._panel.show()
```

The `show` method first clears the window and draws the borders around it with the `box` method. Then, we set the `title` again. The `cursers.curs_set(0)` call will disable the cursor; we do that here because we don't want the cursor visible when we are selecting the items in the list. Finally, we call the `show` method in the panel.

It would also be nice to have a way to know whether the current panel is visible or not. So, let's add a method called `is_visible`:

```
def is_visible(self):
    return not self._panel.hidden()
```

Here, we can use the `hidden` method on the panel, which returns `true` if the panel is hidden and `false` if the panel is visible.

The last touch in this class is to add the possibility of comparing panels. We can achieve this by overriding some special methods; in this case, we want to override the `__eq__` method, which will be invoked every time we use the `==` operator. Remember that we created an `id` for every panel? We can use that `id` now to test the equality:

```
def __eq__(self, other):
    return self._id == other._id
```

Perfect! Now that we have the `Panel` base class, we are ready to create a special implementation of the panel that will contain menus to select items.

Adding menus for albums and track selection

Now, we are going to create a file called `menu_item.py` in the `musicterminal/client/` directory and we will start by importing some functions that we will need:

```
from uuid import uuid1
```

We only need to import the `uuid1` function from the `uuid` module because, like the panels, we are going to create an `id` (GUID) for every menu item in the list.

Let's start by adding the class and the constructor:

```
class MenuItem:
    def __init__(self, label, data, selected=False):
        self.id = str(uuid1())
        self.data = data
        self.label = label

        def return_id():
            return self.data['id'], self.data['uri']

        self.action = return_id
        self.selected = selected
```

The `MenuItem` initializer gets three arguments, the `label` item, the `data` which will contain the raw data returned by the Spotify REST API, and a flag stating whether the item is currently selected or not.

We start off by creating an id for the item, then we set the values for the data and label properties using the argument values that are passed in the class initializer.

Every item in the list will have an action that will be executed when the item is selected on the list, so we create a function called `return_id` that returns a tuple with the item id (not the same as the id that we just created). This is the id for the item on Spotify, and the URI is the URI for the item on Spotify. The latter will be useful when we select and play a song.

Now, we are going to implement some special methods that will be useful for us when performing item comparisons and printing items. The first method that we are going to implement is `__eq__`:

```
def __eq__(self, other):
    return self.id == other.id
```

This will allow us to use the index function to find a specific `MenuItem` in a list of `MenuItem` objects.

The other special method that we are going to implement is the `__len__` method:

```
def __len__(self):
    return len(self.label)
```

It returns the length of the `MenuItem` label and it will be used when measuring the length of the menu item labels on the list. Later, when we are building the menu, we are going to use the `max` function to get the menu item with the longest label, and based on that, we'll add extra padding to the other items so that all the items in the list look aligned.

The last method that we are going to implement is the `__str__` method:

```
def __str__(self):
    return self.label
```

This is just for convenience when printing menu items; instead of doing `print(menuitem.label)`, we can just do `print(menuitem)` and it will invoke `__str__`, which will return the value of the `MenuItem` label.

Implementing the menu panel

Now, we are going to implement the menu panel, which will be the container class that will accommodate all the menu items, handle events, and perform rendering on the terminal screen.

Before we start with the implementation of the menu panel, let's add an enumeration that will represent different item alignment options, so we can have a bit more flexibility on how to display the menu items inside the menu.

Create a file called `alignment.py` in the `musicterminal/client` directory with the following contents:

```
from enum import Enum, auto


class Alignment(Enum):
    LEFT = auto()
    RIGHT = auto()
```

You should be an enumeration expert if you followed the code in the first chapter. There's nothing as complicated here; we define a class `Alignment` inheriting from Enum and define two attributes, `LEFT` and `RIGHT`, both with their values set to `auto()`, which means that the values will be set automatically for us and they will be 1 and 2, respectively.

Now, we are ready to create the menu. Let's go ahead and create a final class called `menu.py` in the `musicterminal/client` directory.

Let's add some imports and the constructor:

```
import curses
import curses.panel

from .alignment import Alignment
from .panel import Panel


class Menu(Panel):

    def __init__(self, title, dimensions, align=Alignment.LEFT,
                 items=[]):
        super().__init__(title, dimensions)
        self._align = align
        self.items = items
```

The `Menu` class inherits from the `Panel` base class that we just created, and the class initializer gets a few arguments: the `title`, the `dimensions` (tuple with `height`, `width`, `y` and `x` values) the `alignment` setting which is `LEFT` by default, and the `items`. The items argument is a list of `MenuItems` objects. This is optional and it will be set to an empty list if no value is specified.

The first thing we do in the class initializer is invoke the __init__ method in the base class. We can do that by using the super function. If you remember, the __init__ method on the Panel class gets two arguments, title and dimension, so we pass it to the base class initializer.

Next, we assign the values for the properties align and items.

We also need a method that returns the currently selected item on the list of menu items:

```
def get_selected(self):
    items = [x for x in self.items if x.selected]
    return None if not items else items[0]
```

This method is very straightforward; the comprehension returns a list of selected items, and it will return None if no items are selected; otherwise, it returns the first item on the list.

Now, we can implement the method that will handle item selection. Let's add another method called _select:

```
def _select(self, expr):
    current = self.get_selected()
    index = self.items.index(current)
    new_index = expr(index)

    if new_index < 0:
        return

    if new_index > index and new_index >= len(self.items):
        return

    self.items[index].selected = False
    self.items[new_index].selected = True
```

Here, we start getting the current item selected, and right after that we get the index of the item in the list of menu items using the index method from the array. This is possible because we implemented the __eq__ method in the Panel class.

Then, we get to run the function passed as the argument, expr, passing the value of the currently selected item index.

expr will determine the next current item index. If the new index is less than 0, it means that we reached the top of the menu item's list, so we don't take any action.

If the new index is greater than the current index, and the new index is greater than or equal to the number of menu items on the list, then we have reached the bottom of the list, so no action is required at this point and we can continue selecting the same item.

However, if we haven't reached to top or the bottom of the list, we need to swap the selected items. To do this, we set the selected property on the current item to `False` and set the selected property of the next item to `True`.

The `_select` method is a `private` method, and it is not intended to be called externally, so we define two methods—`next` and `previous`:

```
def next(self):
    self._select(lambda index: index + 1)

def previous(self):
    self._select(lambda index: index - 1)
```

The next method will invoke the `_select` method and pass a lambda expression that will receive an index and add one to it, and the previous method will do the same thing, but instead of increasing the index by 1, it will subtract it. So, in the `_select` method when we call:

```
new_index = expr(index)
```

We are calling either `lambda index: index + 1` or `lambda index: index + 1`.

Great! Now, we are going to add a method that will be responsible for formatting menu items before we render them on the screen. Create a method called `_initialize_items`, which is shown as follows:

```
def _initialize_items(self):
    longest_label_item = max(self.items, key=len)

    for item in self.items:
        if item != longest_label_item:
            padding = (len(longest_label_item) - len(item)) * ' '
            item.label = (f'{item}{padding}'
                          if self._align == Alignment.LEFT
                          else f'{padding}{item}')

        if not self.get_selected():
            self.items[0].selected = True
```

First, we get the menu item that has the largest label; we can do that by using the built-in function `max` and passing the `items`, and, as the key, another built-in function called `len`. This will work because we implemented the special method `__len__` in the menu item.

After discovering the menu item with the largest label, we loop through the items of the list, adding padding on the `LEFT` or `RIGHT`, depending on the alignment options. Finally, if there's no menu item in the list with the selected flag set to `True`, we select the first item as selected.

We also want to provide a method called `init` that will initialize the items on the list for us:

```
def init(self):
    self._initialize_items()
```

We also need to handle keyboard events so we can perform a few actions when the user specifically presses the *Up* and *Down* arrow keys, as well as *Enter*.

First, we need to define a few constants at the top of the file. You can add these constants between the imports and the class definition:

```
NEW_LINE = 10
CARRIAGE_RETURN = 13
```

Let's go ahead and include a method called `handle_events`:

```
def handle_events(self, key):
    if key == curses.KEY_UP:
        self.previous()
    elif key == curses.KEY_DOWN:
        self.next()
    elif key == curses.KEY_ENTER or key == NEW_LINE or key ==
      CARRIAGE_RETURN:
        selected_item = self.get_selected()
        return selected_item.action
```

This method is pretty simple; it gets a `key` argument, and if the key is equal to `curses.KEY_UP`, then we call the `previous` method. If the key is equal to `curses.KEY_DOWN`, then we call the `next` method. Now, if the key is `ENTER`, then we get the selected item and return its action. The action is a function that will execute another function; in our case, we might be selecting an artist or song on a list or executing a function that will play a music track.

In addition to testing whether the key is curses.KEY_ENTER, we also need to check whether the key is a new line \n or a carriage return \r. This is necessary because the code for the *Enter* key can differ depending on the configuration of the terminal the application is running in.

We are going to implement the __iter__ method, which will make our Menu class behave like an iterable object:

```
def __iter__(self):
    return iter(self.items)
```

The last method of this class is the update method. This method will do the actual work of rendering the menu items and refreshing the window screen:

```
def update(self):
    pos_x = 2
    pos_y = 2

    for item in self.items:
        self._win.addstr(
                pos_y,
                pos_x,
                item.label,
                curses.A_REVERSE if item.selected else
                curses.A_NORMAL)
        pos_y += 1

    self._win.refresh()
```

First, we set the x and y coordinates to 2, so the menu on this window will start at line 2 and column 2. We loop through the menu items and call the addstr method to print the item on the screen.

The `addstr` method gets a `y` position, the `x` position, the string that will be written on the screen, in our case `item.label`, and the last argument is the `style`. If the item is selected, we want to show it highlighted; otherwise, it will display with normal colors. The following screenshot illustrates what the rendered list will look like:

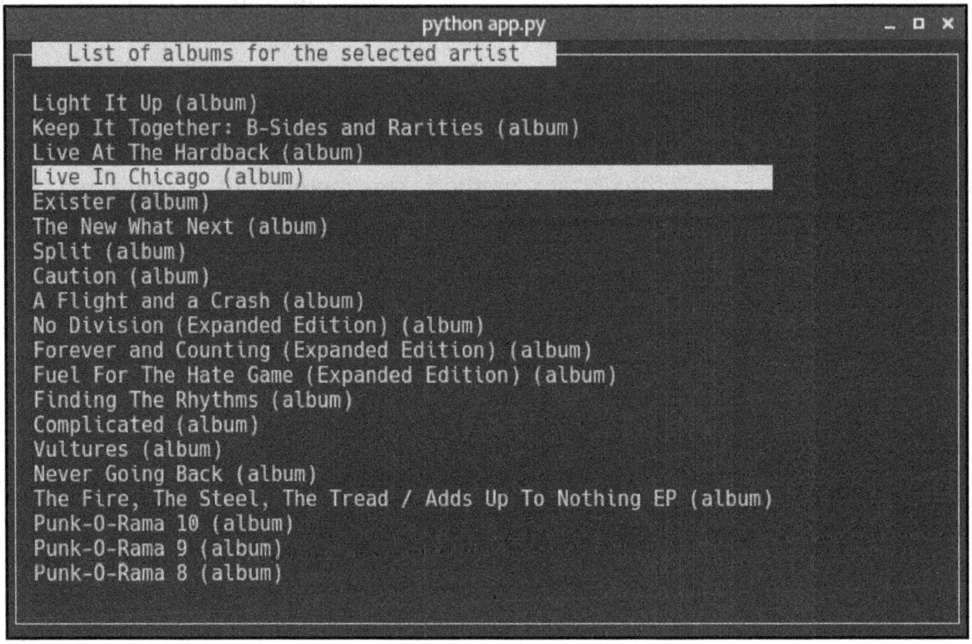

Creating the DataManager class

We have implemented the base functionality to authenticate and consume data from the Spotify REST API, but now we need to create a class that will make use of this functionality so we get the information that we need to be displayed in the client.

Our Spotify terminal client will perform the following actions:

- Search an artist by name
- List the artist's albums
- List the album's tracks
- Request a track to be played

The first thing we are going to add is a custom exception that we can raise, and no result is returned from the Spotify REST API. Create a new file called `empty_results_error.py` in the `musicterminal/client` directory with the following contents:

```
class EmptyResultsError(Exception):
    pass
```

To make it easier for us, let's create a `DataManager` class that will encapsulate all these functionalities for us. Create a file called `data_manager.py` in the `musicterminal/client` directory:

```
from .menu_item import MenuItem

from pytify.core import search_artist
from pytify.core import get_artist_albums
from pytify.core import get_album_tracks
from pytify.core import play

from .empty_results_error import EmptyResultsError

from pytify.auth import authenticate
from pytify.core import read_config


class DataManager():

    def __init__(self):
        self._conf = read_config()
        self._auth = authenticate(self._conf)
```

First, we import the `MenuItem`, so we can return `MenuItem` objects with the request's results. After that, we import functions from the `pytify` module to search artists, get albums, list albums tracks, and play tracks. Also, in the `pytify` module, we import the `read_config` function and authenticate it.

Lastly, we import the custom exception that we just created, `EmptyResultsError`.

The initializer of the `DataManager` class starts reading the configuration and performs the authentication. The authentication information will be stored in the `_auth` property.

Next up, we are going to add a method to search for artists:

```
def search_artist(self, criteria):
    results = search_artist(criteria, self._auth)
    items = results['artists']['items']

    if not items:
        raise EmptyResultsError(f'Could not find the artist:
        {criteria}')

    return items[0]
```

The _search_artist method will get criteria as an argument and call the
search_artist function from the python.core module. If no items are returned, it will
raise an EmptyResultsError; otherwise, it will return the first match.

Before we continue creating the methods that will fetch the albums and the tracks, we need
two utility methods to format the labels of the MenuItem objects.

The first one will format the artist label:

```
def _format_artist_label(self, item):
    return f'{item["name"]} ({item["type"]})'
```

Here, the label will be the name of the item and the type, which can be an album, single, EP,
and so on.

And the second one formats the name of the tracks:

```
def _format_track_label(self, item):

    time = int(item['duration_ms'])
    minutes = int((time / 60000) % 60)
    seconds = int((time / 1000) % 60)

    track_name = item['name']

    return f'{track_name} - [{minutes}:{seconds}]'
```

Here, we extract the duration of the track in milliseconds, convert is to minutes: seconds,
and format the label with the name of the track and its duration between square brackets.

After that, let's create a method to get the artist's albums:

```
def get_artist_albums(self, artist_id, max_items=20):

    albums = get_artist_albums(artist_id, self._auth)['items']

    if not albums:
        raise EmptyResultsError(('Could not find any albums for'
                                 f'the artist_id: {artist_id}'))

    return [MenuItem(self._format_artist_label(album), album)
            for album in albums[:max_items]]
```

The get_artist_albums method gets two arguments, the artist_id and the max_item, which is the maximum number of albums that will be returned by the method. By default, it is set to 20.

The first thing we do here is use the get_artist_albums method from the pytify.core module, passing the artist_id and the authentication objects, and we get the item's attribute from the results, assigning it to the variable albums. If the albums variable is empty, it will raise an EmptyResultsError; otherwise, it will create a list of MenuItem objects for every album.

And we can add another method for the tracks:

```
def get_album_tracklist(self, album_id):

    results = get_album_tracks(album_id, self._auth)

    if not results:
        raise EmptyResultsError('Could not find the tracks for this
        album')

    tracks = results['items']

    return [MenuItem(self._format_track_label(track), track)
            for track in tracks]
```

The get_album_tracklist method gets album_id as an argument and the first thing we do is get the tracks for that album using the get_album_tracks function in the pytify.core module. If no result is returned, we raise an EmptyResultsError; otherwise, we build a list of MenuItem objects.

The last method is the one that will actually send a command to the Spotify REST API to play a track:

```
def play(self, track_uri):
    play(track_uri, self._auth)
```

Very straightforward. Here, we just get `track_uri` as an argument and pass it down the `play` function in the `pytify.core` module, along with the `authentication` object. That will make the track start playing on the available device; it can be a mobile phone, Spotify's client on your computer, the Spotify web player, or even your games console.

Next up, let's put together everything we have built and run the Spotify player terminal.

Time to listen to music!

Now, we have all the pieces we need to start building the terminal player. We have the `pytify` module, which provides a wrapper around the Spotify RESP API and will allow us to search for artists, albums, tracks, and even control the Spotify client running on a mobile phone or a computer.

The `pytify` module also provides two different types of authentication—client credentials and authorization code—and in the previous sections, we implemented all the infrastructures necessary to build an application using curses. So, let's glue all the parts together and listen to some good music.

On the `musicterminal` directory, create a file called `app.py`; this is going to be the entry point for our application. We start by adding import statements:

```
import curses
import curses.panel
from curses import wrapper
from curses.textpad import Textbox
from curses.textpad import rectangle

from client import Menu
from client import DataManager
```

We need to import `curses` and `curses.panel` of course, and this time, we are also importing `wrapper`. This is used for debugging purposes. When developing curses applications, they are extremely hard to debug, and when something goes wrong and some exception is thrown, the terminal will not go back to its original state.

The wrapper takes a `callable` and it returns the terminal original state when the `callable` function returns.

The wrapper will run the callable within a try-catch block and it will restore the terminal in case something goes wrong. It is great for us while developing the application. Let's use the wrapper so we can see any kind of problem that may occur.

We are going to import two new functions, `Textbox` and `rectangle`. We are going to use those to create a search box where the users can search for their favorite artist.

Lastly, we import the `Menu` class and the `DataManager` that we implemented in the previous sections.

Let's start implementing some helper functions; the first one is `show_search_screen`:

```
def show_search_screen(stdscr):
    curses.curs_set(1)
    stdscr.addstr(1, 2, "Artist name: (Ctrl-G to search)")

    editwin = curses.newwin(1, 40, 3, 3)
    rectangle(stdscr, 2, 2, 4, 44)
    stdscr.refresh()

    box = Textbox(editwin)
    box.edit()

    criteria = box.gather()
    return criteria
```

It gets an instance of the window as an argument, so we can print text and add our textbox on the screen.

The `curses.curs_set` function turns the cursor on and off; when set to 1, the cursor will be visible on the screen. We want that in the search screen so the user knows where he/she can start typing the search criteria. Then, we print help text so the user knows that the name of the artist should be entered; then, to finish, they can press *Ctrl + G* or just *Enter* to perform the search.

To create the textbox, we create a new small window with a height that equals 1 and a width that equals 40, and it starts at line 3, column 3 of the terminal screen. After that, we use the `rectangle` function to draw a rectangle around the new window and we refresh the screen so the changes we made take effect.

Then, we create the `Textbox` object, passing the window that we just created, and call the method `edit`, which will set the box to the textbox and enter edit mode. That will `stop` the application and let the user enter some text in the textbox; it will exit when the user clicks *Ctrl + G* or *Enter*.

When the user is done editing the text, we call the `gather` method that will collect the data entered by the user and assign it to the `criteria` variable, and finally, we return `criteria`.

We also need a function to clean the screen easily Let's create another function called `clean_screen`:

```
def clear_screen(stdscr):
    stdscr.clear()
    stdscr.refresh()
```

Great! Now, we can start with the main entry point of our application, and create a function called main with the following contents:

```
def main(stdscr):

    curses.cbreak()
    curses.noecho()
    stdscr.keypad(True)

    _data_manager = DataManager()

    criteria = show_search_screen(stdscr)

    height, width = stdscr.getmaxyx()

    albums_panel = Menu('List of albums for the selected artist',
                        (height, width, 0, 0))

    tracks_panel = Menu('List of tracks for the selected album',
                        (height, width, 0, 0))

    artist = _data_manager.search_artist(criteria)

    albums = _data_manager.get_artist_albums(artist['id'])

    clear_screen(stdscr)

    albums_panel.items = albums
    albums_panel.init()
    albums_panel.update()
```

```
    albums_panel.show()

current_panel = albums_panel

is_running = True

while is_running:
    curses.doupdate()
    curses.panel.update_panels()

    key = stdscr.getch()

    action = current_panel.handle_events(key)

    if action is not None:
        action_result = action()
        if current_panel == albums_panel and action_result is
        not None:
            _id, uri = action_result
            tracks = _data_manager.get_album_tracklist(_id)
            current_panel.hide()
            current_panel = tracks_panel
            current_panel.items = tracks
            current_panel.init()
            current_panel.show()
        elif current_panel == tracks_panel and action_result is
        not None:
            _id, uri = action_result
            _data_manager.play(uri)

    if key == curses.KEY_F2:
        current_panel.hide()
        criteria = show_search_screen(stdscr)
        artist = _data_manager.search_artist(criteria)
        albums = _data_manager.get_artist_albums(artist['id'])

        clear_screen(stdscr)
        current_panel = albums_panel
        current_panel.items = albums
        current_panel.init()
        current_panel.show()

    if key == ord('q') or key == ord('Q'):
        is_running = False

    current_panel.update()
```

```
try:
    wrapper(main)
except KeyboardInterrupt:
    print('Thanks for using this app, bye!')
```

Let's break this down into its constituent parts:

```
curses.cbreak()
curses.noecho()
stdscr.keypad(True)
```

Here, we do some initialization. Usually, curses don't register the key immediately. When it is typed, this is called buffered mode; the user has to type something and then hit *Enter*. In our application, we don't want this behavior; we want the key to be registered right after the user types it. This is what `cbreak` does; it turns off the curses buffered mode.

We also use the `noecho` function to be able the read the keys and to control when we want to show them on the screen.

The last curses setup we do is to turn on the keypad so curses will do the job of reading and processing the keys accordingly, and returning constant values representing the key that has been pressed. This is much cleaner and easy to read than trying to handle it yourself and test key code numbers.

We create an instance of the `DataManager` class so we can get the data we need to be displayed on the menus and perform authentication:

```
_data_manager = DataManager()
```

Now, we create the search dialog:

```
criteria = show_search_screen(stdscr)
```

We call the `show_search_screen` function, passing the instance of the window; it will render the search field on the screen and return the results to us. When the user is done typing, the user input will be stored in the `criteria` variable.

After we get the criteria, we call `get_artist_albums`, which will first search an artist and then get a list of the artist's albums and return a list of `MenuItem` objects.

When the list of albums is returned, we can create the other panels with the menus:

```
height, width = stdscr.getmaxyx()

albums_panel = Menu('List of albums for the selected artist',
                    (height, width, 0, 0))

tracks_panel = Menu('List of tracks for the selected album',
                    (height, width, 0, 0))

artist = _data_manager.search_artist(criteria)

albums = _data_manager.get_artist_albums(artist['id'])

clear_screen(stdscr)
```

Here, we get the height and the width of the main window so we can create panels with the same dimensions. `albums_panel` will display the albums and `tracks_panel` will display the tracks; as I mentioned before, it will have the same dimensions as the main window and both panels will start at row 0, column 0.

After that, we call `clear_screen` to prepare the window to render the menu window with the albums:

```
albums_panel.items = albums
albums_panel.init()
albums_panel.update()
albums_panel.show()

current_panel = albums_panel

is_running = True
```

We first set the item's properties with the results of the albums search. We also call `init` on the panel, which will internally run `_initialize_items`, format the labels and set the currently selected item. We also call the `update` method, which will do the actual work of printing the menu items in the window; lastly, we show how to set the panel to visible.

We also define the `current_panel` variable, which will hold the instance of the panel that is currently being displayed on the terminal.

The `is_running` flag is set to `True` and it will be used in the application's main loop. We will set it to `False` when we want to stop the application's execution.

Now, we enter the main loop of the application:

```
while is_running:
    curses.doupdate()
    curses.panel.update_panels()

    key = stdscr.getch()

    action = current_panel.handle_events(key)
```

To start off, we call `doupdate` and `update_panels`:

- `doupdate`: Curses keeps two data structures representing the physical screen (the one you see on the terminal screen) and a virtual screen (the one keeping the next updated). `doupdate` updates the physical screen so it matches the virtual screen.
- `update_panels`: Updates the virtual screen after changes in the panel stack, changes like hiding, show panels, and so on.

After updating the screen, we wait until a key is pressed using the `getch` function, and assign the key pressed value to the `key` variable. The `key` variable is then passed to the current panel's `handle_events` method.

If you remember the implementation of `handle_events` in the Menu class, it looks like this:

```
def handle_events(self, key):
    if key == curses.KEY_UP:
        self.previous()
    elif key == curses.KEY_DOWN:
        self.next()
    elif key == curses.KEY_ENTER or key == NEW_LINE or key ==
    CARRIAGE_RETURN:
        selected_item = self.get_selected()
    return selected_item.action
```

It handles KEY_DOWN, KEY_UP, and KEY_ENTER. If the key is KEY_UP or KEY_DOWN, it will just update the position in the menu and set a newly selected item, and that will be updated on the screen on the next loop interaction. If the key is KEY_ENTER, we get the selected item and return its action function.

Remember that, for both panels, it will return a function that, when executed, will return a tuple containing the item id and the item URI.

Moving on, we handle if the action is returned:

```
if action is not None:
    action_result = action()
    if current_panel == albums_panel and action_result is not None:
        _id, uri = action_result
        tracks = _data_manager.get_album_tracklist(_id)
        current_panel.hide()
        current_panel = tracks_panel
        current_panel.items = tracks
        current_panel.init()
        current_panel.show()
    elif current_panel == tracks_panel and action_result is not
    None:
        _id, uri = action_result
        _data_manager.play(uri)
```

If the `handle_events` method of the current panel returned a callable `action`, we execute it and get the result. Then, we check if the active panel is the first panel (with the albums). In this case, we need to get a list of tracks for the selected album, so we call `get_album_tracklist` in the `DataManager` instance.

We hide the `current_panel`, switch the current panel to the second panel (the tracks panel), set the items property with the list of tracks, call the init method so the items are formatted properly and a first item in the list is set as selected, and finally we call `show` so the track's panel is visible.

In the event the current panel is the `tracks_panel`, we get the action results and invoke play on the `DataManager`, passing the track URI. It will request the selected track to be played on the device you have active on Spotify.

Now, we want a way of returning to the search screen. We do that when the user hits the *F12* function `key`:

```
if key == curses.KEY_F2:
    current_panel.hide()
    criteria = show_search_screen(stdscr)
    artist = _data_manager.search_by_artist_name(criteria)
    albums = _data_manager.get_artist_albums(artist['id'])

    clear_screen(stdscr)
    current_panel = albums_panel
    current_panel.items = albums
    current_panel.init()
    current_panel.show()
```

For the `if` statement above, test if the user pressed the *F12* function `key`; in this case, we want to return to the search screen so that the user can search for a new artist. When the *F12* key is pressed, we hide the current panel. Then, we call the `show_search_screen` function so the search screen is rendered and the textbox will enter in edit mode, waiting for the user's input.

When the user is done typing and hits *Ctrl+ G* or *Enter*, we search the artist. Then, we get the artist's albums and we show the panel with a list of albums.

The last event that we want to handle is when the user press either the `q` or `Q` key, which sets the `is_running` variable to `False` and the application closes:

```
if key == ord('q') or key == ord('Q'):
    is_running = False
```

Finally, we call `update` on the current panel, so we redraw the items to reflect the changes on the screen:

```
current_panel.update()
```

Outside the main function, we have the code snippet where we actually execute the `main` function:

```
try:
    wrapper(main)
except KeyboardInterrupt:
    print('Thanks for using this app, bye!')
```

We surround it with a `try` catch so if the user presses *Ctrl + C*, a `KeyboardInterrupt` exception will be raised and we just finish the application gracefully without throwing the exception on the screen.

We are all done! Let's try it out!

Open a terminal and type the command—`python app.py`.

The first screen you will see is the search screen:

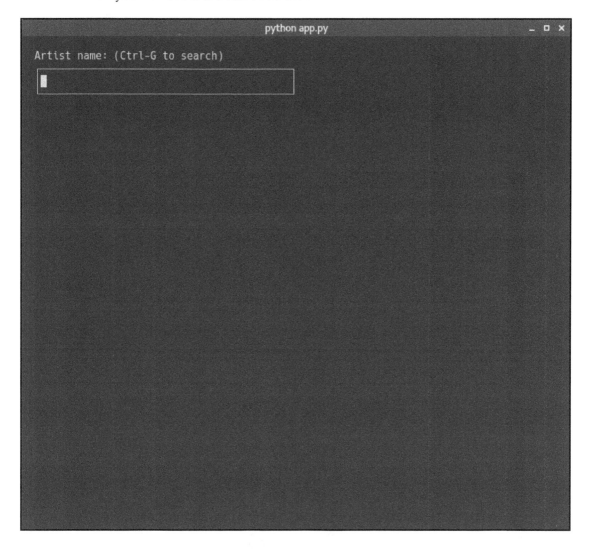

Let me search for one of my favorite artists:

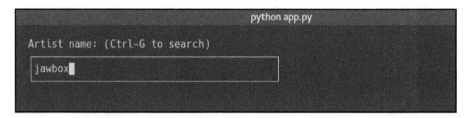

After pressing *Enter* or *Ctrl + G,* you should see a list of albums:

```
                              python app.py                        _ □ ✕
  ┌ List of albums for the selected artist ┐
  My Scrapbook Of Fatal Accidents (album)
  Jawbox (album)
  For Your Own Special Sweetheart (album)
  For Your Own Special Sweetheart (2009 Remaster) (album)
  Novelty (album)
  Grippe (album)
  Jackpot Plus! / Motorist (album)
  Absenter b/w Chinese Fork Tie (album)
  Jawbox (album)
  Dope, Guns & Fucking In The Streets: 1988-1998 Volume 1-11 (album)
  Tribute to the Avengers (album)
  Slamdek A to Z (album)
  Edsel / Jawbox split (album)
```

Here, you can use the arrow keys (*Up* and *Down*) to navigate albums, and press *Enter* to select an album. Then, you will see the screen showing all the tracks of the selected album:

```
                              python app.py                        _ □ ×
   List of tracks for the selected album

Mirrorful - [3:2]
Livid - [3:55]
Iodine - [3:35]
His Only Trade - [1:58]
Chinese Fork Tie - [2:29]
Won't Come Off - [2:46]
Excandescent - [4:25]
Spoiler - [2:28]
Desert Sea - [3:5]
Empire Of One - [2:47]
Mule / Stall - [1:54]
Nickel Nickel Millionaire - [2:35]
Capillary Life - [3:22]
Absenter - [9:22]
```

If this screen is the same, you can use the arrow keys (*Up* and *Down*) to select the track, and *Enter* will send a request to play the song on the device you have Spotify active on.

Summary

We have covered a lot of ground in this chapter; we started by creating an application on Spotify and learning our way around its developer's website. Then, we learned how to implement the two types of authentication flow that Spotify supports: the client credentials flow and the authorization flow.

In this chapter, we also implemented a whole module wrapper with some of the functionality available from Spotify's REST API.

Then, we implemented a simple terminal client where users can search for artists, browse the artist's albums and tracks, and finally play a song in the user's active device, which can be a computer, mobile phone, or even a video game console.

In the next chapter, we are going to create a desktop application that shows the number of votes given through Twitter hashtags.

3
Casting Votes on Twitter

In the previous chapter, we implemented a Terminal application that serves as a remote control for the popular music service Spotify. In this application, we could search for artists, browse albums, and browse the tracks in each album. Lastly, we could even request the track to be played on the user's active device.

This time, we are going to develop an application that will integrate with Twitter, making use of its REST API. Twitter is a social network that has been around since 2006 and there are over 300 million active users. Private users, companies, artists, soccer clubs, you can find almost everything on Twitter. But what makes Twitter so popular, I believe, is its simplicity.

Unlike blog posts, Twitter posts or *tweets* have to be short and get right to the point, and it doesn't require too much time to prepare something to post. Another point that makes Twitter so popular is the fact that the service is a great news source. If you want to keep updated with what's going on in the world, politics, sports, technology, you name it, Twitter is the place to be.

Apart from all that, Twitter has a fairly decent API for us developers and, to take advantage of that, we are going to develop an application where users can cast votes using hashtags. In our application, we are going to configure which hashtags we are going to monitor and it will automatically, from time to time, fetch the latest tweets matching that hashtag, count them, and display them in a user interface.

In this chapter, you will learn how to do the following:

- Create a tweet application
- Use the OAuth library and implement a three-legged authentication flow
- Search for the latest tweets using the Twitter API
- Build a simple user interface using Tkinter
- Learn the basics of multiprocessing and reactive programming

Setting up the environment

The first thing we have to do is, as usual, set up our development environment and the first step is to create a virtual environment for our application. Our application will be called twittervotes, so let's go ahead and create a virtual environment called twittervotes:

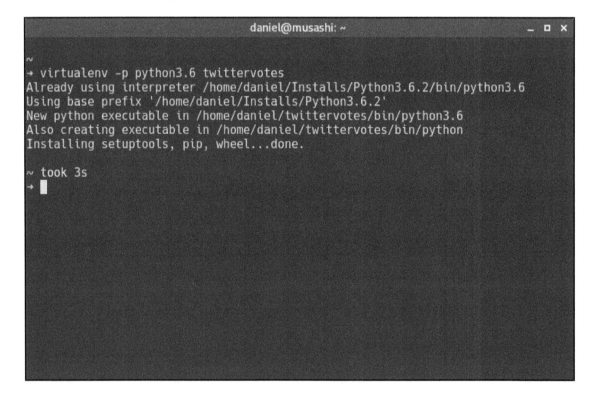

When the `virtualenv` environment has been created, you can activate it with the following command:

`. twittervotes/bin/activate`

Great! Now let's set up the project's directory structure. It should look like the following:

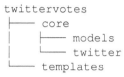

```
twittervotes
├──── core
│     ├──── models
│     └──── twitter
└──── templates
```

Let's dive into the structure a bit:

twittervotes	**The application's root directory. Here, we will create the application's entry point as well as a small helper application to perform the Twitter authentication.**
twittervotes/core	This will contain all the core functionality of our project. It will contain the code to authenticate, read config files, send requests to the Twitter API, and so on.
twittervotes/core/models	Directory in which to keep the application's data models.
twittervotes/core/twitter	In the `twitter` directory, we are going to keep `helper` functions to interact with the Twitter API.
twittervotes/templates	Here, we are going to keep all the HTML templates that will be used by our application.

Next, it is time to add our project's dependencies. Go ahead and create a file called `requirements.txt` in the `twittervotes` directory with the following content:

```
Flask==0.12.2
oauth2==1.9.0.post1
PyYAML==3.12
requests==2.18.4
Rx==1.6.0
```

The following table explains what the preceding dependencies mean:

Flask	**We are going to use Flask here to create a simple web application to perform the authentication with Twitter.**
oauth2	This is a great package that will abstract a lot of the complexity when performing OAuth authentication.
PyYAML	We are going to use this package to create and read config files in YAML format.
Requests	Allow us to access the Twitter API over HTTP.
Rx	Finally, we are going to use Reactive Extensions for Python so we can reactively update our UI soon as a new tweet count arrives.

When the file has been created, run the command `pip install -r requirements.txt`, and you should see an output similar to the following:

```
                              daniel@musashi: ~/projects/twittervotes                                    _ □ ×
~/projects/twittervotes via twittervotes
→ pip install -r requirements.txt
Collecting Flask==0.12.2 (from -r requirements.txt (line 1))
  Using cached Flask-0.12.2-py2.py3-none-any.whl
Collecting oauth2==1.9.0.post1 (from -r requirements.txt (line 2))
  Using cached oauth2-1.9.0.post1-py2.py3-none-any.whl
Collecting PyYAML==3.12 (from -r requirements.txt (line 3))
Collecting requests==2.18.4 (from -r requirements.txt (line 4))
  Using cached requests-2.18.4-py2.py3-none-any.whl
Collecting Rx==1.6.0 (from -r requirements.txt (line 5))
  Using cached Rx-1.6.0-py2.py3-none-any.whl
Collecting click>=2.0 (from Flask==0.12.2->-r requirements.txt (line 1))
  Using cached click-6.7-py2.py3-none-any.whl
Collecting itsdangerous>=0.21 (from Flask==0.12.2->-r requirements.txt (line 1))
Collecting Jinja2>=2.4 (from Flask==0.12.2->-r requirements.txt (line 1))
  Downloading Jinja2-2.10-py2.py3-none-any.whl (126kB)
    100% |████████████████████████████████| 133kB 450kB/s
Collecting Werkzeug>=0.7 (from Flask==0.12.2->-r requirements.txt (line 1))
  Using cached Werkzeug-0.12.2-py2.py3-none-any.whl
Collecting httplib2 (from oauth2==1.9.0.post1->-r requirements.txt (line 2))
Collecting idna<2.7,>=2.5 (from requests==2.18.4->-r requirements.txt (line 4))
  Using cached idna-2.6-py2.py3-none-any.whl
Collecting certifi>=2017.4.17 (from requests==2.18.4->-r requirements.txt (line 4))
  Downloading certifi-2017.11.5-py2.py3-none-any.whl (330kB)
    100% |████████████████████████████████| 337kB 668kB/s
Collecting chardet<3.1.0,>=3.0.2 (from requests==2.18.4->-r requirements.txt (line 4))
  Using cached chardet-3.0.4-py2.py3-none-any.whl
Collecting urllib3<1.23,>=1.21.1 (from requests==2.18.4->-r requirements.txt (line 4))
  Using cached urllib3-1.22-py2.py3-none-any.whl
Collecting MarkupSafe>=0.23 (from Jinja2>=2.4->Flask==0.12.2->-r requirements.txt (line 1))
Installing collected packages: click, itsdangerous, MarkupSafe, Jinja2, Werkzeug, Flask, httplib2, oauth2, PyYAML, idna, certifi, chardet
, urllib3, requests, Rx
Successfully installed Flask-0.12.2 Jinja2-2.10 MarkupSafe-1.0 PyYAML-3.12 Rx-1.6.0 Werkzeug-0.12.2 certifi-2017.11.5 chardet-3.0.4 click
-6.7 httplib2-0.10.3 idna-2.6 itsdangerous-0.24 oauth2-1.9.0.post1 requests-2.18.4 urllib3-1.22

~/projects/twittervotes via twittervotes took 4s
→ █
```

If you run the command `pip freeze`, you will get a list of dependencies in pip format and you will notice that the output lists more dependencies that we actually added to the `requirements` file. The reason for that is that the packages that our project requires also have dependencies and they will also be installed. So do not worry if you have more packages installed than you specified in your `requirements` file.

Now that our environment is set up, we can start creating our Twitter application. As usual, before you start coding, make sure that you have your code under a source control system such as Git; there are plenty of online services that will host your repositories for free.

In this way, you can roll back different versions of your projects and you don't have the risk of losing your work if you have problems with your computers. With that said, let's create our Twitter application.

Creating a Twitter application

In this section, we are going to create our first Twitter application so we can consume the Twitter REST API. You will need to create an account if you don't already have one. If you are not using Twitter, I would strongly recommend it; it is a great way of getting up-to-date with all the news and what is going on in the development world, and it is a great way of making new friends in the Python community.

After you create an account, head over to `https://apps.twitter.com/`, sign in with your login credentials, and you will land on a page where you can see a list of apps that you have already created (the first time, you will probably have an empty list of apps), and on the same page you will have the possibility of creating new apps. Click on the **Create new app** button in the top-right corner and it will open up the following page:

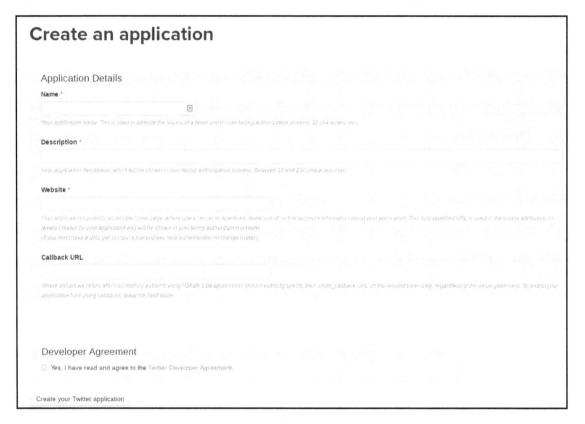

In this form, there are three fields that are required—name, description, and website:

- **Name**: This is the name of your application; it is also the name that will be presented to the users of your application when performing authorization. The name doesn't need to follow any specific naming convention, you can have anything you want.
- **Description**: As the name suggests, this is the description of your application. This field will also be presented to the users of your application, so it is good to have nice text describing your application. In this case, here we don't need much text. Let's add `Application to cast votes on Twitter using hashtags.`

- **Website**: Specify your application's website; it is also going to be presented to the users during authorization and it is the site where your users can go to download or get more information about your application. Since we are in the development phase, we can just add a placeholder such as `http://www.example.com`.
- **Callback URL**: This works the same way as the callback URL in the previous application (the Spotify Terminal app) in the previous chapter. It is a URL that Twitter will call to send the authorization code. It is not a required field but we are going to need it, so let's go ahead and add `;http://localhost:3000/callback`.

After filling in all the fields, you just need to check the Twitter Developer Agreement and click the **Create your Twitter application** button.

If everything went well, you will be directed to another page where you can see more details of your newly created application. Just below the name of the application, you will see an area with tabs that shows settings and different pieces of information about the application:

On the first tab, **Details**, we want to copy all the URLs that we are going to use to perform the authentication. Scroll down to **Application settings**, and copy **Request token URL**, **Authorize URL**, and **Access token URL**:

Request token URL	https://api.twitter.com/oauth/request_token
Authorize URL	https://api.twitter.com/oauth/authorize
Access token URL	https://api.twitter.com/oauth/access_token

Great! Now let's head over to the **Keys and Access Tokens** tab and copy **Consumer Key** and **Consumer Secret**:

Details	Settings	Keys and Access Tokens	Permissions

Application Settings

Keep the "Consumer Secret" a secret. This key should never be human-readable in your application.

Consumer Key (API Key)

Consumer Secret (API Secret)

Now that we have copied all the necessary information, we can create a configuration file that is going to be used by our application. It is always good practice to keep all this in a configuration file so we don't need to hardcode those URLs in our code.

 We are going to add the *consumer key* and *consumer secret* to a configuration file in our project; as the name suggests, this key is *secret* so if you are planning to create a repository for your code in a service such as GitHub, make sure to add the configuration file to the .gitignore file so the keys are not pushed to the cloud repository. Never share these keys with anyone; if you suspect that someone has the keys, you can generate new keys for your application on the Twitter app's website.

Adding the configuration file

In this section, we are going to create the configuration file for our application; the configuration file will be in YAML format. If you would like to know more about YAML, you can check the site http://yaml.org/, where you will find examples, the specification, and also a list of libraries in different programming languages that can be used to manipulate YAML files.

For our application, we are going to use PyYAML, which will allow us to read and write YAML files in a very simple manner. Our configuration file is quite simple so we will not need to use any advanced features of the library, we just want to read the content and write, and the data that we are going to add is quite flat; we will not have any nested objects or lists of any kind.

Let's get the information that we obtained from Twitter when we created our app and add it to the configuration file. Create a file called `config.yaml` in the application's `twittervotes` directory with the following content:

```
consumer_key: '<replace with your consumer_key>'
consumer_secret: '<replace with your consumer secret>'
request_token_url: 'https://api.twitter.com/oauth/request_token'
authorize_url: 'https://api.twitter.com/oauth/authorize'
access_token_url: 'https://api.twitter.com/oauth/access_token'
api_version: '1.1'
search_endpoint: 'https://api.twitter.com/1.1/search/tweets.json'
```

Great! Now we are going to create the first Python code in our project. If you have followed the previous chapters, the functions to read the configuration file will be familiar to you. The idea is simple: we are going to read the configuration file, parse it, and create a model that we can easily use to access the data we added to the config. First, we need to create the configuration model.

Create a file called `models.py` in `twittervotes/core/models/` with the following content:

```python
from collections import namedtuple

Config = namedtuple('Config', ['consumer_key',
                               'consumer_secret',
                               'request_token_url',
                               'access_token_url',
                               'authorize_url',
                               'api_version',
                               'search_endpoint', ])
```

There was a more extensive introduction to `namedtuple` in the previous chapter, so I will not go into as much detail about it again; if you haven't been going through the second chapter, it will suffice to know that `namedtuple` is a kind of class and this code will define a `namedtuple` called `Config` with the fields specified in the array in the second argument.

Great, now let's create another file called `__init__.py` in `twittervotes/core/models` and import the `namedtuple` that we just created:

```python
from .models import Config
```

Now it is time to create the functions that will do the actual work of reading the YAML file and returning it to us. Create a file called `config.py` in `twittervotes/core/`. Let's get started by adding the import statements:

```
import os
import yaml

from .models import Config
```

We are going to use the `os` package to easily obtain the user's current directory and manipulate paths. We also import PyYAML so we can read the YAML files and, lastly, from the `models` module, we import the `Config` model that we just created.

Then we define two functions, starting with the `_read_yaml_file` function. This function gets two arguments—the `filename`, which is the name of the config file that we want to read, and also `cls`, which can be a `class` or `namedtuple` that we will use to store the configuration data.

In this case, we are going to pass the `Config`—namedtuple, which has the same properties as the YAML configuration file that we are going to read:

```
def _read_yaml_file(filename, cls):
    core_dir = os.path.dirname(os.path.abspath(__file__))
    file_path = os.path.join(core_dir, '..', filename)
    with open(file_path, mode='r', encoding='UTF-8') as file:
        config = yaml.load(file)
        return cls(**config)
```

First, we use the `os.path.abspath` function, passing as an argument the special variable `__file__`. When a module is loaded, the variable `__file__` will be set to the same name as the module. That will allow us to easily find where to load the configuration file. So the following snippet will return the path of the core module

`/projects/twittervotes/core`:

```
core_dir = os.path.dirname(os.path.abspath(__file__)) will return
```

We know that the configuration file will live in `/projects/twittervotes/` so we need to join `..` to the path to go up one level in the directory structure so we can read the file. That's why we build the complete configuration file's path as follows:

```
file_path = os.path.join(core_dir, '..', filename)
```

That will give us the flexibility of running this code from any location in our system.

We open the file in the reading mode using UTF-8 encoding and pass it to the `yaml.load` function, assigning the results to the `config` variable. The `config` variable will be a dictionary with all the data we have in the `config` file.

The last line of this function is the interesting part: if you recall, the `cls` argument was a `class` or a `namedtuple` so we spread the values of the config dictionary as an argument. Here, we are going to use the `Config`—namedtuple so `cls(**config)` is the same as `Config, (**config)` and passing the arguments with `**` will be the same as passing all the arguments one by one:

```
Config(
    consumer_key: ''
    consumer_secret: ''
    app_only_auth: 'https://api.twitter.com/oauth2/token'
    request_token_url:
'https://api.twitter.com/oauth/request_token'
    authorize_url: 'https://api.twitter.com/oauth/authorize'
    access_token_url: 'https://api.twitter.com/oauth/access_token'
    api_version: '1.1'
    search_endpoint: '')
```

Now we are going to add the second function we are going to need, the `read_config` function:

```
def read_config():
    try:
        return _read_yaml_file('config.yaml', Config)
    except IOError as e:
        print(""" Error: couldn\'t file the configuration file
        `config.yaml`
        'on your current directory.

        Default format is:',

        consumer_key: 'your_consumer_key'
        consumer_secret: 'your_consumer_secret'
        request_token_url:
        'https://api.twitter.com/oauth/request_token'
        access_token_url:
        'https://api.twitter.com/oauth/access_token'
        authorize_url: 'https://api.twitter.com/oauth/authorize'
        api_version: '1.1'
        search_endpoint: ''
        """)
        raise
```

This function is pretty straightforward; it just makes use of the `_read_yaml_file` function that we just created, passing the `config.yaml` file in the first argument and also the `Config`, `namedtuple` in the second argument.

We catch the `IOError` exception that will be thrown if the file doesn't exist in the application's directory; in that case, we throw a help message showing the users of your application how the config file should be structured.

The final touch is to import it into the `__init__.py` in the `twittervotes/core` directory:

```
from .config import read_config
```

Let's try this out in the Python REPL:

Great, it worked just like we wanted! In the next section, we can start creating the code that will perform the authentication.

Performing authentication

In this section, we are going to create the program that will perform authentication for us so we can use the Twitter API. We are going to do that using a simple Flask application that will expose two routes. The first is the root `/`, which will just load and render a simple HTML template with a button that will redirect us to the Twitter authentication dialog.

The second route that we are going to create is `/callback`. Remember when we specified the callback URL in the Twitter app configuration? This is the route that will be called after we authorize the app. It will return an authorization token that will be used to perform requests to the Twitter API. So let's get right into it!

Before we start implementing the Flask app, we need to add another model to our model's module. This model will represent the request authorization data. Open the `models.py` file in `twittervotes/core/models` and add the following code:

```
RequestToken = namedtuple('RequestToken', ['oauth_token',
                                           'oauth_token_secret',
    'oauth_callback_confirmed'])
```

This will create a `namedtuple` called `RequestToken` with the fields `oauth_token`, `oauth_token_secret`, and `outh_callback_confirmed`; this data will be necessary for us to perform the second step of the authentication.

Lastly, open the `__init__.py` file in the `twittervotes/core/models` directory and let's import the `RequestToken namedtuple` that we just created, as follows:

```
from .models import RequestToken
```

Now that we have the model in place, let's start creating the Flask application. Let's add a very simple template to show a button that will start the authentication process.

Create a new directory in the `twittervotes` directory called `templates` and create a file called `index.html` with the following content:

```
<html>
    <head>
    </head>
    <body>
        <a href="{{link}}"> Click here to authorize </a>
    </body>
</html>
```

Creating the Flask application

Perfect, now let's add another file called `twitter_auth.py` in the `twittervotes` directory. We are going to create three functions in it but, first, let's add some imports:

```
from urllib.parse import parse_qsl

import yaml

from flask import Flask
from flask import render_template
from flask import request
```

```
import oauth2 as oauth

from core import read_config
from core.models import RequestToken
```

First, we import the `parser_qls` from the `urllib.parse` module to parse the returned query string, and the `yaml` module so we can read and write `YAML` configuration files. Then we import everything we need to build our Flask application. The last third-party module that we are going to import here is the `oauth2` module, which will help us to perform the `OAuth` authentication.

Lastly, we import our function `read_config` and the `RequestToken` `namedtuple` that we just created.

Here, we create our Flask app and a few global variables that will hold values for the client, consumer, and the `RequestToken` instance:

```
app = Flask(__name__)

client = None
consumer = None
req_token = None
```

The first function that we are going to create is a function called `get_req_token` with the following content:

```
def get_oauth_token(config):

    global consumer
    global client
    global req_token

    consumer = oauth.Consumer(config.consumer_key,
      config.consumer_secret)
    client = oauth.Client(consumer)

    resp, content = client.request(config.request_token_url, 'GET')

    if resp['status'] != '200':
        raise Exception("Invalid response
        {}".format(resp['status']))

    request_token = dict(parse_qsl(content.decode('utf-8')))

    req_token = RequestToken(**request_token)
```

This function gets as argument an instance to the configuration and the global statements say to the interpreter that the consumer, client, and `req_token` used in the function will be referencing the global variables.

We create a consumer object using the consumer key and the consumer secret that we obtained when the Twitter app was created. When the consumer is created, we can pass it to the client function to create the client, then we call the function request, which, as the name suggests, will perform the request to Twitter, passing the request token URL.

When the request is complete, the response and the content will be stored in the variables `resp` and `content`. Right after that, we test whether the response status is not 200 or `HTTP.OK`; in that case, we raise an exception, otherwise we parse the query string to get the values that have been sent back to us and create a `RequestToken` instance.

Creating the application routes

Now we can start creating the routes. First, we are going to add the root route:

```
@app.route('/')
def home():
    config = read_config()

    get_oauth_token(config)

    url = f'{config.authorize_url}?oauth_token=
    {req_token.oauth_token}'

    return render_template('index.html', link=url)
```

We read the configuration file and pass it the `get_oauth_token` function. This function will populate the global variable `req_token` with the `oauth_token` value; we need this token to start the authorization process. Then we build the authorization URL with the values of `authorize_url` obtained from the configuration file and the `OAuth` request token.

Lastly, we use the `render_template` to render the `index.html` template that we created and we also pass to the function a second argument, which is the context. In this case, we are creating an item called `link` with the value set to `url`. If you remember the `index.html` template, there is an "`{{url}}`" placeholder. This placeholder will be replaced by the value that we assigned to `link` in the `render_template` function.

By default, Flask uses Jinja2 as a template engine but that can be changed to the engine of your preference; we are not going into the details of how to do this in this book because it is beyond our scope.

The last route that we are going to add is the /callback route and that will be the route that will be called by Twitter after the authorization:

```
@app.route('/callback')
def callback():

    global req_token
    global consumer

    config = read_config()

    oauth_verifier = request.args.get('oauth_verifier', '')

    token = oauth.Token(req_token.oauth_token,
                        req_token.oauth_token_secret)

    token.set_verifier(oauth_verifier)

    client = oauth.Client(consumer, token)

    resp, content = client.request(config.access_token_url, 'POST')
    access_token = dict(parse_qsl(content.decode('utf-8')))

    with open('.twitterauth', 'w') as req_auth:
        file_content = yaml.dump(access_token,
        default_flow_style=False)
        req_auth.write(file_content)

    return 'All set! You can close the browser window and stop the
    server.'
```

The implementation of the callback route starts off by using global statements so we can use the global variables req_token and consumer.

Now we get to the interesting part. After the authorization, Twitter will return an outh_verifier so we get it from the request arguments and set it to the variable oauth_verifier; we create a Token instance using the oauth_token and oauth_token_secret that we obtained in the first part of our authorization process.

And we set the oauth_verifier in the Token object and finally create a new client that we are going to use to perform a new request with.

We decode the data received from the request and add it to the access token variable and, to wrap things up, we write the content of `access_token` to a file `.twitterauth` in the `twittervotes` directory. This file is also in YAML format so we are going to add another model and one more function in the `config.py` file to read the new settings.

Note that this process needs to be done just once. That is the reason that we store the data in the `.twitterauth` file. Further requests need only to use the data contained in this file.

If you check the contents of the `.twitterauth` file, you should have something similar to the following:

```
oauth_token: 31******95-***************************rt*****io
oauth_token_secret: NZH*****************************************ze8v
screen_name: the8bitcoder
user_id: '31******95'
x_auth_expires: '0'
```

To finish the Flask application, we need to add the following code at the end of the file:

```
if __name__ == '__main__':
    app.run(host='localhost', port=3000)
```

Let's add a new model to the `models.py` file in `twittervotes/core/models/` with the following content:

```
RequestAuth = namedtuple('RequestAuth', ['oauth_token',
                                         'oauth_token_secret',
                                         'user_id',
                                         'screen_name',
                                         'x_auth_expires', ])
```

Great! One more thing—we need to import the new model in the `__init__.py` file in the `twittervotes/core/models` directory:

```
from .models import RequestAuth
```

Also, let's add a function to read the `.twittervotes` file in `config.py` in `twittervotes/core`. First, we need to import the `RequestAuth`—namedtuple that we just created:

```
from .models import RequestAuth
```

Then we create a function called `read_reqauth` shown as follows:

```
def read_reqauth():
    try:
        return _read_yaml_file('.twitterauth', RequestAuth)
    except IOError as e:
        print(('It seems like you have not authorized the
        application.\n'
                'In order to use your twitter data, please run the '
                'auth.py first.'))
```

This function is very straightforward: we just call the `_read_yaml_file`, passing as arguments the `.twitterauth` file and the new `namedtuple`, `RequestAuth`, that we just created. Again, if some error occurs, we raise an exception and show a help message.

Now we can try the authentication. In the `twittervotes` directory, execute the script `twitter_auth.py`. You should see the following output:

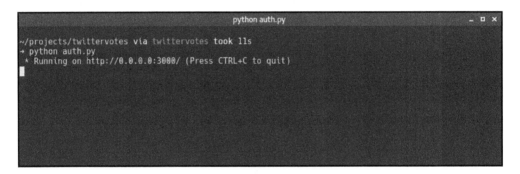

Great! The server is up and running so we can open a browser and go to `http://localhost:3000`. You should see a very simple page with a link to perform the authentication:

If you inspect the link with the browser development tools, you will see that the link is pointing to the authorize endpoint and it is passing the `oauth_token` that we created:

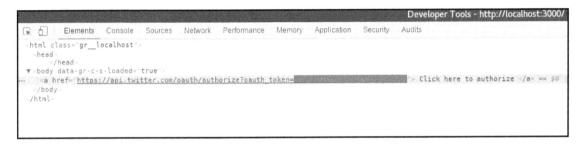

Go ahead and click on the link and you will be sent to the authorization page:

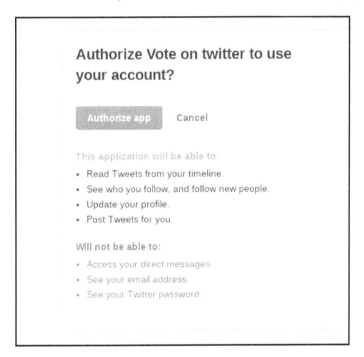

If you click on the **Authorize app** button, you will be redirected back to localhost and a success message will be displayed:

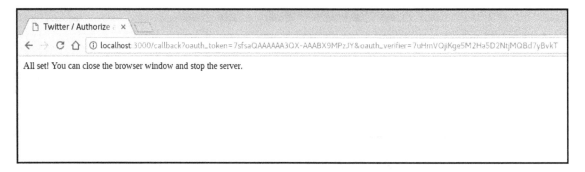

If you pay attention to the URL Twitter has sent back to us, you will find some information. The important point here is the `oauth_verifier` that we will set to the request token and we perform one last request to get the access token. Now you can close the browser, stop the Flask app, and see the results in the file `.twitterauth` in the `twittervotes` directory:

```
oauth_token: 31*******5-KNAbN*********************K40
oauth_token_secret: d***********************************Y3
screen_name: the8bitcoder
user_id: '31******95'
x_auth_expires: '0'
```

Now, all the functionality that we implemented here is very useful if other users are going to use our application; however, there's an easier way to obtain the access token if you are authorizing your own Twitter app. Let's have a look at how that is done.

Go back to the Twitter application settings in `https://apps.twitter.com/`; select the **Keys and Access Tokens** tab and scroll all the way down. If you have already authorized this application, you will see the same information we have now in the file `.twitterauth` but if you haven't authorized the application yet, you will see a **Your Access Token** section looking like the following:

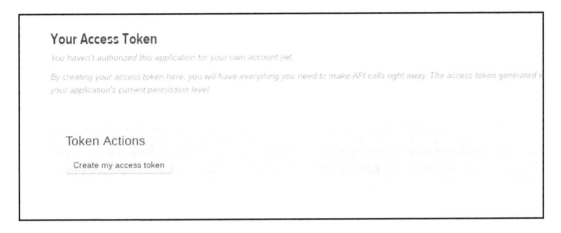

If you click on **Create my access token**, Twitter will generate the access token for you:

After the access token is created, you can just copy the data into the `.twitterauth` file.

Building the Twitter voting application

Now we have our environment set up and we have seen how to create an app on Twitter and perform three-legged authentication, it is time to get right into building the actual application that will count the Twitter votes.

We start off by creating a model class that will represent a hashtag. Create a file called hashtag.py in the twittervotes/core/twitter directory with the following content:

```
class Hashtag:
    def __init__(self, name):
        self.name = name
        self.total = 0
        self.refresh_url = None
```

This is a very simple class. We can pass a name as an argument to the initializer; the name is the hashtag without the hash sign (#). In the initializer, we define a few properties: the name, which will be set to the argument that we pass to the initializer, then a property called total that will keep the hashtag usage count for us.

Finally, we set the refresh_url. The refresh_url is going to be used to perform queries to the Twitter API, and the interesting part here is that the refresh_url already contains the id of the latest tweet that has been returned, so we can use that to fetch only tweets that we haven't already fetched, to avoid counting the same tweet multiple times.

The refresh_url looks like the following:

```
refresh_url':
'?since_id=963341767532834817&q=%23python&result_type=mixed&include
_entities=1
```

Now we can open the file __init__.py in the twittervotes/core/twitter directory and import the class that we just created, as follows:

```
from .hashtag import Hashtag
```

Perfect! Now go ahead and create a file called request.py in the twittervotes/core/ directory.

As usual, we start adding some imports:

```
import oauth2 as oauth
import time
from urllib.parse import parse_qsl
import json

import requests

from .config import read_config
from .config import read_reqauth
```

First, we import the `oauth2` package that we are going to use to perform authentication; we prepare the request, signing it with the `SHA1` key. We also import `time` to set the `OAuth` timestamp setting. We import the function `parse_qsl`, which we are going to use to parse a query string so we can prepare a new request to search for the latest tweets, and the `json` module so we can deserialize the JSON data that the Twitter API sends back to us.

Then, we import our own functions, `read_config` and `read_req_auth`, so we can read both configuration files. Lastly, we import the `json` package to parse the results and the `requests` package to perform the actual request to the Twitter search endpoint:

```
def prepare_request(url, url_params):
    reqconfig = read_reqauth()
    config = read_config()

    token = oauth.Token(
        key=reqconfig.oauth_token,
        secret=reqconfig.oauth_token_secret)

    consumer = oauth.Consumer(
        key=config.consumer_key,
        secret=config.consumer_secret)

    params = {
        'oauth_version': "1.0",
        'oauth_nonce': oauth.generate_nonce(),
        'oauth_timestamp': str(int(time.time()))
    }

    params['oauth_token'] = token.key
    params['oauth_consumer_key'] = consumer.key

    params.update(url_params)

    req = oauth.Request(method="GET", url=url, parameters=params)

    signature_method = oauth.SignatureMethod_HMAC_SHA1()
    req.sign_request(signature_method, consumer, token)

    return req.to_url()
```

This function will read both configuration files—the `config.org` configuration file contains all the endpoint URLs that we need, and also the consumer keys. The `.twitterauth` file contains the `oauth_token` and `oauth_token_secret` that we will use to create a `Token` object that we will pass along with our request.

After that, we define some parameters. `oauth_version` should, according to the Twitter API documentation, always be set to `1.0`. We also send `oauth_nonce`, which is a unique token that we must generate for every request, and lastly, `oauth_timestamp`, which is the time at which the request was created. Twitter will reject a request that was created too long before sending the request.

The last thing that we attach to the parameters is `oauth_token`, which is the token that is stored in the `.twitterath` file, and the consumer key, which is the key that was stored in the `config.yaml` file.

We perform a request to get an authorization and if everything goes right, we sign the request with an SHA1 key and return the URL of the request.

Now we are going to add the function that will perform a request to search for a specific hashtag and return the results to us. Let's go ahead and add another function called `execute_request`:

```
def execute_request(hashtag):
    config = read_config()

    if hashtag.refresh_url:
        refresh_url = hashtag.refresh_url[1:]
        url_params = dict(parse_qsl(refresh_url))
    else:
        url_params = {
            'q': f'#{hashtag.name}',
            'result_type': 'mixed'
        }

    url = prepare_request(config.search_endpoint, url_params)

    data = requests.get(url)

    results = json.loads(data.text)

    return (hashtag, results, )
```

This function will get a `Hashtag` object as an argument and the first thing we do in this function is to read the configuration file. Then we check whether the `Hashtag` object has a value in the `refresh_url` property; in that case, we are going remove the `?` sign in the front of the `refresh_url` string.

After that, we use the function `parse_qsl` to parse the query string and return a list of tuples where the first item in the tuple is the name of the parameter and the second is its value. For example, let's say we have a query string that looks like this:

```
'param1=1&param2=2&param3=3'
```

If we use the `parse_qsl`, passing as an argument this query string, we will get the following list:

```
[('param1', '1'), ('param2', '2'), ('param3', '3')]
```

And then if we pass this result to the `dict` function, we will get a dictionary like this:

```
{'param1': '1', 'param2': '2', 'param3': '3'}
```

As I showed before, the `refresh_url` has the following format:

```
refresh_url':
'?since_id=963341767532834817&q=%23python&result_type=mixed&include
_entities=1
```

And after parsing and transforming it into a dictionary, we can use it to get refreshed data for the underlying hashtag.

If the `Hashtag` object does not have the property `refresh_url` set, then we simply define a dictionary where the `q` is the hashtag name and the result type is set to `mixed` to tell the Twitter API that it should return popular, recent, and real-time tweets.

After defining the search parameters, we use the `prepare_request` function that we created above to authorize the request and sign it; when we get the URL back, we perform the request using the URL we get back from the `prepare_request` function.

We make use of the `json.loads` function to parse the JSON data and return a tuple containing the first item, the hashtag itself; the second item will be the results we get back from the request.

The final touch, as usual, is to import the `execute_request` function in the `__init__.py` file in the core module:

```
from .request import execute_request
```

Let's see how that works in the Python REPL:

```
                                    python                              _ □ ✕
(twittervotes-CGzwc7tX) twittervotes git:master > python            ✷ ★
Python 3.6.2 (default, Dec 22 2017, 15:38:46)
[GCC 6.3.0 20170516] on linux
Type "help", "copyright", "credits" or "license" for more information.
>>> from core.twitter import HashTag
>>> from core import execute_request
>>> from pprint import pprint as pp
>>> hashtag = HashTag('python')
>>> result = execute_request(hashtag)
>>> pp(result)
(<core.twitter.hashtag.HashTag object at 0x7f01caba7588>,
 {'search_metadata': {'completed_in': 0.04,
                       'count': 15,
                       'max_id': 963345304836820993,
                       'max_id_str': '963345304836820993',
                       'query': '%23python',
                       'refresh_url': '?since_id=963345304836820993&q=%23python&result_type=mixed&include_entities=1',
                       'since_id': 0,
                       'since_id_str': '0'},
  'statuses': [{'contributors': None,
                'coordinates': None,
                'created_at': 'Mon Feb 12 03:42:18 +0000 2018',
                'entities': {'hashtags': [{'indices': [27, 39],
                                           'text': 'DataScience'},
                                          {'indices': [45, 52],
                                           'text': 'Python'},
                                          {'indices': [78, 84],
                                           'text': 'abdsc'},
                                          {'indices': [85, 93],
                                           'text': 'BigData'},
                                          {'indices': [94, 110],
                                           'text': 'MachineLearning'}],
```

The output above is much bigger than this but a lot of it has been omitted; I just wanted to demonstrate how the function works.

Enhancing our code

We also want to give our users a good experience so we are going to add a command-line parser so the users of our application can specify some parameters before starting the voting process. There will be only one argument that we are going to implement and that is `--hashtags`, where users can pass a space-separated list of hashtags.

With that said, we are going to define some rules for these arguments. First, we will limit the maximum number of hashtags that we are going to monitor, so we are going to add a rule that no more than four hashtags can be used.

If the user specifies more than four hashtags, we will simply display a warning on the Terminal and pick the first four hashtags. We also want to remove the duplicated hashtags.

When showing these warning messages that we talked about, we could simply print them on the Terminal and it would definitely work; however, we want to make things more interesting, so we are going to use the logging package to do it. Apart from that, implementing a proper logging will give us much more control over what kind of log we want to have and also how we want to present it to the users.

Before we start implementing the command-line parser, let's add the logger. Create a file called `app_logger.py` in the `twittervotes/core` directory with the following content:

```
import os
import logging
from logging.config import fileConfig


def get_logger():
    core_dir = os.path.dirname(os.path.abspath(__file__))
    file_path = os.path.join(core_dir, '..', 'logconfig.ini')
    fileConfig(file_path)
    return logging.getLogger('twitterVotesLogger')
```

This function doesn't do much but first we import the `os` module, then we import the logging package, and lastly, we import the function `fileConfig`, which reads the logging configuration from a config file. This configuration file has to be in the `configparser` format and you can get more information about this format at `https://docs.python.org/3.6/library/logging.config.html#logging-config-fileformat`.

After we read the configuration file, we just return a logger called `twitterVotesLogger`.

Let's see what the configuration file for our application looks like. Create a file called `logconfig.ini` in the `twittervotes` directory with the following content:

```
[loggers]
keys=root,twitterVotesLogger

[handlers]
keys=consoleHandler

[formatters]
keys=simpleFormatter

[logger_root]
level=INFO
handlers=consoleHandler

[logger_twitterVotesLogger]
level=INFO
```

```
handlers=consoleHandler
qualname=twitterVotesLogger


[handler_consoleHandler]
class=StreamHandler
level=INFO
formatter=simpleFormatter
args=(sys.stdout,)

[formatter_simpleFormatter]
format=[%(levelname)s] %(asctime)s - %(message)s
datefmt=%Y-%m-%d %H:%M:%S
```

So here we define two loggers, `root` and `twitterVotesLogger`; the loggers are responsible for exposing methods that we can use at runtime to log messages. It is also through the loggers that we can set the level of severity, for example, INFO, DEBUG and so on. Lastly, the logger passes the log messages along to the appropriated handler.

In the definition of our `twitterVotesLogger`, we set the level of severity to INFO, we set the handler to `consoleHandler` (we are going to describe this very soon), and we also set a qualified name that will be used when we want to get hold of the `twitterVotesLogger`.

The last option for `twitterVotesLoggers` is `propagate`. Since the `twitterVotesLogger` is a child logger, we don't want the log message sent through the `twittersVotesLogger` to propagate to its ancestors. Without `propagate` set to 0, every log message would be shown twice since the `twitterVotesLogger`'s ancestor is the `root` logger.

The next component in the logging configuration is the handler. Handlers are the component that sends the log messages of a specific logger to a destination. We defined a handler called `consoleHandler` of type `StreamHandler`, which is a built-in handler of the logging module. The `StreamHandler` sends out log messages to streams such as `sys.stdout`, `sys.stderr`, or a file. This is perfect for us because we want to send messages to the Terminal.

In the `consoleHandler`, we also set the severity level to INFO and also we set the formatter which is set to the `customFormatter`; then we set the value for args to `(sys.stdout, )`. Args specify where the log messages will be sent to; in this case, we set only `sys.stdout` but you can add multiple output streams if you need.

The last component of this configuration is the formatter `customFormatter`. Formatters simply define how the log message should be displayed. In our `customFormatter`, we just define how the message should be displayed and show the date format.

Now that we have the logging in place, let's add the functions that will parse the command line. Create a file `cmdline_parser.py` in `twittervotes/core` and add some imports:

```
from argparse import ArgumentParser

from .app_logger import get_logger
```

Then we will need to add a function that will validate the command-line arguments:

```
def validated_args(args):

    logger = get_logger()

    unique_hashtags = list(set(args.hashtags))

    if len(unique_hashtags) < len(args.hashtags):
        logger.info(('Some hashtags passed as arguments were '
                        'duplicated and are going to be ignored'))

        args.hashtags = unique_hashtags

    if len(args.hashtags) > 4:
        logger.error('Voting app accepts only 4 hashtags at the
        time')
        args.hashtags = args.hashtags[:4]

    return args
```

`validate_args` functions have only one parameter and it is the arguments that have been parsed by the `ArgumentParser`. The first thing we do in this function is to get hold of the logger that we just created, so we can send log messages to inform the user about possible problems in the command-line arguments that have been passed to the application.

Next, we transform the list of hashtags into a set so all the duplicated hashtags are removed and then we transform it back to a list. After that, we check whether the number of unique hashtags is less than the original number of hashtags that have been passed on the command line. That means that we had duplication and we log a message to inform the user about that.

The last verification we do is to make sure that a maximum of four hashtags will be monitored by our application. If the number of items in the hashtag list is greater than four, then we slice the array, getting only the first four items, and we also log a message to inform the user that only four hashtags will be displayed.

Let's add another function, `parse_commandline_args`:

```
def parse_commandline_args():
    argparser = ArgumentParser(
        prog='twittervoting',
        description='Collect votes using twitter hashtags.')

    required = argparser.add_argument_group('require arguments')

    required.add_argument(
        '-ht', '--hashtags',
        nargs='+',
        required=True,
        dest='hashtags',
        help=('Space separated list specifying the '
                'hashtags that will be used for the voting.\n'
                'Type the hashtags without the hash symbol.'))

    args = argparser.parse_args()

    return validated_args(args)
```

We saw how the `ArgumentParser` works when we were developing the application in the first chapter, the weather application. However, we can still go through what this function does.

First, we define an `ArgumentParser` object, defining a name and a description, and we create a subgroup called `required` that, as the name suggests, will have all the required fields.

Note that we don't really need to create this extra group; however, I find that it helps to keep the code more organized and easier to maintain in case it is necessary to add new options in the future.

We define only one argument, `hashtags`. In the definition of the `hashtags` argument, there is an argument called `nargs` and we have set it to +; this means that I can pass an unlimited number of items separated by spaces, as follows:

```
--hashtags item1 item2 item3
```

The last thing we do in this function is to parse the arguments with the `parse_args` function and run the arguments through the `validate_args` function that has been shown previously.

Let's import the `parse_commandline_args` function in the `__init__.py` file in the `twittervotes/core` directory:

```
from .cmdline_parser import parse_commandline_args
```

Now we need to create a class that will help us to manage hashtags and perform tasks such as keeping the score count of hashtags, updating its value after every request. So let's go ahead and create a class called `HashtagStatsManager`. Create a file called `hashtagstats_manager.py` in `twittervotes/core/twitter` with the following content:

```python
from .hashtag import Hashtag


class HashtagStatsManager:

    def __init__(self, hashtags):

        if not hashtags:
            raise AttributeError('hashtags must be provided')

        self._hashtags = {hashtag: Hashtag(hashtag) for hashtag in
            hashtags}
    def update(self, data):

        hashtag, results = data
        metadata = results.get('search_metadata')
        refresh_url = metadata.get('refresh_url')
        statuses = results.get('statuses')

        total = len(statuses)

        if total > 0:
            self._hashtags.get(hashtag.name).total += total
            self._hashtags.get(hashtag.name).refresh_url =
            refresh_url

    @property
    def hashtags(self):
        return self._hashtags
```

This class is also very simple: in the constructor, we get a list of hashtags and initialize a property, _hashtags, which will be a dictionary where the key is the name of the hashtag and the value is an instance of the Hashtag class.

The update method gets a tuple containing a Hashtag object and the results are returned by the Twitter API. First, we unpack the tuple values and set it to the hashtag and results variables. The results dictionary has two items that are interesting to us. The first is the search_metadata; in this item, we will find the refresh_url and the statuses contain a list of all tweets that used the hashtag that we were searching for.

So we get the values for the search_metadata, the refresh_url, and lastly the statuses. Then we count how many items there are in the statuses list. If the number of items on the statuses list is greater than 0, we update the total count for the underlying hashtag as well as its refresh_url.

Then we import the HashtagStatsManager class that we just created in the __init__.py file in the twittervotes/core/twitter directory:

```
from .hashtagstats_manager import HashtagStatsManager
```

The heart of this application is the class Runner. This class will perform the execution of a function and queue it in the process pool. Every function will be executed in parallel in a different process, which will make the program much faster than if I executed these functions one by one.

Let's have a look at how the Runner class is implemented:

```
import concurrent.futures

from rx import Observable


class Runner:

    def __init__(self, on_success, on_error, on_complete):
        self._on_success = on_success
        self._on_error = on_error
        self._on_complete = on_complete

    def exec(self, func, items):

        observables = []

        with concurrent.futures.ProcessPoolExecutor() as executor:
            for item in items.values():
```

```
    _future = executor.submit(func, item)
    observables.append(Observable.from_future(_future))
all_observables = Observable.merge(observables)
all_observables.subscribe(self._on_success,
                          self._on_error,
                          self._on_complete)
```

The class `Runner` has an initializer taking three arguments; they are all functions that will be called in different statuses of the execution. `on_success` will be called when the execution of the item has been successful, `on_error` when the execution of one function has failed for some reason, and finally `on_complete` will be called when all the functions in the queue have been executed.

There is also a method called `exec` that takes a function as the first argument, which is the function that will be executed, and the second argument is a list of `Hashtag` instances.

There are a few interesting things in the `Runner` class. First, we are using the `concurrent.futures` module, which is a really nice addition to Python and has been around since Python 3.2; this module provides ways of executing callables asynchronously.

The `concurrent.futures` module also provides the `ThreadPoolExecutor`, which will perform asynchronous executions using threads, and the `ProcessPollExecutor`, which uses a process. You can easily switch between these execution strategies according to your needs.

The rule of thumb is if your function is CPU-bound, it is a good idea to use `ProcessPollExecutor`, otherwise, you will suffer big performances issues because of the Python **Global Interpreter Lock** (**GIL**). For I/O-bound operations, I prefer using `ThreadPoolExecutor`.

If you want to read more about the GIL, you can check out the following wiki page: `https://wiki.python.org/moin/GlobalInterpreterLock`.

Since we are not doing any I/O-bound operations, we use `ProcessPoolExecutor`. Then, we loop through the values of the items, which is a dictionary containing all the hashtags that our application is monitoring. And for every hashtag, we pass it to the `submit` function of the `ProcessPollExecutor` along with the function that we want to execute; in our case, it will be the `execute_request` function defined in the core module of our application.

The submit function, instead of returning the value returned by the execute_request function, will return a future object, which encapsulates the asynchronous execution of the execute_request function. The future object provides methods to cancel an execution, check the status of the execution, get the results of the execution, and so on.

Now, we want a way to be notified when the executions change state or when they finish. That is where reactive programming comes in handy.

Here, we get the future object and create an Observable. Observables are the core of reactive programming. An Observable is an object that can be observed and emit events at any given time. When an Observable emits an event, all observers that subscribed to that Observable will be notified and react to those changes.

This is exactly what we are trying to achieve here: we have an array of future executions and we want to be notified when those executions change state. These states will be handled by the functions that we passed as an argument to the Runner initializer—_on_sucess, _on_error, and _on_complete.

Perfect! Let's import the Runner class into __init__.py in the twittervotes/core directory:

```
from .runner import Runner
```

The last piece of our project is to add the entry point of our application. We are going to add the user interface using the Tkinter package from the standard library. So let's start implementing it. Create a file called app.py in the twittervotes directory, and let's start by adding some imports:

```
from core import parse_commandline_args
from core import execute_request
from core import Runner

from core.twitter import HashtagStatsManager

from tkinter import Tk
from tkinter import Frame
from tkinter import Label
from tkinter import StringVar
from tkinter.ttk import Button
```

Here, we import the command-line argument parser that we created, execute_request to perform the requests to the Twitter API, and also the Runner class that will help us execute the requests to the Twitter API in parallel.

We also import the `HashtagStatsManager` to manage the hashtag voting results for us.

Lastly, we have all the imports related to `tkinter`.

In the same file, let's create a class called `Application` as follows:

```
class Application(Frame):

    def __init__(self, hashtags=[], master=None):
        super().__init__(master)

        self._manager = HashtagStatsManager(hashtags)

        self._runner = Runner(self._on_success,
                                self._on_error,
                                self._on_complete)

        self._items = {hashtag: StringVar() for hashtag in
hashtags}
        self.set_header()
        self.create_labels()
        self.pack()

        self.button = Button(self, style='start.TButton',
                                text='Update',
                                command=self._fetch_data)
        self.button.pack(side="bottom")
```

So here, we create a class, `Application`, that inherits from `Frame`. The initializer takes two arguments: hashtags, which are the hashtags that we are going to monitor, and the master argument, which is an object of type `Tk`.

Then we create an instance of `HashtagStatsManager`, passing the list of hashtags; we also create an instance of the `Runner` class passing three arguments. These arguments are functions that will be called when one execution finishes successfully, when the execution fails, and when all the executions are complete.

Then we have a dictionary comprehension that will create a dictionary where the keys are the hashtags and the values are a `Tkinter` variable of type string, which in the `Tkinter` world is called `StringVar`. We do that so it will be easier to update the labels with the results later on.

We call the methods `set_header` and `create_labels` that we are going to implement shortly and finally we call `pack`. The `pack` function will organize widgets such as buttons and labels and place them in the parent widget, in this case, the `Application`.

Then we define a button that will execute the function `_fetch_data` when clicked and we use `pack` to place the button at the bottom of the frame:

```
def set_header(self):
    title = Label(self,
                    text='Voting for hasthags',
                    font=("Helvetica", 24),
                    height=4)
    title.pack()
```

Here's the `set_header` method that I mentioned earlier; it simply creates `Label` objects and places them at the top of the frame.

Now we can add the `create_labels` method:

```
def create_labels(self):
    for key, value in self._items.items():
        label = Label(self,
                        textvariable=value,
                        font=("Helvetica", 20), height=3)
        label.pack()
        self._items[key].set(f'#{key}\nNumber of votes: 0')
```

The `create_labels` method loops through `self._items`, which, if you remember, is a dictionary where the key is the name of the hashtag and the value is a `Tkinter` variable of type string.

First, we create a `Label`, and the interesting part is the `textvariable` argument; we set it to `value`, which is a `Tkinter` variable related to a specific hashtag. Then we place the `Label` in the frame and, lastly, we set the value of the label using the function `set`.

Then we need to add a method that will update the `Labels` for us:

```
def _update_label(self, data):
    hashtag, result = data

    total = self._manager.hashtags.get(hashtag.name).total

    self._items[hashtag.name].set(
        f'#{hashtag.name}\nNumber of votes: {total}')
```

The `_update_label`, as the name suggests, updates the label of a specific hashtag. The data argument is the results returned by the Twitter API and we get the total number of the hashtags from the manager. Finally, we use the `set` function again to update the label.

Let's add another function that will actually do the work of sending the requests to the Twitter API:

```
def _fetch_data(self):
    self._runner.exec(execute_request,
                      self._manager.hashtags)
```

This method will call the method `exec` of the `Runner` to execute the function that performs the requests to the Twitter API.

Then we need to define the methods that will handle the events emitted by the `Observables` created in the `Runner` class; we start by adding the method that will handle execution errors:

```
def _on_error(self, error_message):
    raise Exception(error_message)
```

This is a `helper` method just to raise an exception in case something goes wrong with the execution of the requests.

Then we add another method that handles when the execution of an `Observable` has been successful:

```
def _on_success(self, data):
    hashtag, _ = data
    self._manager.update(data)
    self._update_label(data)
```

The `_on_success` method is going to be called when one execution from the `Runner` finished successfully, and it will just update the manager with the new data and also update the label in the UI.

Lastly, we define a method that will handle when all the executions have been completed:

```
def _on_complete(self):
    pass
```

The `_on_complete` will be called when all the executions of the `Runner` finish. We are not going to be using it so we just use the `pass` statement.

Now it is time to implement the function that will set up the application and initialize the UI—the function `start_app`:

```
def start_app(args):
    root = Tk()

    app = Application(hashtags=args.hashtags, master=root)
    app.master.title("Twitter votes")
    app.master.geometry("400x700+100+100")
    app.mainloop()
```

This function creates the root application, sets the title, defines its dimensions, and also calls the `mainloop` function so the application keeps running.

The last piece is to define the `main` function:

```
def main():
    args = parse_commandline_args()
    start_app(args)


if __name__ == '__main__':
    main()
```

The `main` function is pretty simple. First, we parse the command-line arguments, then we start the application, passing the command-line arguments to it.

Let's see the application in action! Run the following command:

```
python app.py --help
```

You will see the following output:

```
daniel@musashi: ~/Projects/twittervotes                                    _ □ ×
~/Projects/twittervotes $ python app.py --help
usage: twittervoting [-h] -t TIME -ht HASHTAGS [HASHTAGS ...]

Collect votes using twitter hashtags.

optional arguments:
  -h, --help            show this help message and exit

require arguments:
  -t TIME, --time TIME  Specify the active voting time
  -ht HASHTAGS [HASHTAGS ...], --hashtags HASHTAGS [HASHTAGS ...]
                        Comma-separated list specifying the hashtags that will
                        be used for the voting. Type the hashtags with the
                        hash symbol.
~/Projects/twittervotes $ █
```

Let's say we want the voting process to run for 3 minutes and it will monitor the hashtags `#debian`, `#ubuntu`, and `#arch`:

```
python app.py --hashtags debian ubuntu arch
```

Then you should see the following UI:

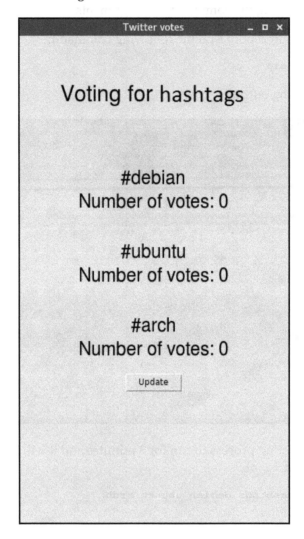

And if you click the **Update** button, the count for every hashtag will be updated.

Summary

In this chapter, we developed an application to cast votes on Twitter and we learned the different concepts and paradigms of the Python programming language.

By creating the hashtag voting application, you have learned how to create and configure a Twitter app and also how to implement a three-legged `OAuth` authentication to consume data from the Twitter API.

We also learned how to use the logging module to show informational messages to the users of our application. Like the previous modules, we also created a command-line parser using the `ArgumentParser` module in the standard library.

We also had an introduction to reactive programming using the `Rx` (Reactive Extensions for Python) module. Then we used the `concurrent.futures` module to enhance the performance of our application, running multiple requests to the Twitter API in parallel.

Lastly, we built a user interface using the `Tkinter` module.

In the next chapter, we are going to build an application that will fetch exchange rate data from the site `http://fixer.io` to perform currency conversion.

4
Exchange Rates and the Currency Conversion Tool

In the previous chapter, we built a really cool application to count votes on Twitter and learned how to authenticate and consume the Twitter API using Python. We also had a good introduction to how to use Reactive Extensions for Python. In this chapter, we are going to create a terminal tool that will fetch exchange rates for the current day from `fixer.io` and use this information to convert the value between different currencies.

`Fixer.io` is a very nice project created by `https://github.com/hakanensari`; on a daily basis, it fetches foreign exchange rate data from the European Central Bank. The API that he created is simple to use and works pretty well.

Our project starts out by creating a framework around the API; when that is in place, we are going to create a terminal application where we can perform currency conversion. All the data that we fetch from the `fixer.io` is going to be stored in a MongoDB database, so we can perform conversions without doing requests to `fixer.io` all the time. This will increase the performance of our application.

In this chapter, we will cover the following:

- How to use `pipenv` to install and manage our project's dependencies
- Working with MongoDB using the PyMongo module
- Consuming REST APIs using Requests

With that said, let's get started!

Setting up the environment

As usual, we will start by setting up our environment; the first thing we need to do is set up a virtual environment that will allow us to easily install our project dependencies without interfering with Python's global installation.

In the previous chapters, we used `virtualenv` to create our virtual environment; however, Kenneth Reitz (the creator of the popular package *requests*) created `pipenv`. `pipenv` is for Python what NPM is for Node.js. However, `pipenv` is used for much more than package management, and it also creates and manages a virtual environment for you. In my opinion, there are a lot of advantages of the old development workflows, but for me, there are two things that stand out: the first is that you no longer need two different tools (`pip`, `virtualenv`), and the second is that it is much simpler to have all these great features in just one place.

Another thing that I really like about `pipenv` is the use of `Pipfile`. Sometimes, it is really hard to work with requirement files. Our production environment and development environment have the same dependencies, and you end up having to maintain two different files; plus, every time you need to remove one dependency, you will need to edit the requirement file manually.

With `pipenv`, you don't need to worry about having multiple requirement files. Development and production dependencies are placed in the same file, and `pipenv` also takes care of updating the `Pipfile`.

Installing `pipenv` is quite simple, just run:

```
pip install pipenv
```

After installing it you can run:

```
pipenv --help
```

You should see an output like the following:

```
                              daniel@musashi: ~                              _ □ ✕
~ ) pipenv --help
Usage: pipenv [OPTIONS] COMMAND [ARGS]...

Options:
  --update          Update Pipenv & pip to latest.
  --where           Output project home information.
  --venv            Output virtualenv information.
  --py              Output Python interpreter information.
  --envs            Output Environment Variable options.
  --rm              Remove the virtualenv.
  --bare            Minimal output.
  --completion      Output completion (to be eval'd).
  --man             Display manpage.
  --three / --two   Use Python 3/2 when creating virtualenv.
  --python TEXT     Specify which version of Python virtualenv should use.
  --site-packages   Enable site-packages for the virtualenv.
  --jumbotron       An easter egg, effectively.
  --version         Show the version and exit.
  -h, --help        Show this message and exit.

Commands:
  check       Checks for security vulnerabilities and against PEP 508 markers
              provided in Pipfile.
  graph       Displays currently-installed dependency graph information.
  install     Installs provided packages and adds them to Pipfile, or (if none
              is given), installs all packages.
  lock        Generates Pipfile.lock.
  open        View a given module in your editor.
  run         Spawns a command installed into the virtualenv.
  shell       Spawns a shell within the virtualenv.
  uninstall   Un-installs a provided package and removes it from Pipfile.
  update      Uninstalls all packages, and re-installs package(s) in [packages]
              to latest compatible versions.
~ )
```

We are not going to go through all the different options because that is beyond the scope of this book, but while we are creating our environment, you will acquire a good knowledge of the basics.

The first step is to create a directory for our project. Let's create a directory called `currency_converter`:

```
mkdir currency_converter && cd currency_converter
```

Now that you are inside the `currency_converter` directory, we are going to use `pipenv` to create our virtual environment. Run the following command:

```
pipenv --python python3.6
```

This will create a virtual environment for the project living in the current directory and will use Python 3.6. The `--python` option also accepts a path to where you installed Python. In my case, I always download the Python source code, build it, and install it in a different location, so this is very useful for me.

You could also use the `--three` option, which would use the default Python3 installation on your system. After running the command, you should see the following output:

```
currency_converter > pipenv --python python3.6
Creating a virtualenv for this project...
Using /home/daniel/Installs/Python3.6/bin/python3.6 to create virtualenv...
"Running virtualenv with interpreter /home/daniel/Installs/Python3.6/bin/python3.6
Using base prefix '/home/daniel/Installs/Python3.6'
New python executable in /home/daniel/Envs/currency_converter-1R21vlbY/bin/python3.6
Also creating executable in /home/daniel/Envs/currency_converter-1R21vlbY/bin/python
Installing setuptools, pip, wheel...done.

Virtualenv location: /home/daniel/Envs/currency_converter-1R21vlbY
currency_converter >
```

If you have a look at the contents of the `Pipfile`, you should have something similar to the following:

```
[[source]]

url = "https://pypi.python.org/simple"
verify_ssl = true
name = "pypi"


[dev-packages]


[packages]


[requires]

python_version = "3.6"
```

This file starts defining where to get the packages from, and in this case, it will download packages from `pypi`. Then, we have a place for the development dependencies of our project, and in `packages`, the production dependencies. Lastly, it says that this project requires Python version 3.6.

Great! Now you can use some commands. For example, if you want to know which virtual environment the project uses, you can run `pipenv --venv`; you will see the following output:

```
daniel@musashi: ~/currency_converter                                          _  □  ×
currency_converter ❯ pipenv --venv
/home/daniel/Envs/currency_converter-1R21vlbY
currency_converter ❯
```

If you want to activate the virtual environment for the project, you can use the `shell` command, as follows:

```
daniel@musashi: ~/currency_converter                                          _  □  ×
currency_converter ❯ pipenv shell
Spawning environment shell (/usr/bin/zsh). Use 'exit' to leave.
source /home/daniel/Envs/currency_converter-1R21vlbY/bin/activate
currency_converter ❯ source /home/daniel/Envs/currency_converter-1R21vlbY/bin/activate
(currency_converter-1R21vlbY) currency_converter ❯
```

Perfect! With the virtual environment in place, we can start adding our project's dependencies.

The first dependency that we are going to add is `requests`.

Run the following command:

```
pipenv install requests
```

We will get the following output:

```
daniel@musashi: ~/currency_converter                                    _ □ ×
(currency_converter-1R21vlbY) currency_converter > pipenv install requests
Installing requests...
Collecting requests
  Using cached requests-2.18.4-py2.py3-none-any.whl
Collecting certifi>=2017.4.17 (from requests)
  Using cached certifi-2018.1.18-py2.py3-none-any.whl
Collecting idna<2.7,>=2.5 (from requests)
  Using cached idna-2.6-py2.py3-none-any.whl
Collecting urllib3<1.23,>=1.21.1 (from requests)
  Using cached urllib3-1.22-py2.py3-none-any.whl
Collecting chardet<3.1.0,>=3.0.2 (from requests)
  Using cached chardet-3.0.4-py2.py3-none-any.whl
Installing collected packages: certifi, idna, urllib3, chardet, requests
Successfully installed certifi-2018.1.18 chardet-3.0.4 idna-2.6 requests-2.18.4 urllib3-1.22

Adding requests to Pipfile's [packages]...
  PS: You have excellent taste! ❀ 🎁 ❀
Locking [dev-packages] dependencies...
Locking [packages] dependencies...
Updated Pipfile.lock (7b8df8)!
(currency_converter-1R21vlbY) currency_converter >
```

As you can see, `pipenv` installs `requests` as well as all its dependencies.

 The author of `pipenv` is the same developer who created the popular `requests` library. In the installation output, you can see an easter egg, saying `PS: You have excellent taste!`.

The other dependency that we need to add to our project is `pymongo` so that we can connect and manipulate data in a MongoDB database.

Run the following command:

```
pipenv install pymongo
```

We will get the following output:

```
                    daniel@musashi: ~/currency_converter                    _ □ ×
(currency_converter-1R21vlbY) currency_converter > pipenv install pymongo
Installing pymongo…
Collecting pymongo
  Using cached pymongo-3.6.0-cp36-cp36m-manylinux1_x86_64.whl
Installing collected packages: pymongo
Successfully installed pymongo-3.6.0

Adding pymongo to Pipfile's [packages]…
Locking [dev-packages] dependencies…
Locking [packages] dependencies…
Updated Pipfile.lock (39cdd0)!
(currency_converter-1R21vlbY) currency_converter >
```

Let's have a look at the `Pipfile` and see how it looks now:

```
[[source]]

url = "https://pypi.python.org/simple"
verify_ssl = true
name = "pypi"


[dev-packages]



[packages]

requests = "*"
pymongo = "*"


[requires]

python_version = "3.6"
```

As you can see, under the `packages` folder, we have now our two dependencies.

Not much has changed in comparison with installing packages with `pip`. The exception is that now installing and removing dependencies will automatically update the `Pipfile`.

Another command that is very useful is the `graph` command. Run the following command:

```
pipenv graph
```

We will get the following output:

```
daniel@musashi: ~/currency_converter                                    _ □ ✕
(currency_converter-1R21vlbY) currency_converter ❯ pipenv graph
pymongo==3.6.0
requests==2.18.4
  - certifi [required: >=2017.4.17, installed: 2018.1.18]
  - chardet [required: <3.1.0,>=3.0.2, installed: 3.0.4]
  - idna [required: <2.7,>=2.5, installed: 2.6]
  - urllib3 [required: >=1.21.1,<1.23, installed: 1.22]

(currency_converter-1R21vlbY) currency_converter ❯
```

As you can see, the `graph` command is very helpful when you want to know what the dependencies of the packages you have installed are. In our project, we can see that `pymongo` doesn't have any extra dependencies. However, `requests` has four dependencies: `certifi`, `chardet`, `idna`, and `urllib3`.

Now that you have had a great introduction to `pipenv`, let's have a look at what this project's structure will look like:

```
currency_converter
└── currency_converter
       ├── config
       ├── core
```

The top `currency_converter` is the application's `root` directory. Then, one level down we have another `currency_converter` and that is the `currency_converter` module that we are going to create.

Inside the `currency_converter` module directory, we have a core which contains the application core functionality, for example, a command line argument parser, helper functions to handle data, and so on.

We have also configured, as with the other projects, which project will contain functions to read YAML configuration files; finally, we have HTTP, which have all the functions that will perform HTTP requests to the `fixer.io` REST API.

Now that we have learned how to use `pipenv` and how it will help us to be more productive, we can install the initial dependencies to our project. We created the project's directory structure, too. The only missing piece of the puzzle is installing MongoDB.

I'm using Linux Debian 9 and I can easily just install this using Debian's package manager tool:

```
sudo apt install mongodb
```

You will find MongoDB in the package repositories of the most popular Linux distributions, and if you are using Windows or macOS, you can see the instructions in the following links:

For macOS: `https://docs.mongodb.com/manual/tutorial/install-mongodb-on-os-x/`

For Windows: `https://docs.mongodb.com/manual/tutorial/install-mongodb-on-windows/`

After installation, you can verify that everything is working properly using the MongoDB client. Open a terminal and just run the `mongo` command.

And you should get into the MongoDB shell:

```
MongoDB shell version: 3.2.11
connecting to: test
```

To exit the MongoDB shell, just type *CTRL + D*.

Perfect! Now we are ready to start coding!

Creating the API wrapper

In this section, we are going to create a set of functions that will wrap the `fixer.io` API and will help us use it in a simple way within our project.

Let's go ahead and create a new file called `request.py` in
the `currency_converter/currency_converter/core` directory. First, we are going to
include some `import` statements:

```
import requests
from http import HTTPStatus
import json
```

We obviously need `requests` so that we can perform requests to the `fixer.io` endpoints,
and we are also importing `HTTPStatus` from the HTTP module so we can return the correct
HTTP status code; also be a bit more verbose in our code. It's much nicer and easier to read
the `HTTPStatus.OK` return than only `200`.

Lastly, we import the `json` package so that we can parse the JSON content that we get from
`fixer.io` into Python objects.

Next, we are going to add our first function. This function will return the current exchange
rates given a specific currency:

```
def fetch_exchange_rates_by_currency(currency):
    response = requests.get(f'https://api.fixer.io/latest?base=
                               {currency}')

    if response.status_code == HTTPStatus.OK:
        return json.loads(response.text)
    elif response.status_code == HTTPStatus.NOT_FOUND:
        raise ValueError(f'Could not find the exchange rates for:
                           {currency}.')
    elif response.status_code == HTTPStatus.BAD_REQUEST:
        raise ValueError(f'Invalid base currency value:
{currency}')
    else:
        raise Exception((f'Something went wrong and we were unable
                          to fetch'
                         f' the exchange rates for: {currency}'))
```

This function gets a currency as an argument and starts off by sending a request to
the `fixer.io` API to get the latest exchange rates using the currency as a base, which was
given as an argument.

If the response was `HTTPStatus.OK` (`200`), we use the load function from the JSON module
to parse the JSON response; otherwise, we raise exceptions depending on the error that
occurs.

We can also create a file called __init__.py in
the currency_converter/currency_converter/core directory and import the function
that we just created:

```
from .request import fetch_exchange_rates_by_currency
```

Great! Let's try it out in the Python REPL:

```
Python 3.6.3 (default, Nov 21 2017, 06:53:07)
[GCC 6.3.0 20170516] on linux
Type "help", "copyright", "credits" or "license" for more information.
>>> from currency_converter.core import fetch_exchange_rates_by_currency
>>> from pprint import pprint as pp
>>> exchange_rates = fetch_exchange_rates_by_currency('BRL')
>>> pp(exchange_rates)
{'base': 'BRL',
 'date': '2017-12-06',
 'rates': {'AUD': 0.40754,
           'BGN': 0.51208,
           'CAD': 0.39177,
           'CHF': 0.30576,
           'CNY': 2.0467,
           'CZK': 6.7122,
           'DKK': 1.9486,
           'EUR': 0.26183,
           'GBP': 0.23129,
           'HKD': 2.4173,
           'HRK': 1.9758,
           'HUF': 82.332,
           'IDR': 4191.1,
           'ILS': 1.0871,
           'INR': 19.963,
           'JPY': 34.697,
           'KRW': 338.15,
           'MXN': 5.8134,
           'MYR': 1.261,
           'NOK': 2.5548,
           'NZD': 0.4488,
           'PHP': 15.681,
           'PLN': 1.1034,
           'RON': 1.2128,
           'RUB': 18.273,
           'SEK': 2.599,
           'SGD': 0.41696,
           'THB': 10.096,
           'TRY': 1.191,
           'USD': 0.3094,
```

```
'ZAR': 4.1853}}
```

Perfect! It works just like we expected.

Next, we are going to start building the database helper class.

Adding the database helper class

Now that we have implemented the function that will fetch the exchange rate information from `fixer.io`, we need to add the class that will retrieve and save the information we fetched into our MongoDB.

So, let's go ahead and create a file called `db.py` inside the `currency_converter/currency_converter/core` directory; let's add some `import` statements:

```
from pymongo import MongoClient
```

The only thing we need to `import` is the `MongoClient`. The `MongoClient` will be responsible for opening a connection with our database instance.

Now, we need to add the `DbClient` class. The idea of this class is to serve as a wrapper around the `pymongo` package functions and provide a simpler set of functions, abstracting some of the repetitive boilerplate code when working with `pymongo`:

```
class DbClient:

    def __init__(self, db_name, default_collection):
        self._db_name = db_name
        self._default_collection = default_collection
        self._db = None
```

a class called `DbClient` and its constructor gets two arguments, `db_name` and `default_collection`. Note that, in MongoDB, we don't need to create the database and the collection before using it. When we try to insert data for the first time, the database and the collection will be created for us.

This might seem strange if you are used to working with SQL databases such as MySQL or MSSQL where you have to connect to the server instance, create a database, and create all the tables before using it.

We aren't concerned about security in this example since MongoDB is beyond the scope of this book and we are only focusing on Python.

Then, we are going to add two methods, `connect` and `disconnect`, to the database:

```
def connect(self):
    self._client = MongoClient('mongodb://127.0.0.1:27017/')
    self._db = self._client.get_database(self._db_name)

def disconnect(self):
    self._client.close()
```

The `connect` method will use the `MongoClient` connecting to the database instance at our localhost, using the port `27017` which is the default port that MongoDB runs right after the installation. These two values might be different for your environment. The `disconnect` method simply calls the method close to the client and, as the name says, it closes the connection.

Now, we are going to add two special functions, __enter__ and __exit__:

```
def __enter__(self):
    self.connect()
    return self

def __exit__(self, exec_type, exec_value, traceback):
    self.disconnect()

    if exec_type:
        raise exec_type(exec_value)

    return self
```

We want the `DbClient` class to be used within its own context, and this is achieved by using a context manager and with the `with` statement. The basic implementation of a context manager is done by implementing these two functions, __enter__ and __exit__. __enter__ will be called when we enter the context that the `DbClient` is running. In this case, we are going to call the `connect` method to connect to our MongoDB instance.

The __exit__ method, on the other hand, is called when the current context is terminated. The context can be terminated by normal causes or by some exception that has been thrown. In our case, we disconnect from the database and, if exec_type is not equal to None, which means that if some exception has occurred, we raise that exception. This is necessary, otherwise, exceptions occurring within the context of the DbClient would be suppressed.

Now, we are going to add a private method called _get_collection:

```
def _get_collection(self):
    if self._default_collection is None:
        raise AttributeError('collection argument is required')

    return self._db[self._default_collection]
```

This method will simply check if we have defined a default_collection. If not, it will throw an exception; otherwise, we return the collection.

We need just two methods to finish this class, one to find items in the database and another to insert or update data:

```
def find_one(self, filter=None):
    collection = self._get_collection()
    return collection.find_one(filter)

def update(self, filter, document, upsert=True):
    collection = self._get_collection()

    collection.find_one_and_update(
        filter,
        {'$set': document},
        upsert=upsert)
```

The find_one method gets one optional argument called filter, which is a dictionary with criteria that will be used to perform the search. If omitted, it will just return the first item in the collection.

There are a few more things going on in the update method. It gets three arguments: filter, document, and the optional argument, upsert.

The filter argument is exactly the same as the find_one method; it is a criterion that will be used to search the collection's item that we want to update.

The document argument is a dictionary with the fields that we want to update in the collection's item or insert.

Lastly, the optional argument `upsert`, when set to `True`, means that if the item that we are trying to update doesn't exist in the database's collection, then we are going to perform an insert operation and add the item to the collection.

The method starts off by getting the default collection and then uses the collection's `find_on_and_update` method, passing the `filter` to the dictionary with the fields that we want to update and also the `upsert` option.

We also need to update the __init__.py file in the `currency_converter/currency_converter/core` directory with the following contents:

```
from .db import DbClient
```

Great! Now, we can start creating the command line parser.

Creating the command line parser

I have to confess one thing: I'm a command-line type of guy. Yes, I know it is considered by some people as outdated, but I love doing work on the terminal. I am definitely more productive and if you are using Linux or macOS, you can combine tools to get the results that you want. That's the reason that we are going to add a command line parser for this project.

There are some things we need to implement in order to start creating the command line parser. One functionality that we are going to add is the possibility of setting a default currency, which will avoid user of our application always having to specify the base currency to perform currency conversions.

To do that, we are going to create an action, We have seen how actions work in `Chapter 1`, *Implementing the Weather Application*, but just to refresh our minds, actions are classes that can be bound to command line arguments to execute a certain task. These actions are called automatically when the argument is used in the command line.

Before going into the development of custom actions, we need to create a function that will fetch the configuration of our application from the database. First, we are going to create a custom exception that will be used to raise errors when we cannot retrieve the configuration from the database. Create a file named `config_error.py` in the `currency_converter/currency_converter/config` directory with the following contents:

```
class ConfigError(Exception):
    pass
```

Perfect! This is all we need to create our custom exception. We could have used a built-in exception, but that would have been too specific to our application. It is always a good practice to create custom exceptions for your application; it will make your life and the life of your colleagues much easier when troubleshooting bugs.

Create a file named `config.py` in the `currency_converter/currency_converter/config/` directory with the following contents:

```
from .config_error import ConfigError
from currency_converter.core import DbClient


def get_config():
    config = None

    with DbClient('exchange_rates', 'config') as db:
        config = db.find_one()

    if config is None:
        error_message = ('It was not possible to get your base
                         currency, that '
                         'probably happened because it have not been
'
                         'set yet.\n Please, use the option '
                         '--setbasecurrency')
        raise ConfigError(error_message)

    return config
```

Here, we start off by adding from the `import` statements. We start importing the `ConfigError` custom exception that we just created and we also import the `DbClient` class so we can access the database to retrieve the configuration for our application.

Then, we define the `get_config` function. This function will not take any argument, and the function starts by defining a variable config with a `None` value. Then, we use the `DbClient` to connect to the `exchange_rate` database and use the collection named `config`. inside the `DbClient` context, we use the `find_one` method without any argument, which means that the first item in that config collection will be returned.

If the `config` variable is still `None`, we raise an exception saying to the user that there's no configuration in the database yet and that it is necessary to run the application again with the `--setbasecurrency` argument. We are going to implement the command line arguments in a short while. If we have the value of the config, we just return it.

We also need to create a __init__.py file in the `currency_converter/currency_converter/config` directory with the following contents:

```
from .config import get_config
```

Now, let's start adding our first action, which will set the default currency. Add a file called `actions.py` in the `currency_converter/currency_converter/core` directory:

```
import sys
from argparse import Action
from datetime import datetime

from .db import DbClient
from .request import fetch_exchange_rates_by_currency
from currency_converter.config import get_config
```

First, we import `sys` so we can terminate the program's execution if something goes wrong. Then, we import the `Action` from the `argparse` module. We need to create a class inheriting from `Action` when creating custom actions. We also import `datetime` because we are going to add functionality to check if the exchange rates that we are going to use are outdated.

Then, we import some of the classes and functions that we created. We start with the `DbClient` so we can fetch and store data in the MongoDB, then `fetch_exchange_rates_by_currency` to fetch fresh data from `fixer.io` when necessary. Finally, we import a helper function called `get_config` so we can get the default currency from the config collection in the database.

Let's start by adding the `SetBaseCurrency` class:

```
class SetBaseCurrency(Action):
    def __init__(self, option_strings, dest, args=None, **kwargs):
        super().__init__(option_strings, dest, **kwargs)
```

Here, we define the `SetBaseCurrency` class, inheriting from `Action`, and we also add a constructor. It doesn't do much; it just all the constructor of the base class.

Now, we need to implement a special method called `__call__`. It will be called when the argument that the action is bound to is parsed:

```
def __call__(self, parser, namespace, value, option_string=None):
    self.dest = value

    try:
        with DbClient('exchange_rates', 'config') as db:
            db.update(
                {'base_currency': {'$ne': None}},
                {'base_currency': value})

        print(f'Base currency set to {value}')
    except Exception as e:
        print(e)
    finally:
        sys.exit(0)
```

This method gets four arguments, and the parser is an instance of the `ArgumentParser` that we are going to create shortly. `namespace` is an object which is the result of the argument parser; we went through namespace objects in detail in Chapter 1, *Implementing the Weather Application*. The value is the value that has been passed to the underlying argument and lastly, the `option_string` is the argument that the action is bound to.

We start the method by setting the value, the destination variable for the argument, and then create an instance of the `DbClient`. Note that we are using the `with` statement here, so we run the update within the DbClient context.

Then, we call the `update` method. Here, we are passing two arguments to the `update` method, the first being `filter`. When we have `{'base_currrency': {'$ne': None}}`, it means that we are going to update an item in the collection where the base currency is not equal to None; otherwise, we are going to insert a new item. This is the default behavior of the `update` method in the `DbClient` class because we have the `upsert` option set to `True` by default.

When we finish updating, we print the message to the user saying that the default currency has been set and we exit the execution of the code when we hit the `finally` clause. If something goes wrong, and for some reason, we cannot update the `config` collection, an error will be displayed and we exit the program.

The other class that we need to create it is the `UpdateForeignerExchangeRates` class:

```
class UpdateForeignerExchangeRates(Action):
    def __init__(self, option_strings, dest, args=None, **kwargs):
        super().__init__(option_strings, dest, **kwargs)
```

As with the class before, we define the class and inherit from `Action`. The constructor only calls the constructor in the base class:

```
    def __call__(self, parser, namespace, value, option_string=None):

        setattr(namespace, self.dest, True)

        try:
            config = get_config()
            base_currency = config['base_currency']
            print(('Fetching exchange rates from fixer.io'
                    f' [base currency: {base_currency}]'))
            response =
            fetch_exchange_rates_by_currency(base_currency)
            response['date'] = datetime.utcnow()

            with DbClient('exchange_rates', 'rates') as db:
                db.update(
                    {'base': base_currency},
                    response)
        except Exception as e:
            print(e)
        finally:
            sys.exit(0)
```

We also need to implement the __call__ method, which will be called when using the argument that this action will be bound to. We are not going through the method arguments again because it is exactly the same as the previous one.

The method starts by setting the value to `True` for the destination property. The argument that we are going to use to run this action will not require arguments and it will default to `False`, so if we use the argument, we set it to `True`. It is just a way of stating that we have used that argument.

Then, we get the configuration from the database and get the `base_currency`. We show a message to the user saying that we are fetching the data from `fixer.io` and then we use our `fetch_exchange_rates_by_currency` function, passing the `base_currency` to it. When we get a response, we change the date to UTC time so it will be easier for us to calculate if the exchange rate for a given currency needs to be updated.

 Remember that `fixer.io` updates its data around 16:00 CET.

Then, we create another instance of the `DbClient` and use the `update` method with two arguments. The first one is `filter`, so it will change any item in the collection that matches the criteria, and the second argument is the response that we get from `fixer.io` API.

After everything is done, we hit the `finally` clause and terminate the program's execution. If something goes wrong, we show a message to the user in the terminal and terminate the program's execution.

Creating the currency enumeration

Another thing we need to do before starting the command line parser is to create an enumeration with the possible currencies that the users of our application will be able to choose from. Let's go ahead and create a file called `currency.py` in the `currency_converter/currency_converter/core` directory with the following contents:

```
from enum import Enum


class Currency(Enum):
    AUD = 'Australia Dollar'
    BGN = 'Bulgaria Lev'
    BRL = 'Brazil Real'
    CAD = 'Canada Dollar'
    CHF = 'Switzerland Franc'
    CNY = 'China Yuan/Renminbi'
    CZK = 'Czech Koruna'
    DKK = 'Denmark Krone'
    GBP = 'Great Britain Pound'
    HKD = 'Hong Kong Dollar'
    HRK = 'Croatia Kuna'
    HUF = 'Hungary Forint'
```

```
IDR = 'Indonesia Rupiah'
ILS = 'Israel New Shekel'
INR = 'India Rupee'
JPY = 'Japan Yen'
KRW = 'South Korea Won'
MXN = 'Mexico Peso'
MYR = 'Malaysia Ringgit'
NOK = 'Norway Kroner'
NZD = 'New Zealand Dollar'
PHP = 'Philippines Peso'
PLN = 'Poland Zloty'
RON = 'Romania New Lei'
RUB = 'Russia Rouble'
SEK = 'Sweden Krona'
SGD = 'Singapore Dollar'
THB = 'Thailand Baht'
TRY = 'Turkish New Lira'
USD = 'USA Dollar'
ZAR = 'South Africa Rand'
EUR = 'Euro'
```

This is pretty straightforward. We have already covered enumerations in Python in the previous chapters, but here we define the enumeration where the key is the currency's abbreviation and the value is the name. This matches the currencies that are available in `fixer.io` as well.

Open the `__init__.py` file in the `currency_converter/currency_converter/core` directory and add the following import statement:

```
from .currency import Currency
```

Creating the command line parser

Perfect! Now, we are all set to create the command line parser. Let's go ahead and create a file called `cmdline_parser.py` in the `currency_converter/currency_converter/core` directory and as usual, let's start importing everything we need:

```
import sys
from argparse import ArgumentParser

from .actions import UpdateForeignerExchangeRates
from .actions import SetBaseCurrency
```

```
from .currency import Currency
```

From the top, we import `sys`, so that can we exit the program if something is not right. We also include the `ArgumentParser` so we can create the parser; we also import the `UpdateforeignerExchangeRates` and `SetBaseCurrency` actions that we just created. The last thing in the `Currency` enumeration is that we are going to use it to set valid choices in some arguments in our parser.

Create a function called `parse_commandline_args`:

```
def parse_commandline_args():

    currency_options = [currency.name for currency in Currency]

    argparser = ArgumentParser(
        prog='currency_converter',
        description=('Tool that shows exchange rated and perform '
                     'currency convertion, using http://fixer.io
                      data.'))
```

The first thing we do here is get only the names of the `Currency` enumeration's keys; this will return a list like this:

```
                                    python                          _ □ ×
(currency_converter-1R21vlbY) currency_converter > python
Python 3.6.2 (default, Dec 22 2017, 15:38:46)
[GCC 6.3.0 20170516] on linux
Type "help", "copyright", "credits" or "license" for more information.
>>> from currency_converter.core import Currency
>>> currency_list = [currency.name for currency in Currency]
>>> currency_list
['AUD', 'BGN', 'BRL', 'CAD', 'CHF', 'CNY', 'CZK', 'DKK', 'GBP', 'HKD', 'HRK', 'HUF', 'IDR', 'ILS
', 'INR', 'JPY', 'KRW', 'MXN', 'MYR', 'NOK', 'NZD', 'PHP', 'PLN', 'RON', 'RUB', 'SEK', 'SGD', 'T
HB', 'TRY', 'USD', 'ZAR', 'EUR']
>>>
```

Here, we finally create an instance of the `ArgumentParser` and we pass two arguments: `prog`, which is the name of the program, we can call it `currency_converter`, and the second is `description`(the description that will be displayed to the user when the `help` argument is passed in the command line).

This is the first argument that we are going to add in `--setbasecurrency`:

```
argparser.add_argument('--setbasecurrency',
                        type=str,
                        dest='base_currency',
                        choices=currency_options,
                        action=SetBaseCurrency,
                        help='Sets the base currency to be
                        used.')
```

The first argument that we define is `--setbasecurrency`. It will store the currency in the database, so we don't need to specify the base currency all the time in the command line. We specify that this argument will be stored as a string and the value that the user enters will be stored in an attribute called `base_currency`.

We also set the argument choices to the `currency_options` that we defined in the preceding code. This will ensure that we can only pass currencies matching the `Currency` enumeration.

`action` specifies which action is going to be executed when this argument is used, and we are setting it to the `SetBaseCurrency` custom action that we defined in the `actions.py` file. The last option, `help`, is the text that is displayed when the application's help is displayed.

Let's add the `--update` argument:

```
argparser.add_argument('--update',
                        metavar='',
                        dest='update',
                        nargs=0,
                        action=UpdateForeignerExchangeRates,
                        help=('Update the foreigner exchange
                                rates '
                              'using as a reference the base
                              currency'))
```

The `--update` argument, as the name says, will update the exchange rates for the default currency. It is meant to be used after the `--setbasecurrency` argument.

Here, we define the argument with the name `--update`, then we set
the `metavar` argument. The `metavar` keyword `--update` will be referenced when the help
is generated. By default, it's the same as the name of the argument but in uppercase. Since
we don't have any value that we need to pass to this argument, we set `metavar` to nothing.
The next argument is `nargs`, which tells the `argparser` that this argument does not require
a value to be passed. Finally, we have the `action` that we set to the other custom action that
we created previously, the `UpdateForeignExchangeRates` action. The last argument
is `help`, which specifies the help text for the argument.

The next argument is the `--basecurrency` argument:

```
argparser.add_argument('--basecurrency',
                       type=str,
                       dest='from_currency',
                       choices=currency_options,
                       help=('The base currency. If specified
it
                           will '
                           'override the default currency set
                           by'
                           'the --setbasecurrency option'))
```

The idea with this argument is that we want to allow users to override the default currency
that they set using the `--setbasecurrency` argument when asking for a currency
conversion.

Here, we define the argument with the name `--basecurrency`. With the `string` type, we
are going to store the value passed to the argument in an attribute called `from_currency`;
we also set the choices to `currency_option` here so we can make sure that only currencies
that exist in the `Currency` enumeration are allowed. Lastly, we set the help text.

The next argument that we are going to add is called `--value`. This argument will receive
the value that the users of our application want to convert to another currency.

Here's how we will write it:

```
argparser.add_argument('--value',
                       type=float,
                       dest='value',
                       help='The value to be converted')
```

Here, we set the name of the argument as `--value`. Note that the type is different from the previous arguments that we defined. Now, we will receive a float value, and the argument parser will store the value passed to the `--value` argument to the attribute called value. The last argument is the `help` text.

Finally, the last argument that we are going to add in the argument that specifies which currency the value will be converted to is going to be called `--to`:

```
argparser.add_argument('--to',
                        type=str,
                        dest='dest_currency',
                        choices=currency_options,
                        help=('Specify the currency that the value
                            will '
                            'be converted to.'))
```

This argument is very similar to the `--basecurrency` argument that we defined in the preceding code. Here, we set the argument's name to `--to` and it is going to be of type `string`. The value passed to this argument will be stored in the attribute called `dest_currency`. Here, we also set a choice of arguments to the list of valid currencies that we extracted from the `Currency` enumeration; last but not the least, we set the help text.

Basic validation

Note that many of these arguments that we defined are required. However, there are some arguments that are dependent on each other, for example, the arguments `--value` and `--to`. You cannot try to convert a value without specifying the currency that you want to convert to and vice versa.

Another problem here is that, since many arguments are required, if we run the application without passing any argument at all, it will just accept it and crash; the right thing to do here is that, if the user doesn't use any argument, we should display the Help menu. With that said, we need to add a function to perform this kind of validation for us, so let's go ahead and add a function called `validate_args`. You can add this function right at the top, after the `import` statements:

```
def validate_args(args):

    fields = [arg for arg in vars(args).items() if arg]

    if not fields:
        return False
```

```
if args.value and not args.dest_currency:
    return False
elif args.dest_currency and not args.value:
    return False

return True
```

So, `args` is going to be passed to this function. `args` is actually an object of `time` and `namespace`. This object will contain properties with the same name that we specified in the `dest` argument in the argument's definitions. In our case, the `namespace` will contain these properties: `base_currency`, `update`, `from_currency`, `value`, and `dest_currency`.

We use a comprehension to get all the fields that are not set to `None`. In this comprehension, we use the built-in function `vars`, which will return the value of the property `__dict__` of `args`, which is an instance of the `Namespace` object. Then, we use the `.items()` function so we can iterate through the dictionary items and one by one test if its value is `None`.

If any argument is passed in the command line, the result of this comprehension will be an empty list, and in that case, we return `False`.

Then, we test the arguments that need to be used in pairs: `--value` (value) and `--to` (`dest_currency`). It will return `False` if we have a value, but `dest_currency` is equal to `None` and vice versa.

Now, we can complete `parse_commandline_args`. Let's go to the end of this function and add the code as follows:

```
args = argparser.parse_args()

if not validate_args(args):
    argparser.print_help()
    sys.exit()

return args
```

Here, we parse the arguments and set them to the variable `args`, and remember that `args` will be of the `namespace` type. Then, we pass `args` to the function that we just created, the `validate_args` function. If the `validate_args` returns `False`, it will print the help and terminate the program's execution; otherwise, it will return `args`.

Next, we are going to develop the application's entry point that will glue together all the pieces that we have developed so far.

Adding the application's entry point

This is the section of this chapter that we all have been waiting for; we are going to create the application entry point and glue together all the pieces of code that we have written so far.

Let's create a file called `__main__.py` in the `currency_converter/currency_converter` directory. We have already used the `_main_` file before in Chapter 1, *Implementing the Weather Application*. When we place a file called `__main__.py` in the module's `root` directory, it means that that file is the entry script of the module. So, if we run the following command:

```
python -m currency_converter
```

It is the same as running:

```
python currency_converter/__main__.py
```

Great! So, let's start adding content to this file. First, add some `import` statements:

```
import sys

from .core.cmdline_parser import parse_commandline_args
from .config import get_config
from .core import DbClient
from .core import fetch_exchange_rates_by_currency
```

We import the `sys` package as usual in case we need to call exit to terminate the execution of the code, then we import all the classes and utility functions that we developed so far. We start by importing the `parse_commandline_args` function for command line parsing, the `get_config` so that we can get hold of the default currency set by the user, the `DbClient` class so we can access the database and fetch the exchange rates; lastly, we also import the `fetch_exchange_rates_by_currency` function, which will be used when we choose a currency that is not in our database yet. We will fetch this from the `fixer.io` API.

Now, we can create the `main` function:

```
def main():
    args = parse_commandline_args()
    value = args.value
    dest_currency = args.dest_currency
    from_currency = args.from_currency

    config = get_config()
    base_currency = (from_currency
                        if from_currency
                        else config['base_currency'])
```

The `main` function starts off by parsing the command line arguments. If everything is entered by the user correctly, we should receive a `namespace` object containing all the arguments with its values. In this stage, we only care about three arguments: `value`, `dest_currency`, and `from_currency`. If you recall from earlier, `value` is the value that the user wants to convert to another currency, `dest_currency` is the currency that the user wants to convert to, and `from_currency` is only passed if the user wishes to override the default currency that is set on the database.

After getting all these values, we call `get_config` to get the `base_currency` from the database, and right after that we check if there is a `from_currency` where we can use the value; otherwise, we use the `base_currency` from the database. This will ensure that if the user specifies a `from_currency` value, then that value will override the default currency stored in the database.

Next, we implement the code that will actually fetch the exchange rates from the database or from the `fixer.io` API, like so:

```
with DbClient('exchange_rates', 'rates') as db:
    exchange_rates = db.find_one({'base': base_currency})

    if exchange_rates is None:
        print(('Fetching exchange rates from fixer.io'
                f' [base currency: {base_currency}]'))

        try:
            response =
            fetch_exchange_rates_by_currency(base_currency)
        except Exception as e:
            sys.exit(f'Error: {e}')

        dest_rate = response['rates'][dest_currency]
        db.update({'base': base_currency}, response)
```

```
    else:
        dest_rate = exchange_rates['rates'][dest_currency]

    total = round(dest_rate * value, 2)
    print(f'{value} {base_currency} = {total} {dest_currency}')
```

We create a connection with the database using the `DbClient` class and also specify that we are going to access the rates collection. inside the context, we first try to find the exchange rated for the base currency. if it is not in the database, we try to fetch it from `fixer.io.`

After that, we extract the exchange rate value for the currency that we are converting to and insert the result in the database so that, the next time that we run the program and want to use this currency as the base, we don't need to send a request to `fixer.io` again.

If we find the exchange rate for the base currency, we simply get that value and assign it to the `dest_rate` variable.

The last thing we have to do is perform the conversion and use the built-in round function to limit the number of digits after the decimal point to two digits, and we print the value in the terminal.

At the end of the file, after the `main()` function, add the following code:

```
    if __name__ == '__main__':
        main()
```

And we're all done!

Testing our application

Let's test our application. First, we are going to show the help message to see which options we have available:

```
                              daniel@musashi: ~/currency_converter                    _  □  x
(currency_converter-1R21vlbY) currency_converter > python -m currency_converter
usage: currency_converter [-h]
                          [--setbasecurrency {AUD,BGN,BRL,CAD,CHF,CNY,CZK,DKK,GBP,HKD,HRK,HUF,IDR,ILS,INR,JPY,KRW,MX
N,MYR,NOK,NZD,PHP,PLN,RON,RUB,SEK,SGD,THB,TRY,USD,ZAR,EUR}]
                          [--update]
                          [--basecurrency {AUD,BGN,BRL,CAD,CHF,CNY,CZK,DKK,GBP,HKD,HRK,HUF,IDR,ILS,INR,JPY,KRW,MXN,M
YR,NOK,NZD,PHP,PLN,RON,RUB,SEK,SGD,THB,TRY,USD,ZAR,EUR}]
                          [--value VALUE]
                          [--to {AUD,BGN,BRL,CAD,CHF,CNY,CZK,DKK,GBP,HKD,HRK,HUF,IDR,ILS,INR,JPY,KRW,MXN,MYR,NOK,NZD
,PHP,PLN,RON,RUB,SEK,SGD,THB,TRY,USD,ZAR,EUR}]

Tool that shows exchange rated and perform currency convertion, using
http://fixer.io data.

optional arguments:
  -h, --help            show this help message and exit
  --setbasecurrency {AUD,BGN,BRL,CAD,CHF,CNY,CZK,DKK,GBP,HKD,HRK,HUF,IDR,ILS,INR,JPY,KRW,MXN,MYR,NOK,NZD,PHP,PLN,RON
,RUB,SEK,SGD,THB,TRY,USD,ZAR,EUR}
                        Sets the base currency to be used.
  --update              Update the foreigner exchange rates using as a
                        reference the base currency
  --basecurrency {AUD,BGN,BRL,CAD,CHF,CNY,CZK,DKK,GBP,HKD,HRK,HUF,IDR,ILS,INR,JPY,KRW,MXN,MYR,NOK,NZD,PHP,PLN,RON,RU
B,SEK,SGD,THB,TRY,USD,ZAR,EUR}
                        The base currency. If specified it will override the
                        default currency set bythe --setbasecurrency option
  --value VALUE         The value to be converted
  --to {AUD,BGN,BRL,CAD,CHF,CNY,CZK,DKK,GBP,HKD,HRK,HUF,IDR,ILS,INR,JPY,KRW,MXN,MYR,NOK,NZD,PHP,PLN,RON,RUB,SEK,SGD,
THB,TRY,USD,ZAR,EUR}
                        Specify the currency that the value will be converted
                        to.
(currency_converter-1R21vlbY) currency_converter >
```

Nice! Just as expected. Now, we can use the `--setbasecurrency` argument to set the base currency:

```
                              daniel@musashi: ~/currency_converter                    _  □  x
(currency_converter-1R21vlbY) currency_converter > python -m currency_converter --setbasecurrency SEK
Base currency set to SEK
(currency_converter-1R21vlbY) currency_converter >
```

Here, I have set the base currency to **SEK** (Swedish Kronor) and, every time I need to perform a currency conversion, I don't need to specify that my base currency is **SEK**. Let's convert 100 **SEK** to **USD** (United States Dollars):

```
                        daniel@musashi: ~/currency_converter                    _ □ ×
(currency_converter-1R21vlbY) currency_converter › python -m currency_converter --value 100 --to USD
Fetching exchange rates from fixer.io [base currency: SEK]
100.0 SEK = 12.36 USD
(currency_converter-1R21vlbY) currency_converter ›
```

As you can see, we didn't have the exchange rate in the database yet, so the first thing the application does is to fetch it from `fixer.io` and save it into the database.

Since I am a Brazilian developer based in Sweden, I want to convert **SEK** to **BRL** (Brazil Real) so that I know how much Swedish Crowns I will have to take to Brazil next time I go to visit my parents:

```
                        daniel@musashi: ~/currency_converter                    _ □ ×
(currency_converter-1R21vlbY) currency_converter › python -m currency_converter --value 100 --to BRL
100.0 SEK = 40.74 BRL
(currency_converter-1R21vlbY) currency_converter ›
```

Note that, since this is the second time that we are running the application, we already have exchange rates with **SEK** as the base currency, so the application does not fetch the data from `fixer.io` again.

Now, the last thing that we want to try is overriding the base currency. At the moment, it is set to **SEK**. We use **MXN** (Mexico Peso) and convert from **MXN** to **SEK**:

```
                            daniel@musashi: ~/currency_converter                    _ □ x
(currency_converter-1R21vlbY) currency_converter > python -m currency_converter --basecurrency MXN --value 100 --to SEK
Fetching exchange rates from fixer.io [base currency: MXN]
100.0 MXN = 43.44 SEK
(currency_converter-1R21vlbY) currency_converter >
```

Summary

In this chapter, we have covered a lot of interesting topics. In the first section, while setting up the environment for our application, you learned how to use the super new and popular tool `pipenv`, which has become the recommend tool at `python.org` for creating virtual environments and also managing project dependencies.

You also learned the basic concepts of object-oriented programming, how to create custom actions for your command line tools, the basics about context managers which is a really powerful feature in the Python language, how to create enumerations in Python, and how to perform HTTP requests using `Requests`, which is one of the most popular packages in the Python ecosystem.

Last but not the least, you learned how to use the `pymongo` package to insert, update, and search for data in a MongoDB database.

In the next chapter, we are going to switch gears and develop a complete, very functional web application using the excellent and very popular Django web framework!

Building a Web Messenger with Microservices

5

In today's application development world, Microservices have become the standard in designing and architecting distributed systems. Companies like Netflix have pioneered this shift and revolutionized the way in which software companies operate, from having small autonomous teams to designing systems that scale with ease.

In this chapter, I will guide you through the process of creating two microservices that will work together to make a messaging web application that uses Redis as a datastore. Messages will automatically expire after a configurable amount of time, so for the purpose of this chapter, let's call it TempMessenger.

In this chapter, we will cover the following topics:

- What is Nameko?
- Creating your first Nameko microservice
- Storing messages
- Nameko Dependency Providers
- Saving messages
- Retrieving all messages
- Displaying messages in the web browser
- Sending messages via POST requests
- Browser polling for messages

TempMessenger Goals

Before starting, let's define some goals for our application:

- A user can go to a website and send messages
- A user can see messages that others have sent
- Messages automatically expire after a configurable amount of time

To achieve this, we will be using Nameko - A microservices framework for Python.

 If at any point during this chapter you would like to refer to all of the code in this chapter in its entirety, feel free to see it, with tests, at: `http://url.marcuspen.com/github-ppb`.

Requirements

In order to partake in this chapter, your local machine will need the following:

- An internet connection
- Docker - If you haven't installed Docker already, see the official documentation: `http://url.marcuspen.com/docker-install`

All other requirements will be installed as we progress through the chapter.

All instructions in this chapter are tailored towards macOS or Debian/Ubuntu systems. I have, however, taken care to only use cross-platform dependencies.

 Throughout this chapter, there will be blocks of code. Different types of code will have their own prefixes, which are as follows:
`$`: To be executed in your terminal, always within your virtualenv
`>>>`: To be executed in your Nameko/Python shell
No prefix: Block of Python code to be used in your editor

What is Nameko?

Nameko is an open-source framework used for building microservices in Python. Using Nameko, you can create microservices that communicate with each other using **RPC (Remote Procedure Calls)** via **AMQP (Advanced Message Queueing Protocol)**.

RPCs

RPC stands for Remote Procedure Call, and I'll briefly explain this with a short example based on a cinema booking system. Within this cinema booking system, there are many microservices, but we will focus on the booking service, which is responsible for managing bookings, and the email service, which is responsible for sending emails. The booking service and email service both exist on different machines and both are unaware of where the other one is. When making a new booking, the booking service needs to send an email confirmation to the user, so it makes a Remote Procedure Call to the email service, which could look something like this:

```
def new_booking(self, user_id, film, time):
    ...
    self.email_service.send_confirmation(user_id, film, time)
    ...
```

Notice in the preceding code how the booking service makes the call as if it were executing code that was local to it? It does not care about the network or the protocol and it doesn't even give details on which email address it needs to send it to. For the booking service, email addresses and any other email related concepts are irrelevant! This allows the booking service to adhere to the **Single Responsibility Principle**, a term introduced by Robert C. Martin in his article *Principles of Object Orientated Design* (http://url.marcuspen.com/bob-ood), which states that:

"A Class should have only one reason to change"

The scope of this quote can also be extended to microservices, and is something we should keep in mind when developing them. This will allow us to keep our microservices self-contained and cohesive. If the cinema decided to change its email provider, then the only service that should need to change is the email service, keeping the work required minimal, which in turn reduces the risk of bugs and possible downtime.

However, RPCs do have their downsides when compared to other techniques such as REST, the main one being that it can be hard to see when a call is remote. One could make unnecessary remote calls without realizing it, which can be expensive since they go over the network and use external resources. So when using RPCs, it's important to make them visibly different.

How Nameko uses AMQP

AMQP stands for Advanced Message Queueing Protocol, which is used by Nameko as the transport for our RPCs. When our Nameko services make RPCs to each other, the requests are placed on the messaging queue, which are then consumed by the destination service. Nameko services use workers to consume and carry out requests; when an RPC is made, the target service will spawn a new worker to carry out the task. Once it's complete, it dies. Since there can be multiple workers executing tasks simultaneously, Nameko can scale up to the amount of workers it has available. If all workers are exhausted, then messages will stay on the queue until a free worker is available.

You can also scale Nameko horizontally by increasing the amount of instances running your service. This is known as clustering, which is also where the name *Nameko* originates, since Nameko mushrooms grow in clusters.

Nameko can also respond to requests from other protocols such as HTTP and websockets.

RabbitMQ

RabbitMQ is used as the message broker for Nameko and allows it to utilize AMQP. Before we start, you will need to install it on your machine; to do so, we will use Docker, which is available on all major operating systems.

For those new to Docker, it allows us to run our code in a standalone, self-contained environment called a container. Within a container is everything that is required for that code to run independently from anything else. You can also download and run pre-built containers, which is how we are going to run RabbitMQ. This saves us from installing it on our local machine and minimizes the amount of issues that can arise from running RabbitMQ on different platforms such as macOS or Windows.

If you do not already have Docker installed, please visit http://url.marcuspen.com/docker-install where there are detailed installation instructions for all platforms. The rest of this chapter will assume that you already have Docker installed.

Starting a RabbitMQ container

In your terminal, execute the following:

```
$ docker run -d -p 5672:5672 -p 15672:15672 --name rabbitmq rabbitmq
```

This will start a RabbitMQ container with the following setup:

- -d: Specifies we want to run the container in daemon mode (background process).
- -p: Allows us to expose ports 5672 and 15672 on the container to our local machine. These are needed for Nameko to communicate with RabbitMQ.
- --name: Sets the container name to rabbitmq.

You can check that your new RabbitMQ container is running by executing:

```
$ docker ps
```

Installing Python requirements

For this project, I'll be using Python 3.6, which, at the time of writing, is the latest stable release of Python. I recommend always using the latest stable version of Python, not only for the new features but to also ensure the latest security updates are applied to your environment at all times.

Pyenv is a really simple way to install and switch between different versions of Python: http://url.marcuspen.com/pyenv.

I also strongly recommend using virtualenv to create an isolated environment to install our Python requirements. Installing Python requirements without a virtual environment can cause unexpected side-effects with other Python applications, or worse, your operating system!

To learn more about virtualenv and how to install it visit: `http://url.marcuspen.com/virtualenv`

Normally, when dealing with Python packages, you would create a `requirements.txt` file, populate it with your requirements and then install it. I'd like to show you a different way that will allow you to easily keep track of Python package versions.

To get started, let's install `pip-tools` within your virtualenv:

```
pip install pip-tools
```

Now create a new folder called `requirements` and create two new files:

```
base.in
test.in
```

The `base.in` file will contain the requirements needed in order for the core of our service to run, whereas the `test.in` file will contain the requirements needed in order to run our tests. It's important to keep these requirements separate, especially when deploying code in a microservice architecture. It's okay for our local machines to have test packages installed, but a deployed version of our code should be as minimal and lightweight as possible.

In the `base.in` file, put the following line:

```
nameko
```

In the `test.in` file, put the following line:

```
pytest
```

Provided you are in the directory containing your `requirements` folder, run the following:

```
pip-compile requirements/base.in
pip-compile requirements/test.in
```

This will generate two files, `base.txt`, and `test.txt`. Here's a small sample of the `base.txt`:

```
...
nameko==2.8.3
path.py==10.5          # via nameko
pbr==3.1.1             # via mock
pyyaml==3.12           # via nameko
redis==2.10.6
```

```
requests==2.18.4        # via nameko
six==1.11.0             # via mock, nameko
urllib3==1.22           # via requests
...
```

Notice how we now have a file that contains all of the latest dependencies and sub-dependencies of Nameko. It specifies which versions are required and also what caused each sub-dependency to be installed. For example, six is required by nameko and mock.

This makes it extremely easy to troubleshoot upgrade issues in the future by being able to easily track version changes between each release of your code.

At the time of writing, Nameko is currently version 2.8.3 and Pytest is 3.4.0. Feel free to use newer versions of these packages if available, but if you have any issues throughout the book then revert back to these by appending the version number in your base.in or test.in file as follows:

```
nameko==2.8.3
```

To install the requirements, simply run:

```
$ pip-sync requirements/base.txt requirements/test.txt
```

The pip-sync command installs all requirements specified in the files while also removing any packages that are in your environment that aren't specified. It's a nice way to keep your virtualenv clean. Alternatively, you can also use:

```
$ pip install -r requirements/base.txt -r requirements/test.txt
```

Creating your first Nameko microservice

Let's start by creating a new folder titled temp_messenger and placing a new file inside, named service.py, with the following code:

```python
from nameko.rpc import rpc

class KonnichiwaService:

    name = 'konnichiwa_service'

    @rpc
    def konnichiwa(self):
        return 'Konnichiwa!'
```

We first start by importing `rpc` from `nameko.rpc`. This will allow us to decorate our methods with the `rpc` decorator and expose them as entrypoints into our service. An entrypoint is any method in a Nameko service that acts as a gateway into our service.

In order to create a Nameko service, we simply create a new class, `KonnichiwaService`, and assign it a `name` attribute. The `name` attribute gives it a namespace; this will be used later when we attempt to make a remote call to the service.

We've written a method on our service which simply returns the word `Konnichiwa!`. Notice how this method is decorated with `rpc`. The `konnichiwa` method is now going to be exposed via RPC.

Before we test this code out we need to create a small `config` file which will tell Nameko where to access RabbitMQ and what RPC exchange to use. Create a new file, `config.yaml`:

```
AMQP_URI: 'pyamqp://guest:guest@localhost'
rpc_exchange: 'nameko-rpc'
```

 The `AMQP_URI` configuration here is correct for users who have started the RabbitMQ container using the instructions given earlier. If you have adjusted the username, password or location, ensure that your changes are reflected here.

You should now have a directory structure that resembles the following:

```
.
├── config.yaml
├── requirements
│   ├── base.in
│   ├── base.txt
│   ├── test.in
│   └── test.txt
├── temp_messenger
    └── service.py
```

Now in your terminal, within the root of your project directory, execute the following:

```
$ nameko run temp_messenger.service --config config.yaml
```

You should have the following output:

```
starting services: konnichiwa_service
Connected to amqp://guest:**@127.0.0.1:5672//
```

Making a call to our service

Our microservice is now running! In order to make our own calls, we can launch a Python shell that has Nameko integrated to allow us to call our entrypoints. To access it, open a new terminal window and execute the following:

```
$ nameko shell
```

This should give you access to a Python shell with the ability to make Remote Procedure Calls. Let's try that out:

```
>>> n.rpc.konnichiwa_service.konnichiwa()
'Konnichiwa!'
```

It worked! We have successfully made a call to our Konnichiwa Service and received some output back. When we executed this code in our Nameko shell, we put a message on the queue, which was then received by our KonnichiwaService. It then spawned a new worker to carry out the work of the konnichiwa RPC.

Unit-testing a Nameko microservice

According to the documentation, `http://url.marcuspen.com/nameko`, Nameko is:

> *"A microservices framework for Python that lets service developers concentrate on application logic and encourages testability."*

We will now focus on the testability part of Nameko; it provides some very useful tools for isolating and testing its services.

Create a new folder, `tests`, and place two new files inside, `__init__.py` (which can be left blank) and `test_service.py`:

```
from nameko.testing.services import worker_factory
from temp_messenger.service import KonnichiwaService

def test_konnichiwa():
    service = worker_factory(KonnichiwaService)
    result = service.konnichiwa()
    assert result == 'Konnichiwa!'
```

When running outside of the test environment, Nameko spawns a new worker for each entrypoint that is called. Earlier, when we tested our `konnichiwa` RPC, the Konnichiwa Service would have been listening for new messages on the Rabbit queue. Once it received a new message for the `konnichiwa` entrypoint, it would spawn a new worker that would carry out that method and then die.

 To learn more about the anatomy of Nameko services, see: `http://url.marcuspen.com/nam-key`.

For our tests, Nameko provides a way to emulate that via a `woker_factory`. As you can see, our test uses `worker_factory`, which we pass our service class, `KonnichiwaService`. This will then allow us to call any entrypoint on that service and access the result.

To run the test, from the root of your code directory, simply execute:

```
pytest
```

That's it. The test suite should now pass. Have a play around and try to make it break.

Exposing HTTP entrypoints

We will now create a new microservice responsible for handling HTTP requests. First of all, let's amend our imports in the `service.py` file:

```
from nameko.rpc import rpc, RpcProxy
from nameko.web.handlers import http
```

Beneath the `KonnichiwaService` we made earlier, insert the following:

```
class WebServer:

    name = 'web_server'
    konnichiwa_service = RpcProxy('konnichiwa_service')

    @http('GET', '/')
    def home(self, request):
        return self.konnichiwa_service.konnichiwa()
```

Notice how the follows a similar pattern to the KonnichiwaService. It has a name attribute and a method decorated in order to expose it as an entrypoint. In this case, it is decorated with the http entrypoint. We specify inside the http decorator that it is a GET request and the location of that request - in this case, the root of our website.

There is also one more crucial difference: This service holds a reference to the Konnichiwa Service via an RpcProxy object. RpcProxy allows us to make calls to another Nameko service via RPC. We instantiate it with the name attribute, which we specified earlier in KonnichiwaService.

Let's try this out - simply restart the Nameko using the command from earlier (this is needed to take into account any changes to the code) and go to http://localhost:8000/ in your browser of choice:

It worked! We've now successfully made two microservices—one responsible for showing a message and one responsible for serving web requests.

Integration testing Nameko microservices

Earlier we looked at testing a service in isolation by spawning a single worker. This is great for unit testing but it is not a viable option for integration testing.

Nameko gives us the ability to test multiple services working in tandem in a single test. Look at the following:

```
def test_root_http(web_session, web_config, container_factory):
    web_config['AMQP_URI'] = 'pyamqp://guest:guest@localhost'

    web_server = container_factory(WebServer, web_config)
    konnichiwa = container_factory(KonnichiwaService, web_config)
    web_server.start()
    konnichiwa.start()

    result = web_session.get('/')

    assert result.text == 'Konnichiwa!'
```

As you can see in the preceding code, Nameko also gives us access to the following test fixtures:

- web_session: Gives us a session in which to make HTTP requests to the service
- web_config: Allows us to access the configuration for the service (outside of testing, this is equivalent to the config.yaml file)
- container_factory: This allows us to simulate a service as a whole rather than just an instance of a worker, which is necessary when integration testing

Since this is running the actual services, we need to specify the location of the AMQP broker by injecting it into the web_config. Using container_factory, we create two containers: web_server and konnichiwa. We then start both containers.

It's then a simple case of using web_session to make a GET request to the root of our site and checking that the result is what we expect.

As we go through the rest of the chapter, I encourage you to write your own tests for the code, as it will not only prevents bugs but also help to solidify your knowledge on this topic. It's also a good way to experiment with your own ideas and modifications to the code as they can tell you quickly if you have broken anything.

For more information on testing Nameko services, see: `http://url.marcuspen.com/nam-test`.

Storing messages

The messages we want our application to display need to be temporary. We could use a relational database for this, such as PostgreSQL, but that would mean having to design and maintain a database for something as simple as text.

An introduction to Redis

Redis is an in-memory data store. The entire dataset can be stored in memory making reads and writes much faster than relational databases, which is useful for data that is not going to need persistence. In addition, we can store data without making a schema, which is fine if we are not going to need complex queries. In our case, we simply need a data store that will allow us to store messages, get messages, and expire messages. Redis fits our use case perfectly!

Starting a Redis container

In your terminal, execute the following:

```
$ docker run -d -p 6379:6379 --name redis redis
```

This will start a Redis container with the following setup:

- -d: Specifies we want to run the container in daemon mode (background process).
- -p: Allows us to expose port 6379 on the container to our local machine. This are needed for Nameko to communicate with Redis.
- --name: Sets the container name to redis.

You can check that your new Redis container is running by executing:

```
$ docker ps
```

Installing the Python Redis client

You will also need to install the Python Redis client to allow you to interact with Redis via Python. To do this, I recommend amending your `base.in` file from earlier to include `redis` and recompiling it to generate your new `base.txt` file. Alternatively, you can run `pip install redis`.

Using Redis

Let's briefly look at the types of Redis commands that could be useful to us for TempMessenger:

- `SET`: Sets a given key to hold a given string. It also allows us to set an expiration in seconds or milliseconds.
- `GET`: Gets the value of the data stored with the given key.
- `TTL`: Gets the time-to-live for a given key in seconds.
- `PTTL`: Gets the time-to-live for a given key in milliseconds.
- `KEYS`: Returns a list of all keys in the data store.

To try them out, we can use `redis-cli` which is a program that ships with our Redis container. To access it, first log in to the container by executing the following in your terminal:

```
docker exec -it redis /bin/bash
```

Then access `redis-cli` in the same terminal window by simply running:

```
redis-cli
```

There are some examples given as follows on how to use `redis-cli`; if you're not familiar with Redis then I encourage you to experiment with the commands yourself.

Set some data, `hello`, to key `msg1`:

```
127.0.0.1:6379> SET msg1 hello
OK
```

Get data stored at key, `msg1`:

```
127.0.0.1:6379> GET msg1
"hello"
```

Set some more data, `hi there`, at key `msg2` and retrieve it:

```
127.0.0.1:6379> SET msg2 "hi there"
OK
127.0.0.1:6379> GET msg2
"hi there"
```

Retrieve all keys currently stored in Redis:

```
127.0.0.1:6379> KEYS *
1) "msg2"
2) "msg1"
```

Save data at `msg3` with an expiry of 15 seconds:

```
127.0.0.1:6379> SET msg3 "this message will die soon" EX 15
OK
```

Get the time-to-live for `msg3` in seconds:

```
127.0.0.1:6379> TTL msg3
(integer) 10
```

Get the time-to-live for `msg3` in milliseconds:

```
127.0.0.1:6379> PTTL msg3
(integer) 6080
```

Retrieve `msg3` before it expires:

```
127.0.0.1:6379> GET msg3
"this message will die soon"
```

Retrieve `msg3` after it expires:

```
127.0.0.1:6379> GET msg3
(nil)
```

Nameko Dependency Providers

When building microservices, Nameko encourages the use of dependency providers to communicate with external resources such as databases, servers, or anything that our application depends on. By using a dependency provider, you can hide away logic that is specific only to that dependency, keeping your service level code clean and agnostic to the ins-and-outs of interfacing with this external resource.

By structuring our microservices like this, we have the ability to easily swap out or re-use dependency providers in other services.

 Nameko provides a list of open source dependency providers that are ready to use: `http://url.marcuspen.com/nam-ext`.

Adding a Redis Dependency Provider

Since Redis is an external resource for our application, we will create a dependency provider for it.

Designing the Client

First, let's create a new folder named `dependencies` inside of our `temp_messenger` folder. Inside, place a new file, `redis.py`. We will now create a Redis client with a simple method that will get a message, given a key:

```
from redis import StrictRedis

class RedisClient:

    def __init__(self, url):
        self.redis = StrictRedis.from_url(
            url, decode_responses=True
        )
```

We start off our code by implementing the __init__ method, which creates our Redis client and assigns it to `self.redis`. `StrictRedis` that can take a number of optional arguments, however, we have only specified the following:

- `url`: Rather than specifying the host, port and database number separately, we can use `StrictRedis'` from_url, which will allow us to specify all three with a single string, like so—`redis://localhost:6379/0`. This is a lot more convenient when it comes to storing it in our `config.yaml` later.
- `decode_responses`: This will automatically convert the data we get from Redis into a Unicode string. By default, data is retrieved in bytes.

Now, in the same class, let's implement a new method:

```
def get_message(self, message_id):
    message = self.redis.get(message_id)

    if message is None:
        raise RedisError(
            'Message not found: {}'.format(message_id)
        )

    return message
```

Outside of our new class, let's also implement a new error class:

```
class RedisError(Exception):
    pass
```

Here we have a method, `get_message`, that takes a `message_id` that will be used as our Redis key. We use the `get` method on our Redis client to retrieve the message with our given key. When retrieving values from Redis, if the key does not exist, it will simply return `None`. Since this method expects there to be a message, we should handle raising an error ourselves. In this case, we've made a simple exception, `RedisError`.

Creating the Dependency Provider

So far we've created a Redis Client with a single method. We now need to create a Nameko Dependency Provider to utilize this client for use with our services. In the same `redis.py` file, update your imports to include the following:

```
from nameko.extensions import DependencyProvider
```

Now, let's implement the following code:

```
class MessageStore(DependencyProvider):

    def setup(self):
        redis_url = self.container.config['REDIS_URL']
        self.client = RedisClient(redis_url)

    def stop(self):
        del self.client

    def get_dependency(self, worker_ctx):
        return self.client
```

In the preceding code, you can see that our new `MessageStore` class inherits from the `DependencyProvider` class. The methods we have specified in our new MessageStore class will be called at certain moments of our microservice lifecycle:

- `setup`: This will be called before our Nameko services starts. Here we get the Redis URL from `config.yaml` and create a new `RedisClient` using the code we made earlier.
- `stop`: When our Nameko services begin to shut down, this will be called.
- `get_dependency`: All dependency providers need to implement this method. When an entrypoint fires, Nameko creates a worker and injects the result of `get_dependency` for each dependency specified in the service into the worker. In our case, this means that our workers will all have access to an instance of `RedisClient`.

 Nameko offers more methods to control how your dependency providers function at different moments of the service lifecycle: `http://url.marcuspen.com/nam-writ`.

Creating our Message Service

In our `service.py`, we can now make use of our new Redis Dependency Provider. Let's start off by creating a new service, which will replace our Konnichiwa Service from earlier. First, we need to update our imports at the top of our file:

```
from .dependencies.redis import MessageStore
```

Now we can create our new service:

```
class MessageService:

    name = 'message_service'
    message_store = MessageStore()

    @rpc
    def get_message(self, message_id):
        return self.message_store.get_message(message_id)
```

This is similar to our earlier services; however, this time we are specifying a new class attribute, `message_store`. Our RPC entrypoint, `get_message`, can now make use of this and call `get_message` in our `RedisClient` and simply return the result.

We could have done all of this by creating a new Redis client within our RPC entrypoint and implementing a Redis GET. However, by creating a dependency provider, we promote reusability and hide away the unwanted behavior of Redis returning None when a key does not exist. This is just a small example of why Dependency Providers are extremely good at decoupling our services from external dependencies.

Putting it all together

Let's try out the code we have just created. Start by saving a new key-value pair to Redis using the redis-cli:

```
127.0.0.1:6379> set msg1 "this is a test"
OK
```

Now start our Nameko services:

```
$ nameko run temp_messenger.service --config config.yaml
```

We can now use nameko shell to make remote calls to our new MessageService:

```
>>> n.rpc.message_service.get_message('msg1')
'this is a test'
```

As expected, we were able to retrieve a message that we set earlier using redis-cli via our MessageService entrypoint.

Let's now try to get a message that does not exist:

```
>>> n.rpc.message_service.get_message('i_dont_exist')
Traceback (most recent call last):
  File "<console>", line 1, in <module>
  File
"/Users/marcuspen/.virtualenvs/temp_messenger/lib/python3.6/site-
packages/nameko/rpc.py", line 393, in __call__
    return reply.result()
  File
"/Users/marcuspen/.virtualenvs/temp_messenger/lib/python3.6/site-
packages/nameko/rpc.py", line 379, in result
    raise deserialize(error)
nameko.exceptions.RemoteError: RedisError Message not found:
i_dont_exist
```

This isn't the prettiest of errors and there are certain things we can do to reduce the traceback with this, but the final line states the exception we defined earlier and clearly shows us why that request failed.

We will now move on to saving messages.

Saving messages

Earlier, I introduced the Redis SET method. This will allow us to save a message to Redis, but first, we need to create a new method in our dependency provider that will handle this.

We could simply create a new method that called `redis.set(message_id, message)`, but how would we handle new message IDs? It would be a bit troublesome if we expected the user to input a new message ID for each message they wanted to send, right? An alternative is to have the message service generate a new random message ID before it calls the dependency provider, but that would clutter our service with logic that could be handled by the dependency itself.

We'll solve this by having the dependency create a random string to be used as the message ID.

Adding a save message method to our Redis client

In `redis.py`, let's amend our imports to include `uuid4`:

```
from uuid import uuid4
```

`uuid4` generates us a unique random string that we can use for our message.

We can now add our new `save_message` method to the `RedisClient`:

```
def save_message(self, message):
    message_id = uuid4().hex
    self.redis.set(message_id, message)

    return message_id
```

First off, we generate a new message ID using `uuid4().hex`. The `hex` attribute gives us the UUID as a 32-character hexadecimal string. We then use it as a key to save the message and return it.

Adding a save message RPC

Let's now create the RPC method that is going to call our new client method. In our `MessageService`, add the following method:

```
@rpc
def save_message(self, message):
    message_id = self.message_store.save_message(message)
    return message_id
```

Nothing fancy here, but notice how easy it is becoming to add new functionality to our service. We are separating logic that belongs in the dependency from our entrypoints, and at the same time making our code reusable. If another RPC method we create in the future needs to save a message to Redis, we can easily do so without having to recreate the same code again.

Let's test this out by only using the `nameko shell` - remember to restart your Nameko service for changes to take effect!

```
>>> n.rpc.message_service.save_message('Nameko is awesome!')
'd18e3d8226cd458db2731af8b3b000d9'
```

The ID returned here is random and will differ from the one you get from your session.

```
>>>n.rpc.message_service.get_message
    ('d18e3d8226cd458db2731af8b3b000d9')
    'Nameko is awesome!'
```

As you can see, we have successfully saved a message and used the UUID that is returned to retrieve our message.

This is all well and good, but for the purposes of our app we don't expect the user to have to supply a message UUID in order to read messages. Let's make this a bit more practical and look at how we can get all of the messages in our Redis store.

Retrieving all messages

Similar to our previous steps, we will need to add a new method to our Redis dependency in order to add more functionality. This time, we will be creating a method that will iterate through all of our keys in Redis and return the corresponding messages in a list.

Adding a get all messages method to our Redis client

Let's add the following to our `RedisClient`:

```
def get_all_messages(self):
    return [
        {
            'id': message_id,
            'message': self.redis.get(message_id)
        }
        for message_id in self.redis.keys()
    ]
```

We start off by using `self.redis.keys()` to gather all keys that are stored in Redis, which, in our case, are the message IDs. We then have a list comprehension that will iterate through all of the message IDs and create a dictionary for each one, containing the message ID itself and the message that is stored in Redis, using `self.redis.get(message_id)`.

 For large scale applications in a production environment, it is not recommended to use the Redis KEYS method, since this will block the server until it has finished completing its operation. For more information, see: http://url.marcuspen.com/rediskeys.

Personally, I prefer to use a list comprehension here to build the list of messages, but if you are struggling to understand this method, I recommend writing it as a standard for loop.

For the sake of this example, see the following code for the same method built as a for loop:

```
def get_all_messages(self):
    message_ids = self.redis.keys()
    messages = []

    for message_id in message_ids:
        message = self.redis.get(message_id)
        messages.append(
            {'id': message_id, 'message': message}
```

```
        )
    return messages
```

Both of these methods do exactly the same thing. Which do you prefer? I'll leave that choice to you...

Whenever I write a list or dictionary comprehension, I always start by having a test that checks the output of my function or method. I then write my code with a comprehension and test it to ensure the output is correct. I'll then change my code to a for loop and ensure the test still passes. After that, I look at both versions of my code and decide which one looks the most readable and clean. Unless the code needs to be super efficient, I always opt for code that reads well, even if that means a few more lines. This approach pays off in the long run when it comes to reading back and maintaining that code later!

We now have a way to obtain all messages in Redis. In the preceding code, I could have simply returned a list of messages with no dictionaries involved, just the string value of the message. But what if we wanted to add more data to each message later? For example, some metadata to say when the message was created or how long the message has until it expires... we'll get to that part later! Using a dictionary here for each message will allow us to easily evolve our data structures later on.

We can now look at adding a new RPC to our `MessageService` that will allow us to get all of the messages.

Adding a get all messages RPC

In our `MessageService` class, simply add:

```
@rpc
def get_all_messages(self):
    messages = self.message_store.get_all_messages()
    return messages
```

I'm sure that by now, I probably do not need to explain what is going on here! We are simply calling the method we made earlier in our Redis dependency and returning the result.

Putting it all together

Within your virtualenv, using `nameko shell`, we can now test this out.:

```
>>> n.rpc.message_service.save_message('Nameko is awesome!')
'bf87d4b3fefc49f39b7dd50e6d693ae8'
>>> n.rpc.message_service.save_message('Python is cool!')
'd996274c503b4b57ad5ee201fbcca1bd'
>>> n.rpc.message_service.save_message('To the foo bar!')
'69f99e5863604eedaf39cd45bfe8ef99'
>>> n.rpc.message_service.get_all_messages()
[{'id': 'd996274...', 'message': 'Python is cool!'},
 {'id': 'bf87d4b...', 'message': 'Nameko is awesome!'},
 {'id': '69f99e5...', 'message': 'To the foo bar!'}]
```

There we have it! We can now retrieve all of the messages in our data store. (For the sake of space and readability, I've truncated the message IDs.)

There is one issue with the messages that are returned here - can you spot what it is? The order in which we put the messages into Redis is not the same order that we have received when we get them out again. We'll come back to this later, but for now, let's move on to displaying these messages in our web browser.

Displaying messages in the web browser

Earlier, we added the `WebServer` microservice to handle HTTP requests; we will now amend this so that when a user lands on the root home page, they are shown all of the messages in our data store.

One way to do this is to use a templating engine such as Jinja2.

Adding a Jinja2 Dependency Provider

Jinja2 is a templating engine for Python that is extremely similar to the templating engine in Django. For those who are familiar with Django, you should feel right at home using it.

Before we start, you should amend your `base.in` file to include `jinja2`, re-compile your requirements and install them. Alternatively, simply run `pip install jinja2`.

Creating the template renderer

When generating a simple HTML template in Jinja2, the following three steps are required:

- Creating a template environment
- Specifying the template
- Rendering the template

With these three steps, it's important to identify which parts are never subject (or at least extremely unlikely) to change while our application is running... and which are. Keep this in mind as I explain through the following code.

In your dependencies directory, add a new file, `jinja2.py` and start with the following code:

```
from jinja2 import Environment, PackageLoader, select_autoescape

class TemplateRenderer:

    def __init__(self, package_name, template_dir):
        self.template_env = Environment(
            loader=PackageLoader(package_name, template_dir),
            autoescape=select_autoescape(['html'])
        )

    def render_home(self, messages):
        template = self.template_env.get_template('home.html')
        return template.render(messages=messages)
```

In our `__init__` method, we require a package name and a template directory. With these, we can then create the template environment. The environment requires a loader, which is simply a way of being able to load our template files from a given package and directory. We've also specified that we want to enable auto-escaping on our HTML files for security.

We've then made a `render_home` method that will allow us to render our `home.html` template once we've made it. Notice how we render our template with `messages`... you'll see why later!

Can you see why I've structured the code this way? Since the `__init__` method is always executed, I've put the creation of our template environment there, since this is unlikely to ever change while our application is running.

However, which template we want to render and the variables we give to that template are always going to change, depending on what page the user is trying to access and what data is available at that given moment in time. With the preceding structure, it becomes trivial to add a new method for each webpage of our application.

Creating our homepage template

Let's now look at the HTML required for our template. Let's start by creating a new directory next to our dependencies, titled `templates`.

Inside our new directory, create the following `home.html` file:

```
<!DOCTYPE html>

<body>
    {% if messages %}
        {% for message in messages %}
            <p>{{ message['message'] }}</p>
        {% endfor %}
    {% else %}
        <p>No messages!</p>
    {% endif %}
</body>
```

This HTML is nothing fancy, and neither is the templating logic! If you are unfamiliar to Jinja2 or Django templating then you're probably thinking that this HTML looks weird with the curly braces everywhere. Jinja2 uses these to allow us to input Python-like syntax into our template.

In the preceding example, we start off with an `if` statement to see if we have any messages (the format and structure of `messages` will be the same as the messages that are returned by the `get_all_messages` RPC we made earlier). If we do, then we have some more logic, including a for loop that will iterate and display the value of `'message'` for each dictionary in our `messages` list.

If there are no messages, then we will just show the `No messages!` text.

 To learn more about Jinja2, visit: `http://url.marcuspen.com/jinja2`.

Creating the Dependency Provider

We will now need to expose our `TemplateRenderer` as a Nameko Dependency Provider. In the `jinja2.py` file we made earlier, update our imports to include the following:

```
from nameko.extensions import DependencyProvider
```

Then add the following code:

```
class Jinja2(DependencyProvider):

    def setup(self):
        self.template_renderer = TemplateRenderer(
            'temp_messenger', 'templates'
        )

    def get_dependency(self, worker_ctx):
        return self.template_renderer
```

This is extremely similar to our previous Redis dependency. We specify a `setup` method that creates an instance of our `TemplateRenderer` and a `get_dependency` method that will inject it into the worker.

This is now ready to be used by our `WebServer`.

Making a HTML response

We can now start to use our new Jinja2 dependency in our `WebServer`. First, we need to include it in our imports of `service.py`:

```
from .dependencies.jinja2 import Jinja2
```

Let's now amend our `WebServer` class to be the following:

```
class WebServer:

    name = 'web_server'
    message_service = RpcProxy('message_service')
    templates = Jinja2()

    @http('GET', '/')
    def home(self, request):
        messages = self.message_service.get_all_messages()
        rendered_template = self.templates.render_home(messages)
```

```
        return rendered_template
```

Notice how we have assigned a new attribute, `templates`, like we did earlier in our `MessageService` with `message_store`. Our HTTP entrypoint now talks to our `MessageService`, retrieves all of the messages in Redis, and uses them to create a rendered template using our new Jinja2 dependency. We then return the result.

Putting it all together

Restart your Nameko services and let's try this out in the browser:

It's worked... sort of! The messages we stored in Redis earlier are present, which means the logic in our template is functioning properly, but we also have all of the HTML tags and indentation from our home.html.

The reason for this is because we haven't yet specified any headers for our HTTP response to indicate that it is HTML. To do this, let's create a small helper function outside of our WebServer class, which will convert our rendered template into a response with proper headers and a status code.

In our service.py, amend our imports to include:

```
from werkzeug.wrappers import Response
```

Then add the following function outside of our classes:

```
def create_html_response(content):
    headers = {'Content-Type': 'text/html'}
    return Response(content, status=200, headers=headers)
```

This function creates a headers dictionary, which contains the correct content type, HTML. We then create and return a Response object with an HTTP status code of 200, our headers, and the content, which in our case will be the rendered template.

We can now amend our HTTP entrypoint to use our new helper function:

```
@http('GET', '/')
def home(self, request):
    messages = self.message_service.get_all_messages()
    rendered_template = self.templates.render_home(messages)
    html_response = create_html_response(rendered_template)

    return html_response
```

Our `home` HTTP entrypoint now makes use of the `create_html_reponse`, giving it the rendered template, and then returns the response that is made. Let's try this out again in our browser:

As you can now see, our messages now display as we expect them with no HTML tags to be found! Have a try at deleting all data in Redis with the `flushall` command using the `redis-cli` and reload the webpage. What happens?

We will now move on to sending messages.

Sending messages via POST requests

So far we've made good progress; we have a site that has the ability to display all of the messages in our data store with two microservices. One microservice handles the storing and retrieval of our messages, and the other acts as a web server for our users. Our `MessageService` already has the ability to save messages; let's expose that in our `WebServer` via a `POST` request.

Adding a send messages POST request

In our `service.py`, add the following import:

```
import json
```

Now add the following to our `WebServer` class:

```
@http('POST', '/messages')
def post_message(self, request):
    data_as_text = request.get_data(as_text=True)

    try:
        data = json.loads(data_as_text)
    except json.JSONDecodeError:
        return 400, 'JSON payload expected'

    try:
        message = data['message']
    except KeyError:
        return 400, 'No message given'

    self.message_service.save_message(message)

    return 204, ''
```

With our new `POST` entrypoint, we start off by extracting the data from the request. We specify the parameter `as_text=True`, because we would otherwise get the data back as bytes.

Once we have that data, we can then attempt to load it from JSON into a Python dictionary. If the data is not valid JSON then this can cause a `JSONDecodeError` in our service, so it's best to handle that nicely and return a bad request status code of `400`. Without this exception handling, our service would return an internal server error, which has a status code of `500`.

Now that the data is in a dictionary format, we can obtain the message inside it. Again, we have some defensive code which will handle any occurrences of an absent `'message'` key and return another `400`.

We then proceed to save the message using the `save_message` RPC we made earlier in our `MessageService`.

With this, TempMessenger now has the ability to save new messages via an HTTP POST request! If you wanted to, you can test this out using curl or another API client, like so:

```
$ curl -d '{"message": "foo"}' -H "Content-Type: application/json" -X POST
http://localhost:8000/messages
```

We will now update our `home.html` template to include the ability to use this new POST request.

Adding an AJAX POST request in jQuery

Now before we start, let me say that at the time of writing, I am in no way a JavaScript expert. My expertise lie more in back-end programming than front-end. That being said, if you have worked in web development for more than 10 minutes, then you know that trying to avoid JavaScript is near impossible. At some point, we will probably have to dabble in some just to deliver a piece of work.

With that in mind, *please do not be scared off!*

The code you are about to read is something that I learned just by reading the jQuery documentation, so it's extremely simple. If you are comfortable with front-end code then I'm sure there are probably a million different and probably better ways to do this in JavaScript, so please amend as you see fit.

You will first need to add the following after the `<!DOCTYPE html>`:

```
<head>
  <script src="https://code.jquery.com/jquery-latest.js"></script>
</head>
```

This will download and run the latest version of jQuery in the browser.

In our `home.html`, before the closing `</body>` tag, add the following:

```
<form action="/messages" id="postMessage">
  <input type="text" name="message" placeholder="Post message">
  <input type="submit" value="Post">
</form>
```

We start off here with some simple HTML to add a basic form. This only has a text input and a submit button. On its own, it will render a text box and a submit button, but it will not do anything.

Let's now follow that code with some jQuery JavaScript:

```
<script>

$( "#postMessage" ).submit(function(event) { # ①
  event.preventDefault(); # ②

  var $form = $(this),
    message = $form.find( "input[name='message']" ).val(),
    url = $form.attr("action"); # ③

  $.ajax({ # ④
    type: 'POST',
    url: url,
    data: JSON.stringify({message: message}), # ⑤
    contentType: "application/json", # ⑥
    dataType: 'json', # ⑦
    success: function() {location.reload();} # ⑧
  });
});
</script>
```

This will now add some functionality to our submit button. Let's briefly cover what is happening here:

1. This will create an event listener for our page that listens for the `postMessage` event.
2. We also prevent the default behavior of our submit button using `event.preventDefault();`. In this case, it would submit our form and attempt to perform a GET on `/messages?message=I%27m+a+new+message`.
3. Once that is triggered, we then find the message and URL in our form.
4. With these, we then construct our AJAX request, which is a POST request.
5. We use `JSON.stringify` to convert our payload into valid JSON data.
6. Remember earlier, when we had to construct a response and supply header information to say that our content type was `text/html`? Well, we are doing the same thing here in our AJAX request, but this time, our content type is `application/json`.
7. We set the `datatype` to `json`. This tells the browser the type of data we are expecting back from the server.
8. We also register a callback that reloads the webpage if the request is successful. This will allow us to see our new message on the page (and any other new ones) since it will get all of the messages again. This forced page reload is not the most elegant way of handling this, but it will do for now.

Provided you haven't cleared the data from Redis (this can be done by manually deleting them or by simply restarting your machine), you should still see the old messages from earlier.

Once you've typed your message, click the **Post** button to submit your new message:

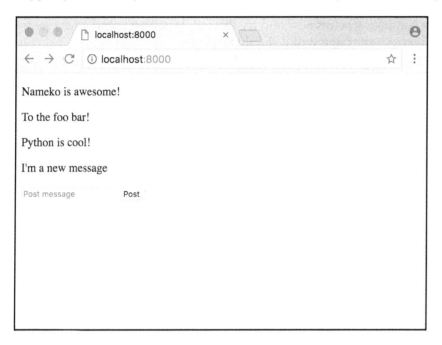

Looks like it worked! Our application now has the ability to send new messages. We will now move onto the last requirement for our application, which is to expire messages after a given period of time.

Expiring messages in Redis

We are now onto the last requirement for our app, expiring messages. Since we are using Redis to store our messages, this becomes a trivial task.

Let's look back at our `save_message` method in our Redis dependency. Redis' `SET` has some optional parameters; the two we are most interested in here are `ex` and `px`. Both allow us to set the expiry of the data we are about to save, with one difference: `ex` is in seconds and `px` is in milliseconds:

```
def save_message(self, message):
    message_id = uuid4().hex
    self.redis.set(message_id, message, ex=10)

    return message_id
```

In the preceding code, you can see that the only amendment to the code I've made is to add `ex=10` to the `redis.set` method; this will cause all of our messages to expire in 10 seconds. Restart your Nameko services now and try this out. When you send a new message, wait 10 seconds and refresh the page, and it should be gone.

> **Please note** that if there were any messages in Redis before you made this change, they will still be present, since they were saved without an expiry. To remove them, delete all data in Redis with the `flushall` command using the `redis-cli`.

Feel free to play around with the expiry time, setting it to whatever you wish with either the `ex` or `px` parameters. One way you could make this better is to move the expiry time constant to the configuration file, which is then loaded whenever you start Nameko, but for now, this will suffice.

Sorting messages

One thing you will quickly notice with the current state of our app is that the messages are not in any order at all. When you send a new message it could be inserted anywhere in the thread of messages, making our app pretty inconvenient, to say the least!

To remedy this, we will sort the messages by the amount of time left before they expire. First, we will have to amend our `get_all_messages` method in our Redis dependency to also get the time-to-live for each message:

```python
def get_all_messages(self):
    return [
        {
            'id': message_id,
            'message': self.redis.get(message_id),
            'expires_in': self.redis.pttl(message_id),
        }
        for message_id in self.redis.keys()
    ]
```

As you can see in the preceding code, we have added a new `expires_in` value to each message. This uses the Redis PTTL command, which returns the time to live in milliseconds for a given key. Alternatively, we could also use the Redis TTL command, which returns the time to live in seconds, but we want this to be as precise as possible to make our sorting more accurate.

Now, when our `MessageService` calls `get_all_messages`, it will also know how long each message has to live. With this, we can create a new helper function to sort the messages.

First, add the following to our imports:

```
from operator import itemgetter
```

Outside of the `MessageService` class, create the following function:

```
def sort_messages_by_expiry(messages, reverse=False):
    return sorted(
        messages,
        key=itemgetter('expires_in'),
        reverse=reverse
    )
```

This uses Python's built-in `sorted` function, which has the ability to return a sorted list from a given iterable; in our case the iterable is `messages`. We use `key` to specify what we want `messages` to be sorted by. Since we want the `messages` to be sorted by `expires_in`, we use an `itemgetter` to extract it to be used as the comparison. We've given the `sort_messages_by_expiry` function an optional parameter, `reverse`, which, if set to `True`, will make `sorted` return the sorted list in a reverse order.

With this new helper function, we can now amend our `get_all_messages` RPC in our `MessageService`:

```
@rpc
def get_all_messages(self):
    messages = self.message_store.get_all_messages()
    sorted_messages = sort_messages_by_expiry(messages)
    return sorted_messages
```

Our app will now return our messages, sorted with the newest messages at the bottom. If you'd like to have the newest messages at the top, then simply change `sorted_messages` to be:

```
sorted_messages = sort_messages_by_expiry(messages, reverse=True)
```

Our app now fits all the acceptance criteria we specified earlier. We have the ability to send messages and get existing messages, and they all expire after a configurable amount of time. One thing that is less than ideal is that we rely on a browser refresh to fetch the latest state of the messages. We can fix this in a number of ways, but I will demonstrate one of the simplest ways to solve this; via polling.

By using polling, the browser can constantly make a request to the server to get the latest messages without forcing a page refresh. We will have to introduce some more JavaScript to achieve this, but so would any other method.

Browser polling for messages

When the browser makes a poll to get the latest messages, our server should return the messages in a JSON format. To achieve this, we'll need to create a new HTTP endpoint that returns the messages as JSON, without using the Jinja2 templating. We will first construct a new helper function to create a JSON response, setting the correct headers.

Outside of our WebServer, create the following function:

```
def create_json_response(content):
    headers = {'Content-Type': 'application/json'}
    json_data = json.dumps(content)
    return Response(json_data, status=200, headers=headers)
```

This is similar to our `create_html_response` from earlier, but here it sets the Content-Type to `'application/json'` and converts our data into a valid JSON object.

Now, within the WebServer, create the following HTTP entrypoint:

```
@http('GET', '/messages')
def get_messages(self, request):
    messages = self.message_service.get_all_messages()
    return create_json_response(messages)
```

This will call our `get_all_messages` RPC and return the result as a JSON response to the browser. Notice how we are using the same URL, `/messages`, as we do in our endpoint, here to send a new message. This is a good example of being RESTful. We use a POST request to `/messages` to create a new message and we use a GET request to `/messages` to get all messages.

Polling with JavaScript

To enable our messages to update automatically without a browser refresh, we will create two JavaScript functions—messagePoll, which will get the latest messages, and updateMessages, which will update the HTML with these new messages.

Start by replacing the Jinja2 if block in our home.html, which iterates through our list of messages, with the following line:

```
<div id="messageContainer"></div>
```

This will be used later to hold our new list of messages generated by our jQuery function.

Inside the <script> tags in our home.html, write the following code:

```
function messagePoll() {
  $.ajax({
    type: "GET", # ①
    url: "/messages",
    dataType: "json",
    success: function(data) { # ②
      updateMessages(data);
    },
    timeout: 500, # ③
    complete: setTimeout(messagePoll, 1000), # ④
  })
}
```

This is another AJAX request, similar to the one we made earlier to send a new message, with a few differences:

1. Here, we are performing a GET request to the new endpoint we made in our WebServer instead of a POST request.
2. If successful, we use the success callback to call the updateMessages function that we will create later.
3. Set timeout to 500 milliseconds - this is the amount of time in which we should expect a response from our server before giving up.
4. Use complete, which allows us to define what happens once the success or error callback has completed - in this case, we set it to call poll again after 1000 milliseconds using the setTimeout function.

We will now create the `updateMessages` function:

```
function updateMessages(messages) {
  var $messageContainer = $('#messageContainer'); # ①
  var messageList = []; # ②
  var emptyMessages = '<p>No messages!</p>'; # ③

  if (messages.length === 0) { # ④
    $messageContainer.html(emptyMessages); #
  } else {
    $.each(messages, function(index, value) {
      var message = $(value.message).text() || value.message;
      messageList.push('<p>' + message + '</p>'); #
    });
    $messageContainer.html(messageList); # ⑤
  }
}
```

By using this function, we can replace all of the code in our HTML template that generates the list of messages in the Jinja2 template. Let's go through this step-by-step:

1. First, we get the `messageContainer` within the HTML so that we can update it.
2. We generate an empty `messageList` array.
3. We generate the `emptyMessages` text.
4. We check if the amount of messages is equal to 0:
    a. If so, we use `.html()` to replace `messageContainer` HTML with "No messages!".
    b. Otherwise, for each message in `messages`, we first strip any HTML tags that could be present using jQuery's built-in `.text()` function. Then we wrap the message in `<p>` tags and append them to the `messageList` using `.push()`.
5. Finally, we use `.html()` to replace the `messageContainer` HTML with the `messagesList`.

In point *4b*, it's important to escape any HTML tags that could be present in the message, as a malicious user could send a nasty script as a message, which would be executed by everyone using the app!

This is by no means the best way to solve the issue of having to force refresh the browser to update the messages, but it is one of the simplest ways for me to demonstrate in this book. There are probably more elegant ways to achieve the polling, and if you really wanted to do this properly then WebSockets is by far your best option here.

Summary

This now brings us to a close with the guide to writing the TempMessenger application. If you have never used Nameko before or written a microservice, I hope I have given you a good base to build on when it comes to keeping services small and to the point.

We started by creating a service with a single RPC method and then used that within another service via HTTP. We then looked at ways in which we can test Nameko services with fixtures that allow us to spawn workers and even the services themselves.

We introduced dependency providers and created a Redis client with the ability to get a single message. With that, we expanded the Redis dependency with methods that allowed us to save new messages, expire messages, and return them all in a list.

We looked at how we can return HTML to the browser using Jinja2, and at creating a dependency provider. We even looked at some JavaScript and JQuery to enable us to make requests from the browser.

One of the main themes you will have probably noticed is the need to keep dependency logic away from your service code. By doing this we keep our services agnostic to the workings that are specific to only that dependency. What if we decided to switch Redis for a MySQL database? In our code, it would just be a case of creating a new dependency provider for MySQL and new client methods that mapped to the ones our `MessageService` expects. We'd then make the minimal change of swapping Redis for MySQL in our `MessageService`. If we did not write our code in this way then we would have to invest more time and effort to make changes to our service. We'd also introduce more scope for bugs to arise.

If you are familiar with other Python frameworks, you should now see how Nameko allows us to easily create scalable microservices while still giving us a more *batteries not included* approach when compared to something like Django. When it comes to writing small services that serve a single purpose that are focused on backend tasks, Nameko can be a perfect choice.

In the next chapter, we will look at extending TempMessenger with a User Authentication microservice using a PostgreSQL database.

6
Extending TempMessenger with a User Authentication Microservice

In the last chapter, we created a web-based messenger, TempMessenger, which consists of two microservices—one that is responsible for storing and retrieving messages and another that is responsible for serving web requests.

In this chapter, we will look to extend our existing TempMessenger platform with a User Authentication microservice. This will consist of a Nameko service with a PostgreSQL database dependency that has the ability to create new users and authenticate existing users.

We will also replace our Nameko Web Server microservice with a more suitable Flask app that will allow us to keep track of web sessions for our users.

It is necessary to have read the last chapter in order to follow this chapter.

We will cover the following topics:

- Creating a Postgres dependency
- Creating a User Service
- Securely storing passwords in a Database
- Authenticating users
- Creating a Flask app
- Web sessions

TempMessenger goals

Let's add some new goals for our new and improved TempMessenger:

- Users can now sign-up for the application
- To send messages, users must be logged in
- Users not logged in can still read all messages

 If at any point you would like to refer to all of the code in this chapter in its entirety, feel free to view it with tests at:
http://url.marcuspen.com/github-ppb.

Requirements

In order to function in this chapter, your local machine will need the following:

- An internet connection
- Docker: If you haven't installed Docker already, please see the official documentation: http://url.marcuspen.com/docker-install
- A virtualenv running Python 3.6 or later; you can reuse your virtualenv from the last chapter.
- pgAdmin: see the official documentation for installation instructions: http://url.marcuspen.com/pgadmin
- A RabbitMQ container running on the default ports: this should be present from the last chapter, Chapter 5, *Building a Web Messenger with Microservices*.
- A Redis container running on the default ports: this should be present from the last chapter, Chapter 5, *Building a Web Messenger with Microservices*.

All other requirements will be installed as we progress through the chapter.

All instructions in this chapter are tailored towards macOS or Debian/Ubuntu systems; however, I have made an effort to only use multi-platform dependencies.

 Throughout this chapter, there will be blocks of code. Different types of code will have their own prefixes, which are as follows:
$: to be executed in your terminal, always within your virtualenv
>>>: to be executed in your Nameko/Python shell
No prefix: block of Python code to be used in your editor

Creating a Postgres dependency

Previously, all the data we wanted to store was temporary. Messages had a fixed lifetime and would expire automatically; if our application had a catastrophic failure then the worst-case scenario would be that our messages would be lost, which for TempMessenger is hardly an issue at all!

However, user accounts are a totally different kettle of fish altogether. They must be stored for as long as the user wishes and they must be stored securely. We also need a proper schema for these accounts to keep the data consistent. We also need to be able to query and update the data with ease.

For these reasons, Redis probably isn't the best solution. One of the many benefits of building microservices is that we aren't tied to a specific technology; just because our Message Service uses Redis for storage doesn't mean that our User Service has to follow suit...

Starting a Postgres Docker container

To begin, you will start a Postgres Docker container in your terminal:

```
$ docker run --name postgres -e POSTGRES_PASSWORD=secret -e
POSTGRES_DB=users -p 5432:5432 -d postgres
```

This will start a Postgres container with some basic setup:

- `--name` sets the name of the container
- `-e` allows us to set environment variables:
    - `POSTGRES_PASSWORD`: The password used to access the database
    - `POSTGRES_DB`: The name of the database
        - `-p` allows us to expose port `5432` on the container to port `5432` on our local machine
        - `-d` allows us to start the container in daemon mode (runs in the background)

 If you are creating a database for a production environment then it is important to set a more secure password and keep it safe!

You can check if the container is up and running by executing the following and ensuring that your `postgres` container is present:

```
$ docker ps
```

Creating the user model

In order to store data about our users in Postgres, we first need to create a model that will define the fields and type of data we want to store.

We will first need to install two new Python packages: SQLAlchemy and Psycopg. SQLAlchemy is a toolkit and object-relational mapper that will serve as our gateway into the world of SQL. Psycopg is a PostgreSQL database adapter for Python.

Start by adding `sqlalchemy` (*version 1.2.1 at the time of writing*) and `psycopg2` (*version 2.7.4 at the time of writing*) to your `base.in` file. From the root of your project folder, within your virtualenv, run:

```
$ pip-compile requirements/base.in
$ pip-sync requirements/base.txt requirements/test.txt
```

This will add `sqlalchemy` and `psycopg2` to our requirements and will ensure that our virtualenv packages match them exactly. Alternatively, you can `pip install` them if you are choosing not to use pip-tools.

In our dependencies folder, create a new file, `users.py`. Usually, you would have a different file for your database models, but for the purpose of simplicity we will embed it within our dependency. To start, let's define our imports and the base class to be used by our model:

```
from sqlalchemy import Column, Integer, Unicode
from sqlalchemy.ext.declarative import declarative_base

Base = declarative_base()
```

We start by importing `Column`, which will be used to declare our database columns, and some basic field types: `Integer` and `Unicode`. As for `declarative_base`, we use that to create our `Base` class, from which our User model will inherit. This will create the mapping between our model and a database table.

Now let's define a basic model for our `users`:

```
class User(Base):
    __tablename__ = 'users'

    id = Column(Integer, primary_key=True)
    first_name = Column(Unicode(length=128))
    last_name = Column(Unicode(length=128))
    email = Column(Unicode(length=256), unique=True)
    password = Column(Unicode(length=512))
```

As you can see, our `User` class inherits from the Base class we defined earlier.
`__tablename__` sets the name of the table. Let's briefly go over some of the database
columns we have defined:

- `id`: A unique identifier and primary key for each user in our database. It's
  common practice for database models to have their IDs as integers for simplicity.
- `first_name` and `last_name`: a maximum length of 128 characters should be
  enough for any name. We've also used `Unicode` as our type to cater for names
  that include symbols such as Chinese.
- `email`: Again, a large field length and `Unicode` to cater for symbols. We've also
  made this field unique, which will prevent multiple users with the same email
  address from being created.
- `password`: We won't be storing passwords in plain text here; we'll come back to
  this later!

> To learn more about SQLAlchemy, see
> `http://url.marcuspen.com/sqlalchemy`.

Creating the user dependency

Now that we have a basic user model defined, we can create a Nameko dependency for it.
Luckily for us, some of the work has already been done for us in the form of `nameko-sqlalchemy`, an open-source Nameko dependency that will handle all of the semantics
around database sessions and also gives us some very useful Pyest fixtures for testing.

Install `nameko-sqlalchemy` (*version 1.0.0 at the time of writing*) by adding it to the
`requirements/base.in` file, and follow the same procedure as earlier to install
`sqlalchemy`.

We will now create a wrapper class that will be used to encapsulate all of the logic around managing users. In `users.py`, add the following code:

```
class UserWrapper:

    def __init__(self, session):
        self.session = session
```

This will be the basis of our wrapper and will require a database session object in the form of `session`. Later, we will add more methods to this class, such as `create` and `authenticate`. In order to create our user dependency, first let's add the following to our imports:

```
from nameko_sqlalchemy import DatabaseSession
```

Now let's create a new class, User Store, which will serve as our dependency:

```
class UserStore(DatabaseSession):

    def __init__(self):
        super().__init__(Base)

    def get_dependency(self, worker_ctx):
        database_session = super().get_dependency(worker_ctx)
        return UserWrapper(session=database_session)
```

To explain this code, first, let's talk about `DatabaseSession`. This pre-made dependency provider for Nameko, given to us by `nameko-sqlalchemy`, already includes methods such as `setup` and `get_dependency`, as covered in the previous chapter. Therefore, our `UserStore` class is simply inheriting from it to use this existing functionality.

The `DatabaseSession` class' `__init__` method takes the declarative base for our models as its only argument. In our `UserStore` class, we override this with our own `__init__` method, which amends it to use our `Base` and carry out the same functionality as it would have originally done by using Python's in-built `super` function.

 To learn more about Python's `super` method, see:
http://url.marcuspen.com/python-super.

The original `get_dependency` method in the `DatabaseSession` class simply returns a database session; however, we want ours to return an instance of our `UserWrapper` so that we can easily call the `create` and `authenticate` methods that we will make later. To override this in an elegant way so that we still keep all of the logic that generates the database session, we again use the `super` function to generate `database_session` and return an instance of our `UserWrapper`.

Creating users

Now that we have our Nameko dependency in place, we can start to add functionality to our `UserWrapper`. We will start by creating users. Add the following to the `UserWrapper` class:

```
def create(self, **kwargs):
    user = User(**kwargs)
    self.session.add(user)
    self.session.commit()
```

This `create` method will create a new `User` object, add it to our database session, commit that change to the database, and return the user. Nothing fancy here! But let's talk about the process of `self.session.add` and `self.session.commit`. When we first `add` the user to the session, this adds the user to our local database session in memory, rather than adding them to our actual database. The new user has been staged but no changes have actually taken place in our database. This is rather useful. Say we wanted to do multiple updates to the database, making a number of calls to the database can be expensive, so we first make all the changes we want in memory, then `commit` them all with a single database transaction.

Another thing you'll notice in the preceding code is that we use `**kwargs` instead of defining the actual arguments to create a new `User`. If we were to change the user model, this minimizes the changes needed since the keyword arguments directly map to the fields.

Creating the User Service

In the last chapter, we simply had two services in the same module, which is fine for any small-scale project. However, now that our platform is starting to grow and new roles are being defined between services, let's start to split these out by keeping them in different modules. Alongside your `service.py`, create a new file, `user_service.py`.

Add the following code:

```
from nameko.rpc import rpc
from .dependencies.users import UserStore

class UserService:

    name = 'user_service'
    user_store = UserStore()

    @rpc
    def create_user(self, first_name, last_name, email, password):
        self.user_store.create(
            first_name=first_name,
            last_name=last_name,
            email=email,
            password=password,
        )
```

If you read the last chapter, then there is nothing new here. We've created a new `UserService`, given it the `UserStore` dependency and made an RPC, which is simply a pass-through to the `create` method on the dependency. However, here we have opted to define the arguments to create a user rather than use `**kwargs` like we did in the dependency method. This is because we want the RPC to define the contract it has with other services that will interface with it. If another service makes an invalid call, then we want the RPC to reject it as soon as possible without wasting time making a call to the dependency or, worse, making a database query.

We are close to the point where we can test this out, but first we need to update our `config.yaml` with our database settings. Provided you used the command supplied earlier to create a Docker Postgres container, append the following:

```
DB_URIS:
  user_service:Base:
    "postgresql+psycopg2://postgres:secret@localhost/
    users?client_encoding=utf8"
```

`DB_URIS` is used by `nameko-sqlalchemy` to map a Nameko service and a declarative base pair to a Postgres database.

We will also have to create the tables in our Postgres database. Usually, you would do this with a database migration tool, such as Alembic. However, for the purposes of this book, we will use a small one-off Python script to do this for us. In the root of your project directory, create a new file, setup_db.py, with the following code:

```
from sqlalchemy import create_engine
from temp_messenger.dependencies.users import User

engine = create_engine(
    'postgresql+psycopg2://postgres:secret@localhost/'
    'users?client_encoding=utf8'
)
User.metadata.create_all(engine)
```

This code takes our user model in our dependency module and creates the required table in our database for us. create_engine is the starting point as it establishes a connection with the database. We then use our user model metadata (which in our case consists of the table name and columns) and call create_all, which issues the CREATE SQL statements to the database using the engine.

If you are going to want to make changes to the User model while retaining your existing user data, then learning how to use a database migration tool, such as Alembic, is a must and I strongly recommend it.

 To learn more about how to use Alembic, see
http://url.marcuspen.com/alembic.

To run, in your terminal with your virtualenv simply execute:

```
$ python setup_db.py
```

Now let's take a look at our new table using a Database Admin tool. There are many Database Admin tools out there, my personal favorite being Postico for Mac, but for the purposes of this book, we will use pgAdmin, which works on all platforms.

Download and install pgAdmin from `http://url.marcuspen.com/pgadmin`. Once installed, open and select **Add new server**, which will bring up the following window:

Simply give it a name of your choice in the **General** tab, then in the **Connection** tab, you can fill out the details of our database with the configuration we set when we created our Postgres Docker screenshot earlier. However, if you did not make any changes to this, you can simply copy the details in the preceding image. Remember that the password was set to `secret`. Once you've filled this out, hit Save and it should connect to our database.

Once connected, we can start to look at the details of our database. To see our table, you'll need to expand out and action the menus like so:

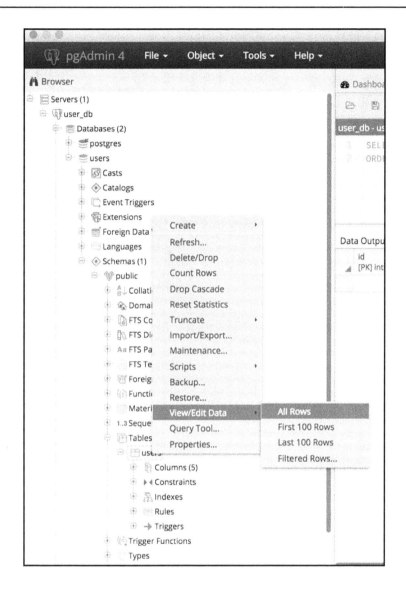

You should now be able to see our table, which represents our user model:

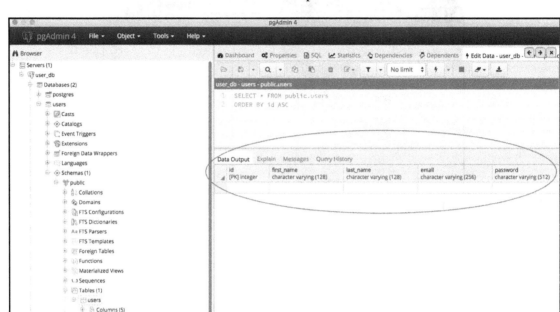

We can now try out creating a user with the Nameko shell. Start our new User Service in the terminal by executing the following, within a virtualenv, in the root of our project folder:

```
$ nameko run temp_messenger.user_service --config config.yaml
```

In another terminal window, within your virtualenv, execute:

```
$ nameko shell
```

Once in your Nameko shell, execute the following to create a new user:

```
>>> n.rpc.user_service.create_user('John', 'Doe', 'john@example.com',
'super-secret')
```

Now let's check **pgAdmin** to see if the user was successfully created. To refresh the data, simply follow the earlier steps to show the user table or click the Refresh button:

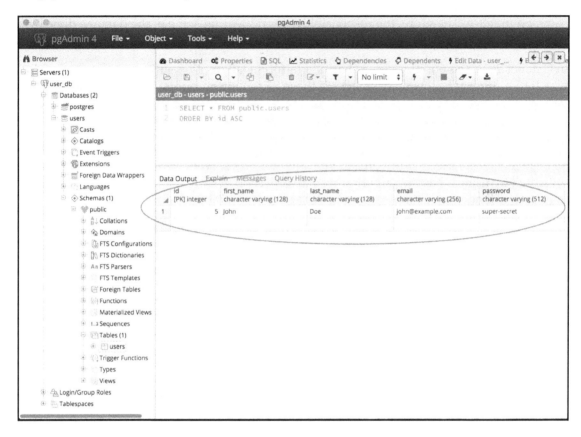

It worked! We now have a functioning User Service that can create new users. However, there is one major issue here... We have just committed one of the worst offenses a software developer can commit—storing passwords in plain text!

Securely storing passwords in the database

The year is 2018 and by now we've probably all heard dozens of stories about companies leaking our sensitive data, including passwords, to hackers. In a lot of these cases, the passwords that were leaked were stored with extremely poor cryptography, meaning that they could be cracked with ease. In some cases, the passwords were even stored in plain text!

Either way, this negligence has led to the leak of millions of users' email and password combinations. This would not be such an issue if we used different passwords for every online account we made... but unfortunately, we are lazy and password reuse is quite common practice. Therefore, the responsibility for mitigating some of the damage done by hackers infiltrating our servers falls to us, the developers.

In October 2016, the popular video sharing platform Dailymotion suffered a data breach in which 85 million accounts were stolen. Of those 85 million accounts, 18 million had passwords attached to them, but luckily they were hashed using Bcrypt. This meant that it would take hackers decades, maybe even centuries, of brute-force computing to crack them with today's hardware (source: `http://url.marcuspen.com/dailymotion-hack`).

So despite hackers successfully breaching Dailymotion's servers, some of the damage was mitigated by using a hashing algorithm, such as Bcrypt, to store the passwords. With this in mind, we will now look at how to implement `bcrypt` hashing for our user passwords, rather than storing them insecurely in plain text.

Using Bcrypt

Start by adding `bcrypt` to your `base.in` file and installing it (*version 3.1.4 at the time of writing*) using the same process as earlier.

 If you have issues installing Bcrypt, please see their installation instructions, which include details on system package dependencies: `http://url.marcuspen.com/pypi-bcrypt`.

In order for `bcrypt` to create a hash of a password, it requires two things—your password and a `salt`. A `salt` is simply a string of random characters. Let's look at how you can create a `salt` in Python:

```
>>> from bcrypt import gensalt
>>> gensalt()
b'$2b$12$fiDoHXkWx6WMOuIfOG4Gku'
```

This is the simplest way to create a `salt` compatible with Bcrypt. The `$` symbols represent different parts of the `salt`, and I'd like to point out the second section: `$12`. This part represents how many rounds of work are required to hash the password, which by default, is `12`. We can configure this like so:

```
>>> gensalt(rounds=14)
b'$2b$14$kOUKDC.05iq1ANZPgBXxYO'
```

Notice how in this `salt`, it has changed to `$14`. By increasing this, we are also increasing the amount of time it would take to create a hash of the password. This will also increase the amount of time it takes to check the password attempt against the hash later on. This is useful since we are trying to prevent hackers from brute-forcing password attempts if they do manage to get hold of our database. However, the default number of rounds, `12`, is plenty enough already! Let's now create a hash of a password:

```
>>> from bcrypt import hashpw, gensalt
>>> my_password = b'super-secret'
>>> salt = gensalt()
>>> salt
b'$2b$12$YCnmXxOcs/GJVTHinSoVs.'
>>> hashpw(my_password, salt)
b'$2b$12$YCnmXxOcs/GJVTHinSoVs.43v/.RVKXQSdOhHffiGNk2nMgKweR4u'
```

Here, we have simply generated a new `salt` using the default amount of rounds and used `hashpw` to generate the hash. Notice how the `salt` is also in the first part of the hash for our password? This is quite convenient as it means we don't also have to store the `salt` separately, which we'll need when it comes to authenticating users later.

Since we used the default number of rounds to generate the `salt`, why not try setting your own amount of rounds? Notice how the amount of time taken by `hashpw` increases the higher you set this. My machine took almost 2 minutes to create a hash when the amount of rounds was set to 20!

Now let's look at how we check passwords against the hash:

```
>>> from bcrypt import hashpw, checkpw, gensalt
>>> my_password = b'super-secret'
>>> salt = gensalt()
>>> hashed_password = hashpw(my_password, salt)
>>> password_attempt = b'super-secret'
>>> checkpw(password_attempt, hashed_password)
True
```

As you can see, `checkpw` takes the password attempt that we are checking and the hashed password as arguments. When we implement this in our dependency, the password attempt will be the part coming from the web request and the hashed password will be stored in the database. Since it was a successful attempt, `checkpw` returns `True`. Let's attempt the same operation with an invalid password:

```
>>> password_attempt = b'invalid-password'
>>> checkpw(password_attempt, hashed_password)
False
```

No surprises here! It returned `False`.

 If you'd like to learn more about storing passwords and the pitfalls of certain methods, I'd suggest you read this short article from Dustin Boswell: `http://url.marcuspen.com/dustwell-passwords`. It explains nicely how hackers can attempt to crack passwords using brute force and rainbow tables. It also goes into a Bcrypt in bit more detail.

Hashing our user passwords

Now that we know how to store passwords more securely, let's amend our `create` method to hash our passwords before storing them in the database. Firstly, at the top of our `users.py` dependency file, let's add `bcrypt` to our imports and add a new constant:

```
import bcrypt

HASH_WORK_FACTOR = 15
```

Our new constant, `HASH_WORK_FACTOR` will be used for the rounds argument that `gensalt` uses. I've set it to 15, which will cause it to take slightly longer to create password hashes and check passwords, but it will be more secure. Please feel free to set this as you wish; just bare in mind that the more you increase this, the longer it will take for our application to create and authenticate users later on.

Now, outside any classes, we will define a new helper function for hashing passwords:

```
def hash_password(plain_text_password):
    salt = bcrypt.gensalt(rounds=HASH_WORK_FACTOR)
    encoded_password = plain_text_password.encode()

    return bcrypt.hashpw(encoded_password, salt)
```

This helper function simply takes our plain text password, generates a `salt`, and returns a hashed password. Now, you may have noticed that when using Bcrypt, we always have to ensure that the passwords we give it are bytestrings. As you'll notice from the preceding code, we had to `.encode()` the password (which by default is UTF-8) before giving it to `hashpw`. Bcrypt also will return the hashed password in the bytestring format. The problem this will bring is that our field for passwords in our database is currently set to Unicode, making it incompatible with our passwords. We have two options here: either call `.decode()` on the password before we store it or amend our password field to something that will accept bytestrings, such as `LargeBinary`. Let's go with the latter, as it is cleaner and saves us from having to convert our data every time we wish to access it.

First, let's amend the line where we import our field types to include `LargeBinary`:

```
from sqlalchemy import Column, Integer, LargeBinary, Unicode
```

Now we can update our `User` model to use our new field type:

```
class User(Base):
    __tablename__ = 'users'

    id = Column(Integer, primary_key=True)
    first_name = Column(Unicode(length=128))
    last_name = Column(Unicode(length=128))
    email = Column(Unicode(length=256), unique=True)
    password = Column(LargeBinary())
```

The only problem we have now is that our existing database is not compatible with our new schema. To solve this, we can either delete the database table or perform a migration. In real-world environments, deleting a whole table is not an option, ever! If you have already taken my advice earlier to study Alembic, then I'd encourage you to put your knowledge to the test and perform a database migration. But for the purposes of this book, I will take advantage of throwaway Docker containers and start from scratch. To do this, in the root of your project, and inside your virtualenv, execute:

```
$ docker rm -f postgres
$ docker run --name postgres -e POSTGRES_PASSWORD=secret -e
POSTGRES_DB=users -p 5432:5432 -d postgres
$ python setup_db.py
```

This will delete your existing Postgres container, create a new one and run the `setup_db.py` script we made earlier. If you check **pgAdmin**, you'll now see that the field type in the column headers for password has changed from `character varying (512)` to `bytea`.

At last, we are now ready to update our `create` method to use our new `hash_password` function:

```
def create(self, **kwargs):
    plain_text_password = kwargs['password']
    hashed_password = hash_password(plain_text_password)
    kwargs.update(password=hashed_password)

    user = User(**kwargs)
    self.session.add(user)
    self.session.commit()
```

As you can see, in the first three lines of the method we:

1. Extract the `plain_text_password` from `kwargs`.
2. Call `hash_password` to create our `hashed_password`.
3. Perform an update on `kwargs` to replace the password with the hashed version.

The rest of the code is unchanged from our previous version.

Let's try this out. In your terminal within your virtualenv, start (or restart) the User Service:

```
$ nameko run temp_messenger.user_service --config config.yaml
```

In another terminal window within your virtualenv, start your Nameko shell:

```
$ nameko shell
```

Inside your Nameko shell, execute the following to add a new user again:

```
>>> n.rpc.user_service.create_user('John', 'Doe', 'john@example.com',
'super-secret')
```

You should notice (depending on how large you set HASH_WORK_FACTOR) that there is now a slight delay compared to last time when creating a new user.

You should now see the following in your **pgAdmin**:

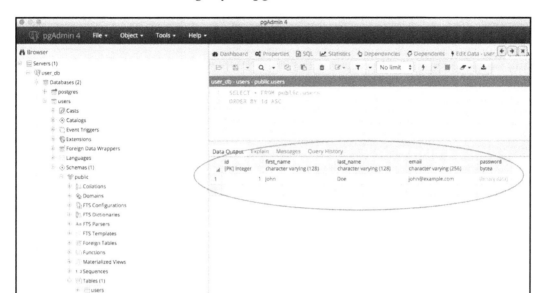

Handling duplicate users

Since we set our email field to be unique, our database already prevents duplicate users. However, if you were to try this for yourself, the output we receive back is not the best. Try it for yourself by adding the same user again in the Nameko shell.

Another problem with this is that, if there were any other errors when creating a new user, there is no nice way for our external services to react to these different types of errors without knowing the type of database we are using, which we want to avoid at all costs.

To solve this, let's start by creating two new exception classes in our `users.py`:

```
class CreateUserError(Exception):
    pass

class UserAlreadyExists(CreateUserError):
    pass
```

We also need to update our imports to include `IntegrityError`, which is the type of error SQLAlchemy raises when there is a unique key violation:

```
from sqlalchemy.exc import IntegrityError
```

Again, we will amend our `create` method, this time to use our two new exceptions:

```
def create(self, **kwargs):
    plain_text_password = kwargs['password']
    hashed_password = hash_password(plain_text_password)
    kwargs.update(password=hashed_password)

    user = User(**kwargs)
    self.session.add(user)

    try:
        self.session.commit()  # ①
    except IntegrityError as err:
        self.session.rollback()  # ②
        error_message = err.args[0]  # ③

        if 'already exists' in error_message:
            email = kwargs['email']
            message = 'User already exists - {}'.format(email)
            raise UserAlreadyExists(message)  # ④
        else:
            raise CreateUserError(error_message)  # ⑤
```

What we have done here is to:

1. Wrap the `self.session.commit()` in a try except block.
2. If an `IntegrityError` occurs, rollback our session, which removes the user from our database session - not completely necessary in this case, but good practice nevertheless.
3. Extract the error message.
4. Check to see if it contains the string `'already exists'`. If so, then we know that the user already exists and we raise the appropriate exception, `UserAlreadyExists`, and give it an error message containing the user's email.
5. If not, then we have an unexpected error and raise the more generic error tailored to our service, `CreateUserError`, and give it the whole error message.

By doing this, our external services will now be able to differentiate between a user error and an unexpected error.

To test this out, restart the User Service and attempt to add the same user again in the Nameko shell.

Authenticating users

We can now look at how to authenticate users. This is a very simple process:

1. Retrieve the user we want to authenticate from the database.
2. Perform a `bcrypt.checkpw` giving it the attempted password and the password hash of the user.
3. Raise an exception if the result is `False`.
4. Return the user if it's `True`.

Retrieving users from the database

Starting with the first point, we will need to add a new dependency method, `get`, which returns the user, given the email, if it exists.

First, add a new exception class in `users.py`:

```
class UserNotFound(Exception):
    pass
```

This is what we will raise in the event of the user not being found. Now we will update our imports to include the following:

```
from sqlalchemy.orm.exc import NoResultFound
```

`NoResultFound`, as the name implies, is raised by SQLAlchemy when a requested object is not found in the database. Now we can add a new method to our `UserWrapper` class:

```
def get(self, email):
    query = self.session.query(User)  # ①

    try:
        user = query.filter_by(email=email).one()  # ②
    except NoResultFound:
        message = 'User not found - {}'.format(email)
```

```
        raise UserNotFound(message)  # ③

    return user
```

Let's understand what we've done in the preceding code:

1. In order to query our database, we first must make a query object using our user model as an argument.
2. Once we have this, we can use `filter_by` and specify some parameters; in this case, we just want to filter by email. `filter_by` always returns an iterable, since you could have multiple results, but since we have a unique constraint on the email field, it's safe to assume that we are only ever going to have one match if it exists. Therefore, we call `.one()`, which returns the single object or raises `NoResultFound` if the filter is empty.
3. We handle `NoResultFound` and raise our own exception, `UserNotFound`, with an error message, which better suits our User Service.

Authenticating a user's password

We will now implement an `authenticate` method that will use the `get` method we just created.

First, let's create a new exception class that will be raised if there is a password mismatch:

```
class AuthenticationError(Exception):
    pass
```

We can now create another method for our `UserWrapper` to authenticate users:

```
def authenticate(self, email, password):
    user = self.get(email)  # ①

    if not bcrypt.checkpw(password.encode(), user.password):  # ②
        message = 'Incorrect password for {}'.format(email)
        raise AuthenticationError(message)  # ③
```

1. We start by using our recently created `get` method to retrieve the user we want to authenticate from our database.

2. We then use `bcrypt.checkpw` to check that the attempted password matches the password stored on the user object retrieved from the database. We call `.encode()` on the password attempt because our external services aren't going to do this for us. Nor should they; this is something specific to Bcrypt and such logic should stay in the dependency.

3. If the password is incorrect, we raise our `AuthenticationError` error with an appropriate message.

All that's left to do now is to create an RPC on our `UserService` class in `user_service.py`:

```
@rpc
def authenticate_user(self, email, password):
    self.user_store.authenticate(email, password)
```

Nothing special here, just a simple pass-through to the `user_store` dependency method we just made.

Let's test this out. Restart the `user_service` and execute the following in your Nameko shell:

```
>>> n.rpc.user_service.authenticate_user('john@example.com', 'super-
secret')
>>>
```

If successful, it should do nothing! Now let's try it with an incorrect password:

```
>>> n.rpc.user_service.authenticate_user('john@example.com', 'wrong')
Traceback (most recent call last):
...
nameko.exceptions.RemoteError: PasswordMismatch Incorrect password for
john@example.com
>>>
```

That's it! That concludes our work on our User Service. We will now look at integrating it with our existing services.

> If you'd like to see how to write some tests for the User Service, you'll find them, plus all the code, in the Github repository mentioned at the start of this chapter.

Splitting out the services

As it stands, we have our `MessageServer` and `WebServer` in the same `service.py` module. It's now time to split these, especially since we will be removing the `WebServer` in favor of a Flask server. At the end of this chapter, the goal is to have a total of three microservices working together, each with its own specific roles:

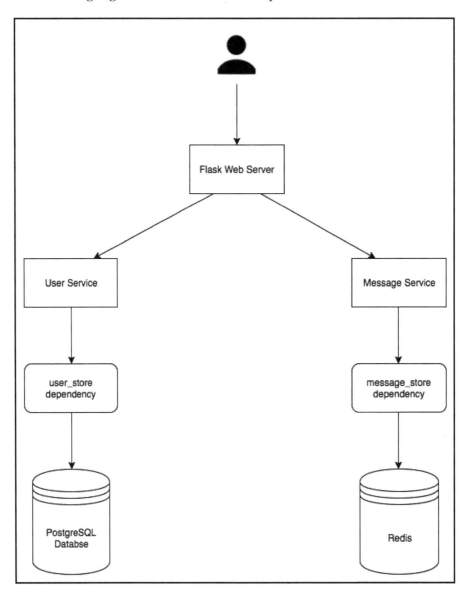

The preceding diagram demonstrates how our services will integrate with each other. Take note of how the Message Service and User Service are totally unaware of each other. A change to the User Service should not require a change to the Message Service and vice versa. By splitting these services, we also gain the advantage of being able to deploy new code to a single service without affecting the others. A bonus from Nameko using RabbitMQ is that, if a service does go down for a short period of time, any work will simply be queued until the service comes back online. We will now begin to reap some of the benefits of a microservice architecture.

To start this refactoring, let's create a new file within our `temp_messenger` folder, `message_service.py`:

```python
from nameko.rpc import rpc
from .dependencies.messages import MessageStore


class MessageService:

    name = 'message_service'

    message_store = MessageStore()

    @rpc
    def get_message(self, message_id):
        return self.message_store.get_message(message_id)

    @rpc
    def save_message(self, message):
        message_id = self.message_store.save_message(message)
        return message_id

    @rpc
    def get_all_messages(self):
        messages = self.message_store.get_all_messages()
        sorted_messages = sort_messages_by_expiry(messages)
        return sorted_messages


def sort_messages_by_expiry(messages, reverse=False):
    return sorted(
        messages,
        key=lambda message: message['expires_in'],
        reverse=reverse
    )
```

All we have done here is take the `MessageService` and all related code from our old `service.py` and place it into our new `message_service.py` module.

Creating a Flask server

We will now create a new Flask web server, which will replace our Nameko Web Server. Flask is better suited to handling web requests than Nameko and comes with a lot more baked in while still being fairly lightweight. One of the features we will take advantage of is Sessions, which will allow our server to keep track of who's logged in. It also works with Jinja2 for templating, meaning that our existing template should already work.

Start by adding `flask` to our `base.in` file, then `pip-compile` and install (*version 0.12.2 at the time of writing*) using the same process as earlier.

Getting started with Flask is quite straightforward; we will start by creating our new home page endpoint. Within your `temp_messenger` directory, create a new file, `web_server.py`, with the following:

```
from flask import Flask, render_template # ①

app = Flask(__name__) # ②

@app.route('/') # ③
def home():
    return render_template('home.html') # ④
```

1. We import the following from `flask`:
   - `Flask`: used to create our Flask app object
   - `render_template`: renders a given template file
2. Create our `app`, the only argument being the name of our module derived from `__name__`.
3. `@app.route` allows you decorate a function with a URL endpoint.

With this, we will be able to get our new Flask web server up and running, albeit with no functionality. To test this, first export some environment variables:

```
$ export FLASK_DEBUG=1
$ export FLASK_APP=temp_messenger/web_server.py
```

The first will set the app to debug mode, one of the features I like about this as it will hot-reload when we update our code, unlike a Nameko service. The second simply tells Flask where our app lives.

 Before we start the Flask app, please ensure that you are not currently running your old Nameko web server as this will cause a port clash.

Within your virtualenv, execute the following in the root of our project to start the server:

```
$ flask run -h 0.0.0.0 -p 8000
```

This will start the Flask server on port 8000, the same port we had our old Nameko web server running on. Provided your local network allows, you can even have other devices on the same network navigate to your machine's IP and use TempMessenger! Now go to http://127.0.0.1:8000 on your browser and you should see the following (albeit with no functionality):

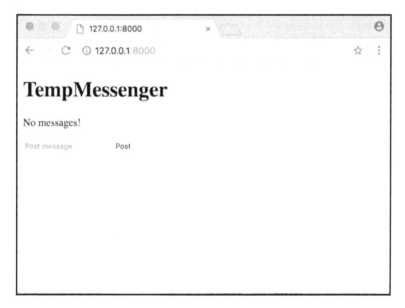

Looks similar to what we had before right? That's because Flask already uses Jinja2 as its default templating engine, so if we want we can delete our old jinja2.py dependency as it's no longer needed. Flask also looks for a folder called templates in the same directory as the app, which is how it automatically knew where to find home.html.

Let's now add the functionality of retrieving messages from our Message Service. This is slightly different from when we were communicating between two Nameko services since Flask does not know how to perform RPC's. First, let's add the following to our imports:

```
from flask.views import MethodView
from nameko.standalone.rpc import ClusterRpcProxy
from flask.json import jsonify
```

We will also need to add some config so that Flask knows where to find our RabbitMQ server. We could just add this in our module as a constant, but since we already have AMQP_URI in our config.yaml, it makes no sense to duplicate it! In our web_server.py module, before app = Flask(__name__), add the following:

```
import yaml
with open('config.yaml', 'r') as config_file:
    config = yaml.load(config_file)
```

This will load all of our config variables from config.yaml. Now add the following class to web_server.py:

```
class MessageAPI(MethodView):

    def get(self):
        with ClusterRpcProxy(config) as rpc:
            messages = rpc.message_service.get_all_messages()

        return jsonify(messages)
```

Whereas our home page endpoint has a function-based view, here we have a class-based view. We've defined a get method, which will be used for any GET requests to this MessageAPI. Take note that the names of the methods are important here since they map to their respective request types. If we were to add a post method (and we will later), then that would map to all POST requests on the MessageAPI.

ClusterRpcProxy allows us to make RPCs outside a Nameko service. It's used as a context manager and allows us to easily call our Message Service. Flask comes with a handy helper function, jsonify, which converts our list of messages into JSON. It's then a simple task of returning that payload, whereby Flask handles the response headers and status code for us.

Let's now add the functionality of sending new messages. First, amend your flask import to include request:

```
from flask import Flask, render_template, request
```

Now add a new post method to the `MessageAPI` class:

```
def post(self): # ①
    data = request.get_json(force=True) # ②

    try:
        message = data['message'] # ③
    except KeyError:
        return 'No message given', 400

    with ClusterRpcProxy(config) as rpc: # ④
        rpc.message_service.save_message(message)

    return '', 204 # ⑤
```

1. You may notice that, rather than obtaining the `request` object from the `post` parameters like we did with our Nameko web server, we are importing it from Flask. In this context, it is a global object that parses all incoming request data for us.
2. We use `get_json`, which is an inbuilt JSON parser that will replace our `get_request_data` function from the last chapter. We specify that `force=True`, which will enforce that the request has valid JSON data; otherwise it will return a `400 Bad Request` error code.
3. Like our old `post_message` HTTP endpoint, we `try` to get `data['message']` or return a `400`.
4. We then again use `ClusterRpcProxy` to make an RPC to save the message.
5. Return a `204` if all went well. We use `204` rather than a `200` here to indicate that, while the request was still successful, there is no content to be returned.

There's one more thing we need to do before this will work, and that is to register our `MessageAPI` with an API endpoint. At the bottom of our `web_server.py`, outside the `MessageAPI` class, add the following:

```
app.add_url_rule(
    '/messages', view_func=MessageAPI.as_view('messages')
)
```

This will direct any requests to `/messages` to the `MessageAPI`.

It's now time to bring our Message Service back online. In a new terminal window and inside your virtualenv, execute:

```
$ nameko run temp_messenger.message_service --config config.yaml
```

Since we now have multiple services, this requires multiple instances running in different terminal windows. If one of your Nameko services is down when you make a request, this can cause functionality to hang indefinitely until that service is back online. This is a side-effect of Nameko using a messaging queue to consume new tasks; the task is simply on the queue, waiting for a service to take it.

Provided that you still have your Flask server running, you should now be able to visit our app in all its former glory at http://127.0.0.1:8000!

Web sessions

Now that we have our old functionality back using our new Flask server, we can start to add some new features such as logging users in and out, creating new users , and allowing only logged in users to send messages. All of these depend heavily on web sessions.

Web sessions allow us to keep track of users between different requests via cookies. In these cookies, we store information that can be passed on from one request to the next. For example, we could store whether a user is authenticated, what their email address is, and so on. The cookies are signed cryptographically using a secret key, which we will need to define before we can use Flask's Sessions. In `config.yaml`, add the following:

```
FLASK_SECRET_KEY: 'my-super-secret-flask-key'
```

Feel free to set your own secret key, this is just an example. In a production-like environment, this would have to be kept safe and secure, otherwise a user could forge their own session cookies.

We will now need to tell our `app` to use this secret key. After `app = Flask(__name__)`, add the following:

```
app.secret_key = config['FLASK_SECRET_KEY']
```

With this done, Flask will now use our `FLASK_SECRET_KEY` from our `config.yaml` to sign cookies.

Creating a sign-up page

We will start these new features by adding the ability for new users to sign up. In `web_server.py`, add the following new class:

```
class SignUpView(MethodView):

    def get(self):
        return render_template('sign_up.html')
```

This new `SignUpView` class will be responsible for dealing with the sign-up process. We've added a get method, which will simply render the `sign_up.html` template that we will create later.

At the end of the `web_server.py` module, create the following URL rule:

```
app.add_url_rule(
    '/sign_up', view_func=SignUpView.as_view('sign_up')
)
```

As you probably already know, this will direct all requests to `/sign_up` to our new `SignUpView` class.

Now let's create our new template. In the `templates` folder, create a new file, `sign_up.html`:

```html
<!DOCTYPE html>
<body>
  <h1>Sign up</h1>
  <form action="/sign_up" method="post">
    <input type="text" name="first_name" placeholder="First Name">
    <input type="text" name="last_name" placeholder="Last Name">
    <input type="text" name="email" placeholder="Email">
    <input type="password" name="password" placeholder="Password">
    <input type="submit" value="Submit">
  </form>
  {% if error_message %}
    <p>{{ error_message }}</p>
  {% endif %}
</body>
```

This is a basic HTML form, consisting of the fields needed to create a new user in our database. The `action` and `method` forms tell it to make a `post` request to the `/sign_up` endpoint. All fields are `text` fields with the exception of password, which is of type `password`, which will cause the user input to be masked. We also have a Jinja `if` statement that will check to see if the template was rendered with an `error_message`. If so, then it will be displayed in a paragraph block. We will use this later to display messages such as **User already exists** to the user.

With these changes made, provided you still have the Flask server running, navigate to `http://127.0.0.1:8000/sign_up` and you should see the new sign-up page:

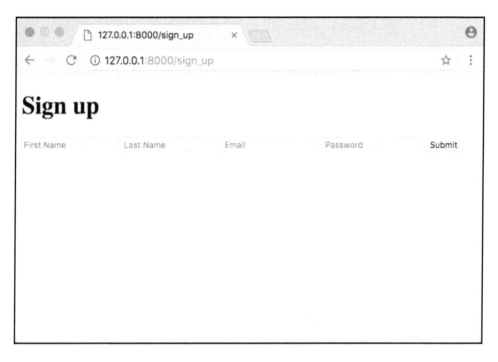

This form will not yet do anything, as we have not defined a post method for our
SignUpView. Let's go ahead and create that. First, update our imports in web_server.py
to include RemoteError from Nameko and session, redirect, and url_for from Flask:

```
from nameko.exceptions import RemoteError
from flask import (
    Flask,
    Redirect,
    render_template,
    request,
    session,
    url_for,
)
```

In your SignUpView class, add the following post method:

```
def post(self):
    first_name = request.form['first_name'] # ①
    last_name = request.form['last_name']
    email = request.form['email']
    password = request.form['password']

    with ClusterRpcProxy(config) as cluster_rpc:
```

```
        try:
            cluster_rpc.user_service.create_user( # ②
                first_name=first_name,
                last_name=last_name,
                email=email,
                password=password,
            )
        except RemoteError as err: # ③
            message = 'Unable to create user {} - {}'.format(
                err.value
            )
            app.logger.error(message)
            return render_template(
                'sign_up.html', error_message=message
            )

    session['authenticated'] = True # ④
    session['email'] = email # ⑤

    return redirect(url_for('home')) # ⑥
```

This is quite a long method, but it's fairly simple. Let's go through it step-by-step:

1. We start by retrieving all relevant fields for a user from `request.form`.
2. We then use `ClusterRpcProxy` to make a `create_user` RPC to our `user_service`.
3. If an error occurs, handle it by:
     - Constructing an error message
     - Logging that message to the console using Flask's `app.logger`
     - Rendering the `sign_up.html` template with the error message
4. If there are no errors, then we continue by adding an `authenticated` Boolean of `True` to the `session` object.
5. Add the user's email to the `session` object.
6. Finally, we redirect the user using `url_for`, which will look for the function endpoint named `home`.

Before we test this out, if you don't already have the User Service running, in a new terminal within your virtualenv execute:

```
nameko run temp_messenger.user_service --config config.yaml
```

With this, you should now have your User Service, Message Service and Flask web server running simultaneously in different terminal windows. If not, then start them using the `nameko` and `flask` commands from earlier.

Navigate to `http://127.0.0.1:8000/sign_up` and attempt to create a new user:

Once you hit **Submit**, it should redirect you to the home page and you should have a new user in your database. Check pgAdmin to ensure that they have been created.

Now go back to `http://127.0.0.1:8000/sign_up` and attempt to add the same user again. It should keep you on the same page and display the error message:

It's all well and good having a sign-up page, but our users need to be able to navigate to it without knowing the URL! Let's make some adjustments to our `home.html` to add a simple **Sign up** link. While we are at it, we can also hide the ability to send new messages unless they are logged in! In our `home.html`, amend our existing `postMessage` form to the following:

```
{% if authenticated %}
  <form action="/messages" id="postMessage">
    <input type="text" name="message" placeholder="Post message">
    <input type="submit" value="Post">
  </form>
{% else %}
  <p><a href="/sign_up">Sign up</a></p>
{% endif %}
```

What we have done here is to wrap our form in a Jinja `if` block. If the user is `authenticated`, then we will show the `postMessage` form; otherwise, we will display a link directing the user to the sign-up page.

We will now also have to update our home endpoint to pass the `authenticated` Boolean from the `session` object to the template renderer. First, let's add a new helper function that gets the authenticated state of a user. This should sit outside any classes inside your `web_server.py` module:

```
def user_authenticated():
    return session.get('authenticated', False)
```

This will attempt to get the `authenticated` Boolean from the `session` object. If it's a brand new `session` then we can't guarantee that the `authenticated` will be there, so we default it to `False` and return it.

In `web_server.py`, update the `home` endpoint to be the following:

```
@app.route('/')
def home():
    authenticated = user_authenticated()
    return render_template(
        'home.html', authenticated=authenticated
    )
```

This will make a call to `user_authenticated` to get the authenticated Boolean of our user. We then render the template by passing it `authenticated`.

Another nice adjustment we can make is to only allow the user to go to the sign up page if they are not authenticated. To do this, we will need to update our `get` method in our `SignUpView` as follows:

```
def get(self):
    if user_authenticated():
        return redirect(url_for('home'))
    else:
        return render_template(sign_up.html')
```

If we are authenticated, then we redirect the user to the `home` endpoint; otherwise, we render the `sign_up.html` template.

If you still have the browser open that you used to create your first user, then if you try to navigate to `http://127.0.0.1:8000/sign_up` it should redirect you to the home page of our site since you are already authenticated.

If you open a different browser, on the home page, you should see the new **Sign up** link we made and the ability to send new messages should have disappeared, since you have a new session.

We now have a new issue. We have prevented users from sending new messages from the app, but they can still send them if they were to use Curl or a REST client. To stop this from happening, we need to make a small tweak to our `MessageAPI`. At the start of the `MessageAPI` post method, add the following:

```
def post(self):
    if not user_authenticated()
        return 'Please log in', 401
    ...
```

Be sure not to adjust any of the other code; the . . . denotes the rest of the code from our `post` method. This will simply reject the user's request with a `401` response that tells the user to log in.

Logging users out

We now need to implement the ability for users to log out. In `web_server.py`, add the following `logout` function endpoint:

```
@app.route('/logout')
def logout():
    session.clear()
    return redirect(url_for('home'))
```

If a user hits this endpoint, Flask will clear their `session` object and redirect them to the home endpoint. Since the session is cleared, the `authenticated` Boolean will be deleted.

In `home.html`, let's update our page to include the link for users to log out. To do this, we will add a new link just after our `postMessage` form:

```
{% if authenticated %}
  <form action="/messages" id="postMessage">
    <input type="text" name="message" placeholder="Post message">
    <input type="submit" value="Post">
  </form>
  <p><a href="/logout">Logout</a></p>
  ...
```

Once saved, and provided we are logged in, we should now have a Logout link underneath our message form:

After clicking the **Logout** link, you should be redirected back to the home page, where you will no longer be able to send messages.

Logging users in

Our app can't be complete without the ability to log a user in! In our `web_server.py`, create a new class, `LoginView`:

```
class LoginView(MethodView):

    def get(self):
        if user_authenticated():
            return redirect(url_for('home'))
        else:
            return render_template('login.html')
```

Like the get in our `SignUpView`, this one will check to see if the user is already `authenticated`. If so, then we will redirect them to the `home` endpoint, otherwise, we will render the `login.html` template.

At the end of our `web_server.py` module, add the following URL rule for the `LoginView`:

```
app.add_url_rule(
    '/login', view_func=LoginView.as_view('login')
)
```

Any request to `/login` will now be directed to our `LoginView`.

Now create a new template, `login.html`, inside our templates folder:

```
<!DOCTYPE html>
<body>
  <h1>Login</h1>
  <form action="/login" method='post'>
    <input type="text" name="email" placeholder="Email">
    <input type="password" name="password" placeholder="Password">
    <input type="submit" value="Post">
  </form>
  {% if login_error %}
    <p>Bad log in</p>
  {% endif %}
</body>
```

As you can see, this is quite similar to our `sign_up.html` template. We create a form, but this time we only have the `email` and `password` fields. We also have a Jinja `if` block for error messages. However, this one has a hardcoded error message rather than one returned from the `LoginView`. This is because it is bad practice to tell a user why they failed to log in. If it was a malicious user and we were telling them things such as *This user does not exist* or *Password incorrect* then this alone would tell them which users exist in our database and they could possibly attempt to brute-force passwords.

In our `home.html` template, let's also add a link for users to log in. To do this, we will add a new link in the `else` statement of our `if authenticated` block:

```
{% if authenticated %}
...
{% else %}
  <p><a href="/login">Login</a></p>
  <p><a href="/sign_up">Sign up</a></p>
{% endif %}
```

We should now be able to navigate to the **Login** page from the home page:

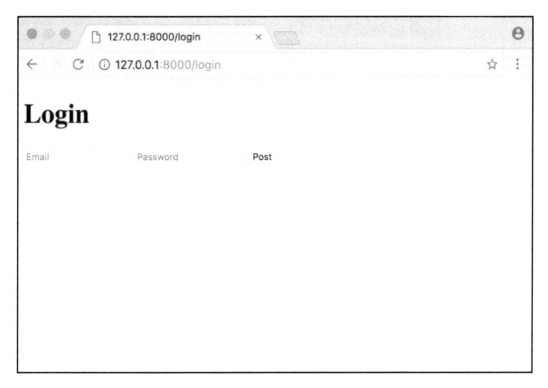

In order for our Login page to work, we will need to create a `post` method in our `LoginView`. Add the following to `LoginView`:

```
def post(self):
    email = request.form['email'] # ①
    password = request.form['password']

    with ClusterRpcProxy(config) as cluster_rpc:
        try:
            cluster_rpc.user_service.authenticate_user( # ②
                email=email,
                password=password,
            )
        except RemoteError as err: # ③
            app.logger.error(
                'Bad login for %s - %s', email, str(err)
            )
            return render_template(
                'login.html', login_error=True
```

```
            )

        session['authenticated'] = True # ④
        session['email'] = email # ⑤

        return redirect(url_for('home')) # ⑥
```

You'll notice that this is quite similar to our `SignUpView` post method. Let's briefly go over what is happening:

1. We retrieve the email and password from `request.form`.
2. We use `ClusterRpcProxy` to make an `authenticate_user` RPC to the `user_service`.
3. If a `RemoteError` occurs, then we:
   - Use Flask's `app.logger` to log the error to the console
   - Render the `login.html` template with `login_error` set to `True`
4. If they authenticate successfully, we set `authenticated` to `True` in the `session` object.
5. Set email to the user's `email` in the `session` object.
6. Redirect the user to the `home` endpoint.

With the preceding code, rather than return the error message to the user, we choose to log the error message to the console where only we can see it. This allows us to see if there are any issues with our authentication system or if a malicious user is up to no good, while still letting the user know that they supplied invalid information.

Provided our services are all still running, you should now be able to test this out! We now have a fully functioning authentication system for TempMessenger and our goals are complete.

Prepending the email to our messages

One thing that our TempMessenger is missing is accountability. We have no idea which users are posting what, which is fine for an anonymous messaging application (and if that is what you want, then skip this section altogether). To do this, when we store our messages, we will want to also store the email of the user who sent it.

Let's start by revisiting the `messages.py` dependency. Update `save_message` in our `RedisClient` to the following:

```
def save_message(self, email, message):
    message_id = uuid4().hex
    payload = {
        'email': email,
        'message': message,
    }
    self.redis.hmset(message_id, payload)
    self.redis.pexpire(message_id, MESSAGE_LIFETIME)

    return message_id
```

The first thing you'll notice is that, in order to call `save_message`, we now require the user's email.

What we have also done here is to change the format of the data we are storing in Redis from a string to a hash. Redis hashes allow us to store dictionary-like objects as the value. They also have the added benefit of being able to pick which key from the dictionary we want to get back out later, as opposed to getting the whole object out.

So here we create a dictionary of the user's email and password and use `hmset` to store it in Redis. `hmset` does not have a `px` or `ex` argument, so instead we make a call to `pexpire`, which expires the given key for the given number of milliseconds. There is also an `expire` equivalent of this for seconds.

> To learn more about Redis hashes and other data types, see:
> http://url.marcuspen.com/redis-data-types.

We will now update our `get_all_messages` method in the `RedisClient` to the following:

```
def get_all_messages(self):
    return [
        {
            'id': message_id,
            'email': self.redis.hget(message_id, 'email'),
            'message': self.redis.hget(message_id, 'message'),
            'expires_in': self.redis.pttl(message_id),
        }
        for message_id in self.redis.keys()
    ]
```

Since the data has changed to a hash, we also have to retrieve it from Redis differently, using the `hget` method. We also get the email corresponding to each message.

Now we will move on to `message_service.py`. Within the `MessageService`, update the `save_message` RPC to the following:

```
@rpc
def save_message(self, email, message):
    message_id = self.message_store.save_message(
        email, message
    )
    return message_id
```

All we have done here is update the arguments for the RPC to include `email` and pass that to the updated `message_store.save_message`.

Back in our `web_server.py`, we will need to update the `MessageAPI` post method to send the user's email when it makes the RPC to the `MessageService`:

```
def post(self):
    if not user_authenticated():
        return 'Please log in', 401

    email = session['email'] # ①
    data = request.get_json(force=True)

    try:
        message = data['message']
    except KeyError:
        return 'No message given', 400

    with ClusterRpcProxy(config) as rpc:
        rpc.message_service.save_message(email, message) # ②

    return '', 204
```

Two small changes we have just made:

1. Obtain the `email` from the `session` object.
2. Update the RPC to also pass the `email`.

In order to see these changes on our page, we will also need to update the `home.html` template. For our JavaScript function, `updateMessages`, update it to the following:

```
function updateMessages(messages) {
    var $messageContainer = $('#messageContainer');
    var messageList = [];
    var emptyMessages = '<p>No messages!</p>';

    if (messages.length === 0) {
      $messageContainer.html(emptyMessages);
    } else {
      $.each(messages, function(index, value) {
        var message = $(value.message).text() || value.message;
        messageList.push(
          '<p>' + value.email + ': ' + message + '</p>'
        );
      });
      $messageContainer.html(messageList);
    }
}
```

This is a minor tweak. If you can't spot it, we've updated the `messageList.push` to include the `email`.

Before you test this, ensure that your Redis store is empty, as old messages will be in the old format and will break our app. You can do this by using `redis-cli` inside of our Redis container:

```
$ docker exec -it redis /bin/bash
$ redis-cli -h redis
redis:6379> flushall
OK
redis:6379>
```

Also, be sure to restart our Message Service so that it takes the new changes into effect. Once you have done that, we can test this new functionality:

Summary

This now concludes our work on the TempMessenger User Authentication system. We started this chapter by using a Postgres database with Python and created a Nameko Dependency to encapsulate it. This was different from our Redis dependency from the last chapter since the data is permanent and required a lot more planning. Despite this, we tucked this logic away and simply exposed two RPC's: `create_user` and `authenticate_user`.

We then looked at how to securely store user passwords in a database. We explored some of the ways you can do this incorrectly, such as by storing passwords in plain text. We used Bcrypt to cryptographically hash our passwords to prevent them from being read if our database was compromised.

When it came to linking the new User Service to the rest of our application, we first split out each service into its own module to allow us to deploy, update, and manage them independently. We reaped some of the benefits of a microservice architecture by showing how easy it was to replace one framework (Nameko) with another (Flask) in the Web Server without affecting the rest of the platform.

We explored the Flask framework and how to create function-based and class-based views. We also looked at Flask session objects and how we could store user data from one request to the next.

As a bonus, we amended our message list to also include the email address of the user who sent it.

I'd encourage you to think of new enhancements to make for TempMessenger and plan accordingly how you would add them, ensuring that logic from our dependencies does not leak outside the service it belongs to—a mistake made by many! Keeping our service boundaries well defined is a hard task and sometimes it helps to start off with a more monolithic approach and separate them out later once they are clear. This is similar to the approach we took with `MessageService` and `WebServer` from the last chapter. *Building Microservices* (O'Reilly) by Sam Newman explains this very well and also covers in more detail the benefits, drawbacks, and challenges associated with building distributed systems.

With this chapter complete, I hope I have given you a deeper insight into how you can benefit from a Microservice architecture in practice. The journey we took creating this application was purposely modular, not only to reflect the modularity of microservices but to demonstrate how we should go about adding new features with minimal impact to the rest of the platform.

7
Online Video Game Store with Django

I was born in the late seventies, which means that I grew up during the birth of the video game industry. My first video game console was the Atari 2600, and it was because of that specific video game console that I decided that I wanted to be a programmer and make video games. I never got a job within the gaming industry, however, but I still love playing video games, and in, my spare time, I try to develop my own games.

To this day, I still go around the internet—especially eBay—buying old video games to bring back my nice childhood memories when all the family, my parents, and my sister, used to play Atari 2600 games together.

Because of my interest in vintage video games, we are going to develop a vintage video game online store; this will be a great way to develop something fun and also learn a lot about web development with the popular Django web framework.

In this chapter, we will cover the following:

- Setting up the environment
- Creating a Django project
- Creating Django apps
- Exploring the Django admin interface
- Learning how to create an application model and perform queries with the Django ORM

Also, as an extra, we will be using the **npm** (**Node Package Manager**) to download the client-side dependencies. We will also cover how to create simple tasks using the task runner Gulp.

To make our application prettier without a lot of effort, we are going to use Bootstrap.

So, let's get started!

Setting up the development environment

As usual, we are going to start setting up the environment for development. In Chapter 4, *Exchange Rates and the Currency Conversion Tool*, you were introduced to pipenv, so in this and the following chapters, we are going to be using pipenv to create our virtual environment and manage our dependencies.

First, we want to create the directory where we are going to keep our project. In your working directory, create a directory called django-project as follows:

```
mkdir django-project && cd django-project
```

Now we can run pipenv to create our virtual environment:

```
pipenv --three
```

If you have Python 3 installed in another location, you can use the argument --python and specify the path where the Python executable is located. If everything went fine, you should see an output such as the following:

Now we can activate our virtual environment using the `pipenv` command shell:

pipenv shell

Great! The only dependency that we are going to add for now is Django.

 At the time of writing this book, Django 2.0 had been released. It has really nice features compared to its predecessor. You can see the list of new features at `https://docs.djangoproject.com/en/2.0/releases/2.0/`.

Let's install Django in our virtual environment:

pipenv install django

Django 2.0 has dropped support for Python 2.0, so if you are planning to develop an application using Python 2, you should install Django 1.11.x or lower. I strongly recommend that you start a new project using Python 3. Python 2 will stop being maintained after a couple of years, and new packages will be created for Python 3. Popular packages of Python 2 will migrate to Python 3.

In my opinion, the best new feature of Django 2 is the new routing syntax, because now it is not necessary to write regular expressions. It is much cleaner and more readable to write something like the following:

path('user/<int:id>/', views.get_user_by_id)

The previous syntax relied more on regular expressions:

url('^user/?P<id>[0-9]/$', views.get_user_by_id)

It is much simpler this way. Another feature that I really like in Django 2.0 is that they have improved the admin UI a little bit and made it responsive; this is a great feature, because I have experienced that creating a new user (while you are on the go with no access to a desktop) on a non-responsive site on a small mobile phone screen can be painful.

Installing Node.js

When it comes to web development, it is almost impossible to stay away from Node.js. Node.js is a project that was released back in 2009. It is a JavaScript runtime that allows us to run JavaScript on the server-side. Why do we care about Node.js if we are developing a website using Django and Python? The reason is that the Node.js ecosystem has several tools that will help us to manage the client-side dependencies in a simple manner. One of these tools that we are going to use is the npm.

Think about npm as the `pip` of the JavaScript world. npm, however, has many more features. One of the features that we are going to use is npm scripts.

So, let's go ahead and install Node.js. Usually, developers need to go over to the Node.js website and download it from there, but I find it much simpler to use a tool called NVM, which allows us to install and switch easily between different versions of Node.js.

To install NVM in our environment, you can follow the instructions at `https://github.com/creationix/nvm`.

 We are covering installation of NVM on Unix/Linux and macOS systems. If you are using Windows, there's an awesome version for Windows that has been developed in the Go language; it can be found at `https://github.com/coreybutler/nvm-windows`.

When NVM is installed, you are ready to install the latest version of Node.js with the following command:

```
nvm install node
```

You can verify if the installation is correct with the command:

```
node --version
```

While writing this book, the latest Node.js version is v8.8.1.

You can also type npm on the terminal, where you should see an output similar to the output that follows:

```
                              daniel@musashi: ~                         _ □ ×

~
→ npm

Usage: npm <command>

where <command> is one of:
    access, adduser, bin, bugs, c, cache, completion, config,
    ddp, dedupe, deprecate, dist-tag, docs, doctor, edit,
    explore, get, help, help-search, i, init, install,
    install-test, it, link, list, ln, login, logout, ls,
    outdated, owner, pack, ping, prefix, prune, publish, rb,
    rebuild, repo, restart, root, run, run-script, s, se,
    search, set, shrinkwrap, star, stars, start, stop, t, team,
    test, tst, un, uninstall, unpublish, unstar, up, update, v,
    version, view, whoami

npm <command> -h     quick help on <command>
npm -l               display full usage info
npm help <term>      search for help on <term>
npm help npm         involved overview

Specify configs in the ini-formatted file:
    /home/daniel/.npmrc
or on the command line via: npm <command> --key value
Config info can be viewed via: npm help config

npm@5.4.2 /home/daniel/.nvm/versions/node/v8.8.1/lib/node_modules/npm

~
→
```

Creating a new Django project

To create a new Django project, run the following command:

```
django-admin startproject gamestore
```

Note that `django-admin` created a directory called `gamestore` that contains some boilerplate code for us. We will go through the files that Django created in a little while, but, first, we are going to create our first Django application. In the Django world, you have the project and the application, and according to the Django documentation, the project describes the web application itself, and the application is a Python package that provides some kind of feature; these applications contain their own set of routes, views, static files and can be reused across different Django projects.

Don't worry if you don't understand it completely; you will learn more as we progress.

With that said, let's create the project's initial application. Run `cd gamestore`, and once you are inside the `gamestore` directory, execute the following command:

```
python-admin startapp main
```

If you list the contents of the `gamestore` directory, you should see a new directory named `main`; that's the directory of the Django application that we are going to create.

Without writing any code at all, you already have a totally functional web application. To run the application and see the results, run the following command:

```
python manage.py runserver
```

You should see the following output:

```
Performing system checks...

System check identified no issues (0 silenced).

You have 14 unapplied migration(s). Your project may not work properly
until you apply the migrations for app(s): admin, auth, contenttypes,
sessions.
Run 'python manage.py migrate' to apply them.

December 20, 2017 - 09:27:48
Django version 2.0, using settings 'gamestore.settings'
Starting development server at http://127.0.0.1:8000/
Quit the server with CONTROL-C.
```

Open your favorite web browser, and go to `http://127.0.0.1:8000`, where you will see the following page:

One thing to note when we start the application for the first time is the following warning:

```
You have 14 unapplied migration(s). Your project may not work properly
until you apply the migrations for app(s): admin, auth, contenttypes,
sessions.
Run 'python manage.py migrate' to apply them.
```

This means that the apps that are registered by default on a Django project, admin, auth, contenttypes, and sessions have migrations (database changes) that haven't been applied to this project. We can run these migrations with the following command:

```
→ python manage.py migrate
Operations to perform:
  Apply all migrations: admin, auth, contenttypes, sessions
Running migrations:
```

```
Applying contenttypes.0001_initial... OK
Applying auth.0001_initial... OK
Applying admin.0001_initial... OK
Applying admin.0002_logentry_remove_auto_add... OK
Applying contenttypes.0002_remove_content_type_name... OK
Applying auth.0002_alter_permission_name_max_length... OK
Applying auth.0003_alter_user_email_max_length... OK
Applying auth.0004_alter_user_username_opts... OK
Applying auth.0005_alter_user_last_login_null... OK
Applying auth.0006_require_contenttypes_0002... OK
Applying auth.0007_alter_validators_add_error_messages... OK
Applying auth.0008_alter_user_username_max_length... OK
Applying auth.0009_alter_user_last_name_max_length... OK
Applying sessions.0001_initial... OK
```

Here Django created all the tables in a SQLite database, you will find the SQLite database file in the application's `root` directory.

The `db.sqlite3` file is the database file that contains the tables for our application. The choice of SQLite is just to make the application simpler for this chapter. Django supports a large set of databases; the most popular databases, such as, Postgres, Oracle, and even MSSQL are supported.

If you run the `runserver` command again, there should not be any migration warnings:

```
→ python manage.py runserver
Performing system checks...

System check identified no issues (0 silenced).
December 20, 2017 - 09:50:49
Django version 2.0, using settings 'gamestore.settings'
Starting development server at http://127.0.0.1:8000/
Quit the server with CONTROL-C.
```

Now there's only one thing that we need to do to wrap this section up; we need to create an administrator user so we can log in to the Django admin UI and administrate our web application.

As with everything else in Django, this is very simple. Just run the following command:

```
python manage.py createsuperuser
```

You will be asked to enter a username and email and to set the password, that is all you have to do to set an administrator account.

In the next section, we are going to have a closer look at the files that the Django created for us.

Exploring the Django project's structure

If you look at the Django website, it says *Django: The Web framework for perfectionists with deadlines,* and I could not agree more with this statement. So far, we haven't written any lines of code, and we already have a site up and running. In just a few commands, we can create a new project with the same directory structure and boilerplate code. Let's start with the development.

We can set up a new database and create a superuser, and, on the top of that, Django comes with a very nice and useful admin UI, where you can visualize our data, , and users.

In this section, we are going to explore the code that Django created for us when starting a new project so that we can get familiar with the structure. Let's go ahead and start adding the other components of our project.

If you have a look inside of the project's root directory, you will find a file called `db.sqlite3`, another file called `manage.py`, and, lastly, a directory with the same name as the project, in our case `gamestore`. The `db.sqlite3` file, as the name suggests, is the database file; this file is created here on the project's root folder because we are working with SQLite. You can explore this file directly from the command line; we are going to demonstrate how to do that shortly.

The second file is `manage.py`. This file is created automatically by the `django-admin` in every Django project. It basically does the same things as `django-admin`, plus two extra things; it will set the `DJANGO_SETTINGS_MODULE` to point to the project's setting file and also put the project's package on the `sys.path`. If you execute `manage.py` without any arguments, you can see the help with all the commands available.

As you can see with `manage.py`, you have many options, such as manage passwords, create a superuser, manage the database, create and execute database migrations, start new apps and projects, and a very important option in `runserver`, which, as the name says, will start the Django development server for you.

Now that we have learned about `manage.py` and how to execute its commands, we are going to take a step back and learn how to inspect the database that we just created. The command to do that is `dbshell`; let's give it a go:

```
python manage.py dbshell
```

Diving into the SQLite

You should get into the SQLite3 command prompt:

```
SQLite version 3.16.2 2017-01-06 16:32:41
Enter ".help" for usage hints.
sqlite>
```

If you want to get a list of all the database's tables, you can use the command `.tables`:

```
sqlite> .tables
auth_group auth_user_user_permissions
auth_group_permissions django_admin_log
auth_permission django_content_type
auth_user django_migrations
auth_user_groups django_session
```

Here you can see that we have all the tables that we created through the `migrate` command.

To look at every table structure, you can use the command `.schema`, and we can use the option `--indent`, so the output will be displayed in a more readable manner:

```
sqlite> .schema --indent auth_group
CREATE TABLE IF NOT EXISTS "auth_group"(
  "id" integer NOT NULL PRIMARY KEY AUTOINCREMENT,
  "name" varchar(80) NOT NULL UNIQUE
  );
```

These are the commands that I use the most when working with SQLite3 databases, but the command-line interface offers a variety of commands. You can use the `.help` command to get a list of all available commands.

SQLite3 databases are very useful when creating prototypes, creating proof of concept projects, or for creating really small projects. If our project does not fall in any of these categories, I would recommend using other SQL databases, such as MySQL, Postgres, and Oracle. There are also non-SQL databases, such as MongoDB. With Django, you can use any of these databases without any problem; if you are using the Django **ORM (Object relation model)**, most of the time you can switch between databases, and the application will continue to work perfectly.

Looking at the project's package directory

Next, let's have a look at the project's package directory. There, you will find a bunch of files. The first file you will see is `settings.py`, which is a very important file, as it is where you are going to put all the settings of our application. In this settings file, you can specify which apps and database you will use, and you can also tell Django where to search for static files and templates, middlewares, and more.

Then you have the `urls.py`; this file is where you specify the URLs that will be available on your application. You can setup URLs on the project level but also for every Django app. If you examine the contents of this `urls.py` file, you won't find much detail. Basically, you will see text explaining how to add new URLs, but Django has defined (out of the box) a URL to the Django admin site:

```
from django.contrib import admin
from django.urls import path

urlpatterns = [
    path('admin/', admin.site.urls),
]
```

We are going to go through the process of adding new URLs to the project, but we can explain this file anyway; remember when I mentioned that in Django you can have diverse apps? So `django.contrib.admin` is also an app, and an app has its own set of URLs, views, templates. So what it is doing here? When we import the admin app and then define a list called `urlpatterns`, in this list we use a function path where the first argument is the URL, and the second argument here can be a view that is going to be executed. But in this case, it is passing the URLs of the `admin.site` app, which means that `admin/` will be the base URL, and all the URLs defined in `admin.site.urls` will be created under it.

For example, if in `admin.site.url`, I have defined two URLs, `users/` and `groups/`, when I have `path('admin/', admin.site.urls)`, I will be actually creating two URLs:

- `admin/users/`
- `admin/groups/`

Lastly, we have the `wsgi.py`, which is a simple WSGI configuration that Django creates for us when creating a new project.

Now that we are a bit more familiar with the Django's project structure, it is time to create our project's first app.

Creating the project's main app

In this section, we are going to create our first Django app. One Django project can contain multiple apps. Splitting the project into apps is a good practice for many reasons; the most obvious is that you can reuse the same app across different projects. Another reason to split the project into multiple apps is that it enforces separation of concerns. Your project will be more organized, easier to reason, and our colleagues will thank you because it will be much easier to maintain.

Let's go ahead and run the command `startapp`, and, as shown before, you can either use the `django-admin` command or use `manager.py`. As we created the project using the `django-admin` command, it is a good opportunity to test the `manager.py` command. To create a new Django app, run the following command:

```
python manager.py startapp main
```

Here, we are going to create an app named `main`. Don't worry that no output is displayed, Django creates the project and the app silently. If you get a list of the directory contents now, you will see that there is a directory named `main`, and inside the `main` directory you will find some files; we are going to explain every file while we are adding changes to it.

So, the first thing we want to do is to add a landing page to our application. To do that, we have to do three things:

- First, we add a new URL to tell Django that when a user of our site browses to the root, it should go the site / and display some content
- The second step is to add a view that will be executed when the user browses to the site's root /

- The last step is to add an HTML template with the content that we want to display to the users

With that said, we need to include a new file called `urls.py` inside of the `main` app directory. First, we add some imports:

```
from django.urls import path
from . import views
```

In the preceding code, we imported the function path from `django.urls`. The path function will return an element to be included in the `urlpatterns` list, and we also import the views file in the same directory; we want to import this view because it is there that we are going to define functions that will be executed when a specific route is accessed:

```
urlpatterns = [
    path(r'', views.index, name='index'),
]
```

Then we use the path function to define a new route. The first argument of the function path is a string that contains the URL pattern that we wish to make available in our application. This pattern may contain angle brackets (for example, `<int:user_id>`) to capture parameters passed on the URL, but, at this point, we are not going use it; we just want to add a URL for the application's root, so we add an empty string `''`. The second argument is the function that is going to be executed, and, optionally, you can add the keyword argument `name`, which sets the URL's name. We will see why this is useful in a short while.

The second part is to define the function called `index` in the `views.py` file, as follows:

```
from django.shortcuts import render


def index(request):
    return render(request, 'main/index.html', {})
```

As there are not too many things going on at this point, we first import the render function from `django.shortcuts`. Django has its own template engine that is built into the framework, and it is possible to change the default template engine to other template engines you like (such as Jinja2, which is one of the most popular template engines in the Python ecosystem), but, for simplicity, we are going to use the default engine. The `render` function gets the request object, the template, and a context object; the latter is an object that contains data to be displayed in the template.

The next thing we need to do is to add a template that will contain the content that we want to display when the user browses to our application. Now, most of the web application's pages contain parts that never change, such as a top menu bar or a page's footer, and these parts can be put into a separate template that can be reused by other templates. Luckily, the Django template engine has this feature. In fact, we can not only inject sub-templates inside a template, but also we can have a base template that will contain the HTML that will be shared between all of the pages. With that said, we are going to create a file called `base.html` inside the `gamestore/templates` directory that has the following contents:

```
<!DOCTYPE html>
<html lang="en">
  <head>
    <meta charset="utf-8">
    <meta http-equiv="X-UA-Compatible" content="IE=edge">
    <meta name="viewport" content="width=device-width,
        initial-scale=1">
    <meta name="description" content="">
    <meta name="author" content="">
    <link rel="icon" href="../../favicon.ico">

    <title>Vintage video games store</title>

    {% load staticfiles %}
    <link href="{% static 'styles/site.css' %}" rel='stylesheet'>
    <link href="{% static 'styles/bootstrap.min.css' %}"
        rel='stylesheet'>
    <link href="{% static 'styles/font-awesome.min.css' %}"
          rel='stylesheet'>
  </head>

  <body>

    <nav class="navbar navbar-inverse navbar-fixed-top">
      <div class="container">
        <div class="navbar-header">
          <button type="button" class="navbar-toggle
            collapsed" data-toggle="collapse" data-
target="#navbar"
            aria-expanded="false" aria-controls="navbar">
            <span class="sr-only">Toggle navigation</span>
            <span class="icon-bar"></span>
            <span class="icon-bar"></span>
            <span class="icon-bar"></span>
          </button>
          <a class="navbar-brand" href="/">Vintage video
          games store</a>
```

```
        </div>
        <div id="navbar" class="collapse navbar-collapse">
          <ul class="nav navbar-nav">
            <li>
              <a href="/">
                <i class="fa fa-home" aria-hidden="true"></i> HOME
              </a>
            </li>
            {% if user.is_authenticated%}
            <li>
              <a href="/cart/">
                <i class="fa fa-shopping-cart"
                   aria-hidden="true"></i> CART
              </a>
            </li>
            {% endif %}
          </ul>
        </div><!--/.nav-collapse -->
      </div>
    </nav>

    <div class="container">

      <div class="starter-template">
        {% if messages %}
          {% for message in messages %}
            <div class="alert alert-info" role="alert">
              {{message}}
            </div>
          {% endfor %}
        {% endif %}

        {% block 'content' %}
        {% endblock %}
      </div>
    </div>
  </body>
</html>
```

We are not going to go through all the HTML parts, just the parts that are the specific syntax of Django's template engine:

```
{% load static %}
<link href="{% static 'styles/site.css' %}" rel='stylesheet'>
<link href="{% static 'styles/bootstrap.min.css' %}"
      rel='stylesheet'>
<link href="{% static 'styles/font-awesome.min.css' %}"
      rel='stylesheet'>
```

The first thing to note here is `{% load static %}`, which will tell Django's template engine that we want to load the static template tag. The static template tag is used to link static files. These files can be images, JavaScript, or Stylesheet files. How does Django find those files, you may ask, and the answer is simple: by magic! No, just kidding; the static template tag will look for the files in the directory specified in the `STATIC_ROOT` variable in the `settings.py` file; in our case we defined `STATIC_ROOT = '/static/'`, so when using the tag `{% static 'styles/site.css' %}` the link `/static/styles/site.css` will be returned.

You may be wondering, why not just write `/static/styles/site.css` instead of using the tag? The reason for this is that the tag gives us much more flexibility for change in case we need to update the path where we serve our static files. Imagine a situation where you have a large application with hundreds of templates, and in all of them, you hardcode `/static/` and then decide to change that path (and you don't have a team). You would need to change every single file to perform this change. If you use the static tag, you can simply move the files to a different location, and the tag changes the value of the `STATIC_ROOT` variable in the settings files.

Another tag that we are using in this template is the `block` tag:

```
{% block 'content' %}
{% endblock %}
```

The `block` tag is very simple; it defines an area in the base template that can be used by children templates to inject content in that area. We are going to see exactly how this works when we create the next template file.

The third part is to add the template. The `index` function is going to render a template stored at `main/index.html`, which means that it will leave it in the directory `main/templates/main/`. Let's go ahead and create the folder `main/templates` and then `main/templates/main`:

```
mkdir main/templates && mkdir main/templates/main
```

Create a file called `index.html` in the directory `main/templates/main/`, with the contents as follows:

```
{% extends 'base.html' %}

{% block 'content' %}
    <h1>Welcome to the gamestore!</h1>
{% endblock %}
```

As you can see, here, we start off by extending the base template, which means that all the content of the `base.html` file will be used by the Django template engine to build the HTML that will be provided back to the browser when the user browses to `/`. Now, we also use the `block` tag; in this context, it means that the engine will search for a block tag named `'content'` in the `base.html` file, and, if it finds it, the engine will insert the `h1 html` tab inside the `'content'` block.

This is all about reusability and maintainability of code, because you don't need to insert the menu markup and tags to load JavaScript and CSS files in every single template of our application; you just need to insert them in the base template and use the `block` tag here. The content will change. A second reason to use base templates is that, again, imagine a situation where you need to change something—let's say the top menu that we defined in the `base.html` file, as the menu is only defined in the `base.html` file. All you need to do to perform changes is to change the markup in the `base.html`, and all the other templates will inherit the changes.

We are almost ready to run our code and see how the application is looking so far, but, first, we need to install some client-side dependencies.

Installing client-side dependencies

Now that we have NodeJS installed, we can install the project's client-side dependencies. As the focus of this chapter is Django and Python, we don't want to spend too much time styling our application and going through huge CSS files. However, we do want our application to look great, and for this reason we are going to install two things: Bootstrap and Font Awesome.

Bootstrap is a very well-known toolkit that has been around for many years. It has a very nice set of components, a grid system, and plugins that will help us make our application look great for our users when they are browsing the application on a desktop, or even a mobile device.

Font Awesome is another project that has been around for a while, and it is a font and icons framework.

To install these dependencies, we could just run the npm's install command. However, we are going to do better. Similar to `pipenv`, which creates a file for our Python dependencies, `npm` has something similar. This file is called `package.json`, and it contains not only the project's dependencies but also scripts and meta information about the package.

So let's go ahead and add the `package.json` file to the `gamestore/` directory, with the following content:

```
{
    "name": "gamestore",
    "version": "1.0.0",
    "description": "Retro game store website",
    "dependencies": {
        "bootstrap": "^3.3.7",
        "font-awesome": "^4.7.0"
    }
}
```

Great! Save the file, and run this command on the terminal:

```
npm install
```

If everything goes well, you should see a message saying that two packages have been installed.

If you list the contents of the `gamestore` directory, you will see that `npm` created a new directory called `node_modules`, and it is there that `npm` installed Bootstrap and Font Awesome.

For simplicity, we are going to just copy the CSS files and fonts that we need to the `static` folder. However, when building an application, I would recommend using tools such as `webpack`, which will bundle all our client-side dependencies and set up a `webpack` dev server to serve the files for your Django application. Since we want to focus on Python and Django we can just go ahead and copy the files manually.

First, we can create the directory of the CSS files as follows:

```
mkdir static && mkdir static/styles
```

Then we need to copy the bootstrap files. First, the minified CSS file:

```
cp node_modules/bootstrap/dist/css/bootstrap.min.css static/styles/
```

Next, we need to copy the Font Awesome files, starting with the minified CSS:

```
cp node_modules/font-awesome/css/font-awesome.min.css static/styles/
```

And the fonts:

```
cp -r node_modules/font-awesome/fonts/ static/
```

We are going to add another CSS file that will contain some custom CSS that we may add to the application to give a personal touch to the application. Add a file called `site.css` in the `gamestore/static/styles` directory with the following contents:

```css
.nav.navbar-nav .fa-home,
.nav.navbar-nav .fa-shopping-cart {
    font-size: 1.5em;
}
.starter-template {
    padding: 70px 15px;
}

h2.panel-title {
    font-size: 25px;
}
```

There are a few things we need to do to run our application for the first time; first, we need to add the main app that we created to the `INSTALLED_APPS` list in the `settings.py` file in the `gamestore/gamestore` directory. It should look like this:

```python
INSTALLED_APPS = [
    'django.contrib.admin',
    'django.contrib.auth',
    'django.contrib.contenttypes',
    'django.contrib.sessions',
    'django.contrib.messages',
    'django.contrib.staticfiles',
    'main',
]
```

In the same settings file you will find the list `TEMPLATES`:

```python
TEMPLATES = [
    {
        'BACKEND':
    'django.templates.backends.django.DjangoTemplates',
        'DIRS': [],
        'APP_DIRS': True,
        'OPTIONS': {
            'context_processors': [
                'django.templates.context_processors.debug',
                'django.templates.context_processors.request',
                'django.contrib.auth.context_processors.auth',
```

```
                    'django.contrib.messages.context_processors.messages',
                        ],
                    },
                },
        ]
```

The value of `DIRS` is an empty list. We need to change it to:

```
'DIRS': [
    os.path.join(BASE_DIR, 'templates')
]
```

That will tell Django to search for templates in the `templates` directory.

Then, at the end of the `settings.py` file, add the following line:

```
STATICFILES_DIRS = [os.path.join(BASE_DIR, 'static'), ]
```

This will tell Django to search for static files in the `gamestore/static` directory.

Now we need to tell Django to register the URLs that we have defined in the `main` app. So, let's go ahead and open the file `urls.py` in the `gamestore/gamestore` directory. We need to include `"main.urls"` in the `urlpatterns` list. After the changes, the `urls.py` file should look like this:

```
from django.contrib import admin
from django.urls import path, include

urlpatterns = [
    path('admin/', admin.site.urls),
    path('', include('main.urls'))
]
```

Note that we also need to import the `include` function of the `django.urls` module.

Great! Now we have all the client-site dependencies in place and ready to be used by our application, and we can start the application for the first time to see the changes that we have implemented so far. Open the terminal, and use the command `runserver` to start Django's development server, like so:

```
python manage.py runserver
```

Browse to `http://localhost:8000`; you should see a page like the one shown in the following screenshot:

Adding login and logout views

Every online store needs some sort of user management. Our application's users should be able to create an account, change their account details, obviously log in to our application so they can place orders, and also log out from the application.

We are going to start adding the login and logout functionality. The good news is that it is super easy to implement in Django.

First, we need to add a Django form to our login page. Django has a built-in form of authentication; however, we want to customize it, so we are going to create another class that inherits from the Django built-in `AuthenticationForm` and add our changes.

Create a file called `forms.py` in `gamestore/main/` with the following content:

```python
from django import forms
from django.contrib.auth.forms import AuthenticationForm


class AuthenticationForm(AuthenticationForm):
    username = forms.CharField(
        max_length=50,
        widget=forms.TextInput({
            'class': 'form-control',
```

```
                    'placeholder': 'User name'
            })
        )

        password = forms.CharField(
            label="Password",
            widget=forms.PasswordInput({
                'class': 'form-control',
                'placeholder': 'Password'
            })
        )
```

This class is quite simple. First, we import `forms` from the `django` module and the `AuthenticationForm` from `django.contrib.auth.forms`, and then we create another class, also called `AuthenticationForm`, which inherits from Django's `AuthenticationForm`. Then we define two properties, the username and the password. We define the username as an instance of `CharField`, and there are some keyword arguments that we pass in its constructor. They are:

- `max_length`, which, as the name suggests limits the size of the string to 50 characters.
- We also use the `widget` argument, which specifies how this property will be rendered on the page. In this case, we want to render it as an input text element, so we pass an instance to `TextInput`. It is possible to pass some options to the `widget`; in our case, here we pass `'class'`, which is the CSS class and the placeholder.

All these options will be used when the template engine renders this property on the page.

The second property that we define here is the password. We also define it as a `CharField`, and, instead of passing `max_length`, this time we set the label to `'Password'`. The `widget` we set to `PasswordInput` so the template engine will render the field on the page as input with a type equal to the password, and, lastly, we define the same settings for this field class and placeholder.

Now we can start registering the new URLs for logging in and out. Open the file `gamestore/main/urls.py`. To start, we are going to add some `import` statements:

```
from django.contrib.auth.views import login
from django.contrib.auth.views import logout
from .forms import AuthenticationForm
```

After the `import` statements, we can start registering the authentication URLs. At the end of the `urlpattens` list, add the following code:

```
path(r'accounts/login/', login, {
    'template_name': 'login.html',
    'authentication_form': AuthenticationForm
}, name='login'),
```

So, here we are creating a new URL, `'accounts/login'`, and when requesting this URL the function view `login` will be executed. The third argument for the path function is a dictionary with some options, and the `template_name` specifies the template that will be rendered on the page when browsing to the underlying URL. We also define the `authetication_form` with the `AuthenticationForm` value that we just created. Lastly, we set the keyword argument `name` to `login`; naming the URL is very helpful when we need to create a link for this URL and also improves maintainability, because changes in the URL itself won't require changes in the templates as the templates reference the URL by its name.

Now that the login is in place, let's add the logout URL:

```
path(r'accounts/logout/', logout, {
    'next_page': '/'
}, name='logout'),
```

Similar to the login URL, in the logout URL we use the path function passing first the URL itself (`accounts/logout`); we pass the function logout that we imported from the Django built-in authentication views, and, as an option, we set `next_page` to `/`. This means that when the user logs out, we redirect the user to the application's root page. Lastly, we also name the URL as logout.

Great. Now it is time to add the templates. The first template that we are going to add is the login template. Create a file named `login.html` at `gamestore/templates/` with the following contents:

```
{% extends 'base.html' %}

{% block 'content' %}

<div>
  <form action="." method="post" class="form-signin">

    {% csrf_token %}

    <h2 class="form-signin-heading">Login</h2>
    <label for="inputUsername" class="sr-only">User name</label>
```

```
            {{form.username}}
            <label for="inputPassword" class="sr-only">Password</label>
            {{form.password}}
            <input class="btn btn-lg btn-primary btn-block"
                type="Submit" value="Login">
        </form>
        <div class='signin-errors-container'>
            {% if form.non_field_errors %}
            <ul class='form-errors'>
                {% for error in form.non_field_errors %}
                    <li>{{ error }}</li>
                {% endfor %}
            </ul>
            {% endif %}
        </div>
    </div>

    {% endblock %}
```

In this template, we also extend the base template, and we add the content of the login template with the content block that has been defined in the base template.

First, we create a `form` tag and set the method to POST. Then, we add the `csrf_token` tag. The reason we add this tag is to prevent cross-site request attacks, where a malicious site performs a request to our site on behalf of the current logged in user.

 If you want to know more about this type of attack, you can visit the site at `https://www.owasp.org/index.php/Cross-Site_Request_Forgery_ (CSRF)`.

After the Cross-Site Request Forgery tag, we add the two fields we need: username and password.

Then we have the following markup:

```
<div class='signin-errors-container'>
    {% if form.non_field_errors %}
    <ul class='form-errors'>
        {% for error in form.non_field_errors %}
        <li>{{ error }}</li>
        {% endfor %}
    </ul>
    {% endif %}
</div>
```

This is where we are going to display possible authentication errors. The forms object has a property called `non_field_error`, which contains errors that are not related to field validation. For example, if your user types the wrong username or password, then the error will be added the to `non_field_error` list.

We create a `ul` element (unordered list) and loop through the `non_field_errors` list adding `li` elements (list items) with the error text.

We have now the login in place, and we need to just include it to the page—more specifically, to the `base.html` template. But, first, we need to create a little partial template that will display the login and logout links on the page. Go ahead and add a file called `_loginpartial.html` to the `gamestore/templates` directory that has the following contents:

```
{% if user.is_authenticated %}
<form id="logoutForm" action="{% url 'logout' %}" method="post"
      class="navbar-right">
    {% csrf_token %}
  <ul class="nav navbar-nav navbar-right">
    <li><span class="navbar-brand">Logged as:
          {{ user.username }}</span></li>
    <li><a href="javascript:document.getElementById('
        logoutForm').submit()">Log off</a></li>
  </ul>

</form>

{% else %}

<ul class="nav navbar-nav navbar-right">
    <li><a href="{% url 'login' %}">Log in</a></li>
</ul>

{% endif %}
```

This partial template will render two different contents depending on whether the user is authenticated or not. If the user is authenticated, it will render the logout form. Note that the action of the form makes use of the named URL; we don't set it to `/accounts/logout` but to `{% url 'logout' %}`. Django's URL tag will replace the URL name with the URL. Again, we need to add the `csrf_token` tag to prevent Cross-Site Request Forgery attacks, and, finally, we define an unordered list with two items; the first item will display the text `Logged as:` and the user's username, and the second item on the list will show the logout button.

Note that we added an anchor tag inside of the list item element, and that the `href` property has some JavaScript code in it. That code is pretty simple; it uses the function `getElementById` to get the form and then call the form's submit function to submit to the server the request to `/accounts/logout`.

This is just a preference for implementation; you could easily have skipped this JavaScript code and added a submit button instead. It would have the same effect.

In case the user is not authenticated, we only show the `login` link. The `login` link also uses the URL tag that will replace the name `login` with the URL.

Great! Let's add the login partial template to the base template. Open the file `base.html` at `gamestore/templates`, and locate the unordered list, shown as follows:

```
<ul class="nav navbar-nav">
  <li>
    <a href="/">
      <i class="fa fa-home" aria-hidden="true"></i> HOME
    </a>
  </li>
</ul>
```

We are going to add the `_loginpartial.html` template using the `include` tag:

```
{% include '_loginpartial.html' %}
```

The include tag will inject the content of the `_loginpartial.html` template in this position in the markup.

The final touch here is to add some styling, so the login page looks nice like the rest of the application. Open the file `site.css` in the `gamestore/static/styles` directory, and include the following contents:

```
/* Signin page */
/* Styling extracted from http://getbootstrap.com/examples/signin/
*/

.form-signin {
    max-width: 330px;
    padding: 15px;
    margin: 0 auto;
}
.form-signin input[type="email"] {
    margin-bottom: -1px;
}
```

```
.form-signin input[type="email"] border-top {
    left-radius: 0;
  right-radius: 0;
}
.form-signin input[type="password"] {
    margin-bottom: 10px;
}

.form-signin input[type="password"] border-top {
    left-radius: 0;
    right-radius: 0;
}

.form-signin .form-signin-heading {
  margin-bottom: 10px;
}

.form-signin .checkbox {
  font-weight: normal;
}

.form-signin .form-control {
  position: relative;
  height: auto;
  -webkit-box-sizing: border-box;
  -moz-box-sizing: border-box;
  box-sizing: border-box;
  padding: 10px;
  font-size: 16px;
}

.form-signin .form-control:focus {
  z-index: 2;
}

.signin-errors-container .form-errors {
  padding: 0;
  display: flex;
  flex-direction: column;
  list-style: none;
  align-items: center;
  color: red;
}

.signin-errors-container .form-errors li {
  max-width: 350px;
  }
```

Testing the login/logout forms

Before we try this out, let's open the file `settings.py` in the `gamestore/gamestore` directory, and at the end of the file add the following setting:

```
LOGIN_REDIRECT_URL = '/'
```

This will tell Django that, after the login, the user will be redirected to "/".

Now we are ready to test the login and logout functionality, although you probably don't have any users in the database. However, we created the superuser while we were setting up our Django project, so go ahead and try logging in with that user. Run the command `runserver` to start the Django development server again:

```
python manage.py runserver
```

Browse to `http://localhost:8000` and note that you now have the login link in the top right corner of the page:

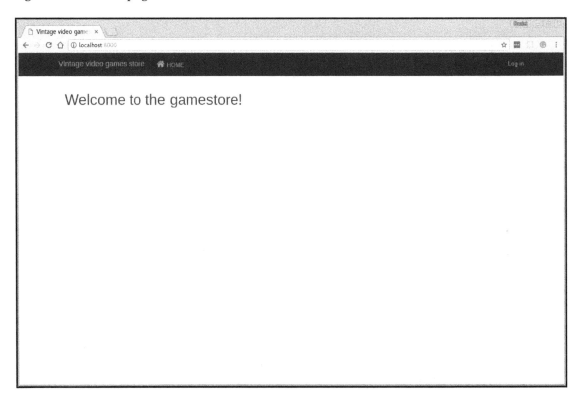

If you click that, you will be redirected to `/accounts/login`, and the login page template that we created will be rendered:

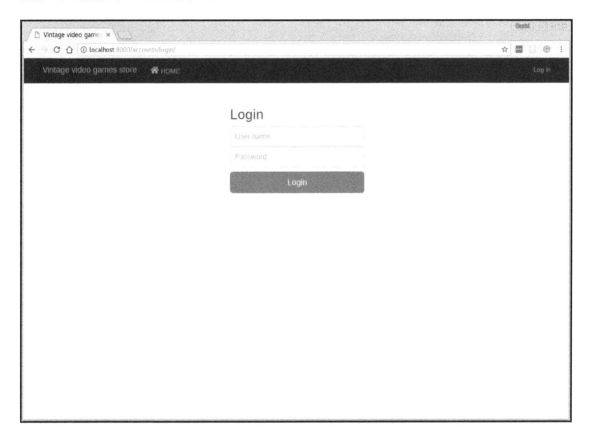

First, try typing the wrong password or username so we can verify that the error message is being displayed correctly:

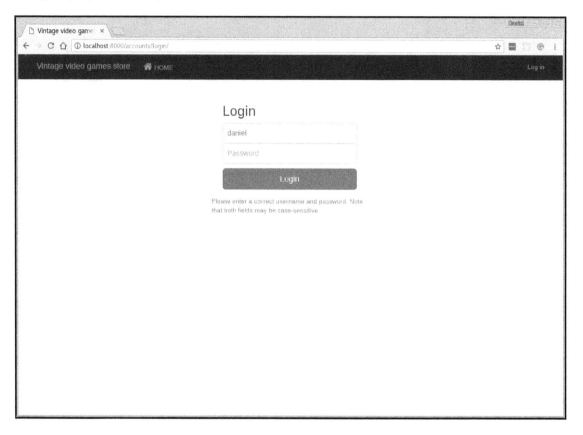

Great! It works!

Now log in with the superuser, and if everything works fine, you should be redirected to the application root's URL. It says, **Logged as** with your username, and right after it there is a logout link. Give it a go, and click on the link **Log off**:

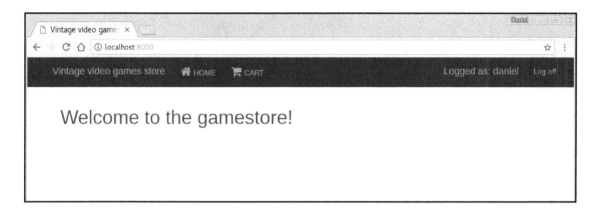

Creating new users

Now that we are able to log in and log out of our application, we need to add another page so the users can create accounts on our application and place orders.

There are some rules that we want to enforce when creating a new account. The rules are:

- The username field is required, and it has to be unique to our application
- The email field is required, and it has to be unique to our application
- The last and first name are required
- Both password fields are required, and they must match

If any of these rules are not followed, we will not create the user account, and an error should be returned to the user.

With that said, let's add a small helper function that will verify whether a field has a value that already exists in the database. Open the file `forms.py` in `gamestore/main`. First, we need to import the User model:

```
from django.contrib.auth.models import User
```

Then, add the `validate_unique_user` function:

```
def validate_unique_user(error_message, **criteria):
    existent_user = User.objects.filter(**criteria)

    if existent_user:
        raise forms.ValidationError(error_message)
```

This function gets an error message and keyword arguments that will be used as a criterion to search for items matching a specific value. We create a variable called `existent_user`, and filter the user models passing the criteria. If the value of the variable `existent_user` is different to `None`, it means that we have found a user who matches our criterion. We then raise a `ValidationError` exception with the error message that we passed to the function.

Nice. Now we can start adding a form that will contain all the fields that we want the user to fill out when creating an account. In the same file, `forms.py` in the `gamestore/main` directory, add the following class:

```python
class SignupForm(forms.Form):
    username = forms.CharField(
        max_length=10,
        widget=forms.TextInput({
            'class': 'form-control',
            'placeholder': 'First name'
        })
    )

    first_name = forms.CharField(
        max_length=100,
        widget=forms.TextInput({
            'class': 'form-control',
            'placeholder': 'First name'
        })
    )

    last_name = forms.CharField(
        max_length=200,
        widget=forms.TextInput({
            'class': 'form-control',
            'placeholder': 'Last name'
        })
    )

    email = forms.CharField(
        max_length=200,
        widget=forms.TextInput({
            'class': 'form-control',
            'placeholder': 'Email'
        })
    )

    password = forms.CharField(
        min_length=6,
        max_length=10,
```

```
        widget=forms.PasswordInput({
            'class': 'form-control',
            'placeholder': 'Password'
        })
    )

    repeat_password = forms.CharField(
        min_length=6,
        max_length=10,
        widget=forms.PasswordInput({
            'class': 'form-control',
            'placeholder': 'Repeat password'
        })
    )
```

So, we start by creating a class called `SignupForm` that will inherit from `Form`, we define a property for every field that is going to be necessary for creating a new account, and we add a username, a first and a last name, an email, and then two password fields. Note that in the password fields we set the min and max length for a password to `6` and `10`, respectively.

Continuing in the same class, `SignupForm`, let's add a method called `clean_username`:

```
def clean_username(self):
    username = self.cleaned_data['username']

    validate_unique_user(
        error_message='* Username already in use',
        username=username)

    return username
```

The prefix `clean` in the name of this method will make Django automatically call this method when parsing the posted data for the field; in this case, it will execute when parsing the field username.

So, we get the username value, and then call the method `validate_unique_user`, passing a default error message and a keyword argument username that will be used as a filter criterion.

Another field that we need to verify for uniqueness is the email ID, so let's implement the `clean_email` method, as follows:

```
def clean_email(self):
    email = self.cleaned_data['email']

    validate_unique_user(
```

```
          error_message='* Email already in use',
          email=email)

    return email
```

It is basically the same as the clean username. First, we get the email from the request and pass it to the `validate_unique_user` function. The first argument is the error message, and the second argument is the email that will be used as the filter criteria.

Another rule that we defined for our create account page is that the password and (repeat) password fields must match, otherwise an error will be displayed to the user. So let's add the same and implement the clean method, but this time we want to validate the `repeat_password` field and not `password`. The reason for that is that if we implement a `clean_password` function, at that point `repeat_password` won't be available in the `cleaned_data` dictionary yet, because the data is parsed in the same order as they were defined in the class. So, to ensure that we will have both values we implement `clean_repeat_password`:

```
    def clean_repeat_password(self):
        password1 = self.cleaned_data['password']
        password2 = self.cleaned_data['repeat_password']

        if password1 != password2:
            raise forms.ValidationError('* Passwords did not match')

        return password1
```

Great. So here we first define two variables; `password1`, which is the request value for the `password` field, and `password2`, the request value for the field `repeat_password`. After that, we just compare if the values are different; if they are, we raise a `ValidationError` exception with the error message to inform the user that the password didn't match and the account will not be created.

Creating the views of the user creation

With the form and validation in place, we can now add the view that will handle the request to create a new account. Open the file `views.py` at `gamestore/main`, and start by adding some `import` statements:

```
    from django.views.decorators.csrf import csrf_protect
    from .forms import SignupForm
    from django.contrib.auth.models import User
```

As we will be receiving data from a POST request, it is a good idea to add Cross-Site Request Forgery checkings, so we need to import the csrf_protect decorator.

We also import the SignupForm that we just created so we can pass it to the view or use it to parse the request data. Lastly, we import the User model.

So, let's create the signup function:

```
@csrf_protect
def signup(request):

    if request.method == 'POST':

        form = SignupForm(request.POST)

        if form.is_valid():
            user = User.objects.create_user(
                username=form.cleaned_data['username'],
                first_name=form.cleaned_data['first_name'],
                last_name=form.cleaned_data['last_name'],
                email=form.cleaned_data['email'],
                password=form.cleaned_data['password']
            )
            user.save()

            return render(request,
            'main/create_account_success.html', {})

    else:
        form = SignupForm()
    return render(request, 'main/signup.html', {'form': form})
```

We start by decorating the signup function with the csrf_protect decorator. The function starts by checking whether the request's HTTP method is equal to POST; in that case, it will create an instance of the SignupForm passing as an argument the POST data. Then we call the function is_valid() on the form, which will return true if the form is valid; otherwise it will return false. If the form is valid, we create a new user and call the save function, and, finally, we render the create_account_success.html.

If the request HTTP method is a GET, the only thing we do is create an instance of a SignupForm without any argument. After that, we call the render function, passing as a first argument the request object, then the template that we are going to render, and, finally, the last argument is the instance of the SignupForm.

We are going to create both templates referenced in this function in a short while, but, first, we need to create a new URL in the url.py file at gamestore/main:

```
path(r'accounts/signup/', views.signup, name='signup'),
```

This new URL can be added right at the end of the urlpatterns list.

We also need to create the templates. We start with the signup template; create a file called signup.html at gamestore/main/templates/main with the following contents:

```
{% extends "base.html" %}

{% block "content" %}

    <div class="account-details-container">
        <h1>Signup</h1>
        <form action="{% url 'signup' %}" method="POST">
            {% csrf_token %}
            {{ form }}
            <button class="btn btn-primary">Save</button>
        </form>
    </div>

{% endblock %}
```

This template is again very similar to the template that we created before, in that it extends the base template and injects some data into the base template's content block. We add an h1 tag with the header text and a form with the action set to {% url 'signup' %}, which the url tag will change to /accounts/signup, and we set the method to POST.

As is usual in forms, we use the csrf_token tag that will work together with the @csrf_protect decorator in the signup function in the views file to protect against Cross-Site Request Forgery.

Then we just call `{{ form }}`, which will render the entire form in this area, and, right after the fields, we add a button to submit the form.

Lastly, we create a template for showing that the account has been successfully created. Add a file called `create_account_success.html` to the `gamestore/main/templates/main` directory with the following contents:

```
{% extends 'base.html' %}

{% block 'content' %}

    <div class='create-account-msg-container'>
        <div class='circle'>
          <i class="fa fa-thumbs-o-up" aria-hidden="true"></i>
        </div>
        <h3>Your account have been successfully created!</h3>
        <a href="{% url 'login' %}">Click here to login</a>
    </div>

{% endblock %}
```

Great! To make it look great, we are going to include some CSS code in the file `site.css` in the `gamestore/static` directory. Add the content shown as follows, at the end of the file:

```
/* Account created page */
.create-account-msg-container {
    display: flex;
    flex-direction: column;
    align-items: center;
    margin-top: 100px;
}

.create-account-msg-container .circle {
    width: 200px;
    height: 200px;
    border: solid 3px;
    display: flex;
    flex-direction: column;
    align-items: center;
    padding-top: 30px;
    border-radius: 50%;
}

.create-account-msg-container .fa-thumbs-o-up {
    font-size: 9em;
}
```

```css
.create-account-msg-container a {
    font-size: 1.5em;
}

/* Sign up page */

.account-details-container #id_password,
.account-details-container #id_repeat_password {
    width:200px;
}

.account-details-container {
    max-width: 400px;
    padding: 15px;
    margin: 0 auto;
}

.account-details-container .btn.btn-primary {
    margin-top:20px;
}

.account-details-container label {
    margin-top: 20px;
}

.account-details-container .errorlist {
    padding-left: 10px;
    display: inline-block;
    list-style: none;
    color: red;
}
```

That's all for the create a user page; let's give it a go! Start the Django developer server again, and browse to http://localhost:8000/accounts/signup, where you should see the create user form, as follows:

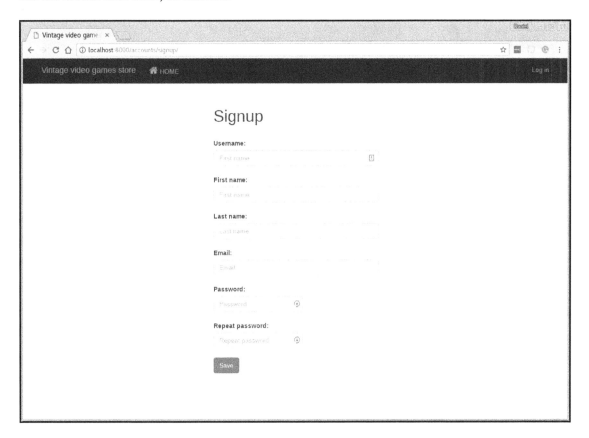

After you fill up all the fields, you should be redirected to a confirmation page, like this:

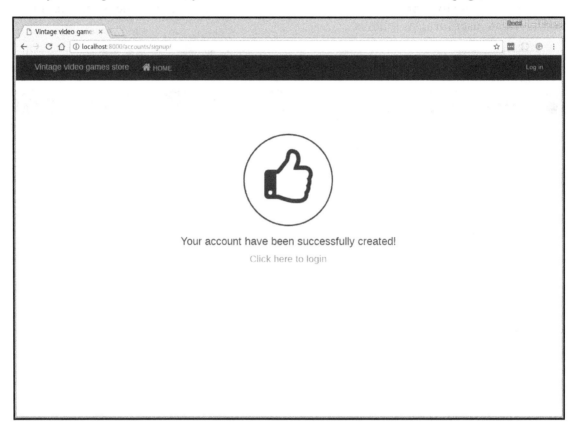

Perform some tests yourself! Try adding invalid passwords, just to verify that the validations we implemented are working properly.

Creating the game data model

Alright, we can log into our application, we can create new users, and we also added the front page template, which is currently blank, but we are going to fix that. We have got to the core of this chapter; we are going to start adding models that will represent the items that we can buy at the store.

The requirements for the game's model that we are going to have on the site is:

- The store is going to sell games for different gaming platforms
- There will be a section on the first page that will list highlighted games
- The users of the store should be able to go to the game's details page and see more information about the game
- The games should be discoverable by different criteria, for example, developer, publisher, release date, and so on
- The administrator of the store should be able to change product details using the Django admin UI.
- The product's picture can be changed, and if not found, it should show a default image

With that said, let's start adding our first model class. Open the file `models.py` in `gamestore/main/`, and add the following code:

```
class GamePlatform(models.Model):
    name = models.CharField(max_length=100)

    def __str__(self):
        return self.name
```

Here, we have added the class `GamePlatform`, and it will represent the gaming platforms that will be available at the store. The class is super simple; we just create a class inheriting from the `Model` class, and we define just one property called `name`. The name property is defined as a `CharField` of a maximum length of 100 characters. Django provides a large variety of data types; you can see the complete list at `https://docs.djangoproject.com/en/2.0/ref/models/fields/`.

Then we override the method `__str__`. This method will dictate how an instance of `GamePlatform` will be displayed when being printed out. The reason that I am overriding this method is that I want to display the name of `GamePlatform` in the list of `GamePlatform` in the Django admin UI.

The second model class that we are going to add here is the `Game` model. In the same file, add the following code:

```
class Game(models.Model):
    class Meta:
        ordering = ['-promoted', 'name']

    name = models.CharField(max_length=100)
```

```
        release_year = models.IntegerField(null=True)

        developer = models.CharField(max_length=100)

        published_by = models.CharField(max_length=100)

        image = models.ImageField(
            upload_to='images/',
            default='images/placeholder.png',
            max_length=100
        )

        gameplatform = models.ForeignKey(GamePlatform,
                                         null=False,
                                         on_delete=models.CASCADE)

        highlighted = models.BooleanField(default=False)
```

Like the previous model class that we created, the `Game` class also inherits from `Model` and we define all the fields that we need according to the specifications. There are some things to note here that are new; the property `release_year` is defined as an integer field, and we set the property `null=True`, which means that this field will not be required.

Another property that used a different type is the image property, which is defined as an `ImageField`, and that will allow us to provide the application's administrators the possibility of changing the game's image. This type inherits from `FileField`, and in the Django Administration UI the field will be rendered as a file picker. The `ImageFile` argument `upload_to` specifies where the image will be stored, and the default is the default image that will be rendered if the game does not have an image. The last argument that we specify here is `max_length`, which is the image path's maximum length.

Then, we define a `ForeignKey`. If you don't know what it is, a foreign key is basically a file that identifies a row in another table. In our case, here we want the game platform to be associated with multiple games. There are a few keyword arguments that we are passing to the definition of the primary key; first we pass the foreign key type, the `null` argument is set to `False`, meaning that the field is required, and, lastly we set the deletion rule to `CASCADE`, so if the application's admin deletes a gaming platform, that operation will cascade and delete all the games associated with that specific gaming platform.

The last property that we define is the `highlighted` property. Do you remember that one of the requirements was to be able to highlight some products and also have them in a more visible area so the users can find them easily? This property does just that. It is a property type Boolean that has the default value set to `False`.

Another detail, that I was saving for last is this: have you noticed that we have a class named `Meta` inside the model class? This is the way that we can add meta information about the model. In this example we are setting a property called `ordering` with the value as an array of strings, where each item represents a property of the `Game` model, so we have first `-highlighted` - the dash sign in front of the property name means descending order—and then we also have the name, which will appear in ascending order.

Let's continue adding more code to the class:

```
objects = GameManager()

def __str__(self):
    return f'{self.gameplatform.name} - {self.name}'
```

Here, we have two things. First, we assign an instance of a class called `GameManager`, which I will go into in more detail in a short while, and we also define the special method `__str__`, which defines that when printing an instance of the `Game` object, it will display the gaming platform and a symbol dash, followed by the name of the name itself.

Before the definition of the `Game`class, let's add another class called `GameManager`:

```
class GameManager(models.Manager):

    def get_highlighted(self):
        return self.filter(highlighted=True)

    def get_not_highlighted(self):
        return self.filter(highlighted=False)

    def get_by_platform(self, platform):
        return self.filter(gameplatform__name__iexact=platform)
```

Before we get into the details of this implementation, I just want to say a few words about `Manager` objects in Django. The `Manager` is the interface between the database and the model classes in Django. By default, every model class has a `Manager`, and it is accessed through the property objects, so why define our own manager? The reason that I implemented a `Manager` for this `models` class is that I wanted to leave all the code concerning database operations within the model, as it makes the code cleaner and more testable.

So, here I defined another class, `GameManager`, that inherits from `Manager`, and so far we defined three methods—`get_highlighted`, which get all games that have the highlighted flag set to `True`, `get_not_highlighted`, which gets all games that highlighted flag is set to `False`, and `get_by_platform`, which gets all the games given a gaming platform.

About the two first methods in this class: I could have just used the filter function and passed an argument where `highlighted` equals `True` or `False`, but, as I mentioned previously, it is much cleaner to have all these methods inside the manager.

Now we are ready to create the database. In the terminal, run the following command:

```
python manage.py makemigrations
```

This command will create a migration file with the changes that we just implemented in the model. When the migrations are created, we can run the command `migrate` and then apply the changes to the database:

```
python manage.py migrate
```

Great! Next up, we are going to create a model to store the game's prices.

Creating the price list data model

Another feature that we want to have in our application is the ability to change the prices of the products as well as knowing when a price was added and, most importantly, when it was last updated. To achieve this, we are going to create another model class, called `PriceList`, in the `models.py` file in the `gamestore/main/` directory, using the following code:

```python
class PriceList(models.Model):
    added_at = models.DateTimeField(auto_now_add=True)

    last_updated = models.DateTimeField(auto_now=True)

    price_per_unit = models.DecimalField(max_digits=9,
                                         decimal_places=2,
                                         default=0)

    game = models.OneToOneField(
        Game,
        on_delete=models.CASCADE,
        primary_key=True)

    def __str__(self):
        return self.game.name
```

As you can see here, you have two datetime fields. The first one is `added_at`, and it has a property `auto_now_add` equals `True`. What it does is get Django to automatically add the current date when we add this price to the table. The `last_update` field is defined with another argument, the `auto_now` equals `True`; this tells Django to set the current date every time an update occurs.

Then, we have a field for the price called `price_per_unit`, which is defined as a `DecimalField` with a maximum of 9 digits and 2 decimal places. This field is not required, and it will always `default` to 0.

Next, we create a `OneToOneField` to create a link between the `PriceList` and the `Game` object. We define that when a game is deleted, the related row in the `PriceList` table will also be removed, and we define this field as the primary key.

Finally, we override the `__str__` method so that it returns the game's name. This will be helpful when updating prices using the Django admin UI.

Now we can make the migration files again:

```
python manage.py makemigrations
```

Apply the changes with the following command:

```
python manage.py migrate
```

Perfect! Now we are ready to start adding the views and the templates to display our games on the page.

Creating the game list and details page

After creating the model for the games and the prices, we have reached the fun part of this section, which is to create the views and templates that will display the games on the page. Let's get started!

So, we have created a template called `index.html` in `main/templates/main`, but we are not displaying anything on it. To make that page more interesting, we are going to add two things:

1. A section on the top of the page that will display the games that we want to highlight. It could be a new game that arrived at the store, a very popular game, or some game that has a good price for the moment.
2. Following the section with the highlighted games, we are going to list all the other games.

The first template that we are going to add is a partial view that will be used to list games. This partial view will be shared to all the templates that we want to display a list of games. This partial view will receive two arguments: `gameslist` and `highlight_games`. Let's go ahead and add a file called `games-list.html` at `gamestore/main/templates/main/` with the following contents:

```
{% load staticfiles %}
{% load humanize %}


<div class='game-container'>
    {% for game in gameslist %}
    {% if game.highlighted and highlight_games %}
      <div class='item-box highlighted'>
    {% else %}
      <div class='item-box'>
    {% endif %}
      <div class='item-image'>
      <img src="{% static game.image.url %}"></img>
</div>
    <div class='item-info'>
      <h3>{{game.name}}</h3>
      <p>Release year: {{game.release_year}}</p>
      <p>Developer: {{game.developer}}</p>
      <p>Publisher: {{game.published_by}}</p>
      {% if game.pricelist.price_per_unit %}
        <p class='price'>
          Price:
          ${{game.pricelist.price_per_unit|floatformat:2|intcomma}}
        </p>
      {% else %}
      <p class='price'>Price: Not available</p>
      {% endif %}
    </div>
    <a href="/cart/add/{{game.id}}" class="add-to-cart btn
```

```
        btn-primary">
        <i class="fa fa-shopping-cart" aria-hidden="true"></i>
        Add to cart
      </a>
    </div>
    {% endfor %}
</div>
```

One thing to note here is that we added at the top of the page `{% load humanize %}`; this is a set of template filters that are built into the Django framework, which we are going to use to format the game price properly. To make use of these filters we need to edit the `settings.py` file in the `gamestore/gamestore` directory and add `django.contrib.humanize` to the `INSTALLED_APPS` setting.

This code will create a container with some boxes containing the game image, details, and an add-to-cart button, similar to the following:

Now we want to modify the `index.html` at `gamestore/main/templates/main`. We can replace the whole content of the `index.html` file with the code, shown as follows:

```
{% extends 'base.html' %}

{% block 'content' %}
  {% if highlighted_games_list %}
    <div class='panel panel-success'>
      <div class='panel-heading'>
        <h2 class='panel-title'><i class="fa fa-gamepad"
        aria-hidden="true"></i>Highlighted games</h2>
      </div>
      <div class='panel-body'>
        {% include 'main/games-list.html' with
          gameslist=highlighted_games_list highlight_games=False%}
```

```
            {% if show_more_link_highlighted %}
            <p>
              <a href='/games-list/highlighted/'>See more items</a>
            </p>
            {% endif %}
          </div>
        </div>
      {% endif %}

      {% if games_list %}
        {% include 'main/games-list.html' with gameslist=games_list
         highlight_games=False%}
        {% if show_more_link_games %}
          <p>
            <a href='/games-list/all/'>See all items</a>
          </p>
        {% endif %}
      {% endif %}

    {% endblock %}
```

Great! The interesting code is:

```
{% include 'main/games-list.html' with
  gameslist=highlighted_games_list
    highlight_games=False%}
```

As you can see, we are including the partial view and passing two parameters: `gameslist` and `highlight_games`. The `gameslist` is obviously a list of games that we want the partial view to render, while `highlight_games` will be used when we want to show the promoted games with a different color so they can be easily identified. In the index page, the `highlight_games` parameter is not used, but when we create a view to list all the games regardless of the fact that it is promoted or not, it may be interesting to change the color of the promoted ones.

Below the promoted games section, we have a section with a list of games that are not promoted, which also makes use of the partial view `games-list.html`.

The last touch on the frontend side is to include the related CSS code, so let's edit the file site.css at gamestore/static/styles/ and add the following code:

```css
.game-container {
    margin-top: 10px;
    display:flex;
    flex-direction: row;
    flex-wrap: wrap;
}

.game-container .item-box {
    flex-grow: 0;
    align-self: auto;
    width:339px;
    margin: 0px 10px 20px 10px;
    border: 1px solid #aba5a5;
    padding: 10px;
    background-color: #F0F0F0;
}

.game-container .item-box .add-to-cart {
    margin-top: 15px;
    float: right;
}

.game-container .item-box.highlighted {
    background-color:#d7e7f5;
}

.game-container .item-box .item-image {
    float: left;
}

.game-container .item-box .item-info {
    float: left;
    margin-left: 15px;
    width:100%;
    max-width:170px;
}

.game-container .item-box .item-info p {
    margin: 0 0 3px;
}

.game-container .item-box .item-info p.price {
    font-weight: bold;
    margin-top: 20px;
```

```
        text-transform: uppercase;
        font-size: 0.9em;
    }

    .game-container .item-box .item-info h3 {
        max-width: 150px;
        word-wrap: break-word;
        margin: 0px 0px 10px 0px;
    }
```

Now we need to modify the index view, so edit the `views.py` file at `gamestore/main/` and perform these changes in the `index` function:

```
def index(request):
    max_highlighted_games = 3
    max_game_list = 9

    highlighted_games_list = Game.objects.get_highlighted()
    games_list = Game.objects.get_not_highlighted()

    show_more_link_promoted = highlighted_games_list.count() >
    max_highlighted_games
    show_more_link_games = games_list.count() > max_game_list

    context = {
        'highlighted_games_list':
         highlighted_games_list[:max_highlighted_games],
        'games_list': games_list[:max_game_list],
        'show_more_link_games': show_more_link_games,
        'show_more_link_promoted': show_more_link_promoted
    }

    return render(request, 'main/index.html', context)
```

Here, we first define how many items of each category of games we want to show; for promoted games, it will be three games, and the non-promoted category will show a maximum of nine games.

Then, we fetch the promoted and non-promoted games, and we create two variables, `show_more_link_promoted` and `show_more_link_games`, which will be set to `True` in case there are more games in the database than the maximum number we defined previously.

We create a context variable that will contain all the data that we want to render in the template, and, lastly, we call the `render` function and pass the `request` to the template we want to render, along with the context.

Because we make use of the `Game` model, we have to import it:

```
from .models import Game
```

Now we are ready to see the results on the page, but, first, we need to create some games. To do that, we first need to register the models in the admin. To do that, edit the `admin.py` file and include the following code:

```
from django.contrib import admin

from .models import GamePlatform
from .models import Game
from .models import PriceList

admin.autodiscover()

admin.site.register(GamePlatform)
admin.site.register(Game)
admin.site.register(PriceList)
```

Registering the models within the Django admin site will allow us to add, edit, and remove games, games platforms, and items in the price list. Because we will be adding images to our games, we need to configure the location where Django should save the images that we upload through the administration site. So, let's go ahead and open the file `settings.py` in the `gamestore/gamestore` directory, and just below the `STATIC_DIRS` setting, add this line:

```
MEDIA_ROOT = os.path.join(BASE_DIR, 'static'</span>)
```

Now, start the site:

```
python manage.py runserver
```

Browse to `http://localhost:8000/admin`, and log in as the superuser account that we created. You should see the models listed on the page:

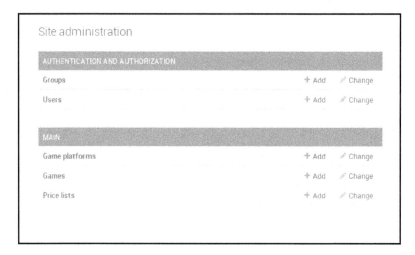

If you click first in `Game` platforms, you will see an empty list. Click on the button **ADD** on the **Game platforms** row on the top right-hand side of the page, and the following form will be displayed:

Just type any name you like, and click on the **SAVE** button to save your changes.

Before we add the games, we need to find a default image and place it at `gamestore/static/images/`. The image should be named `placeholder.png`.

The layout that we build will work better with images that are of the size 130x180. To make it simpler, when I am creating prototypes, and I don't want to spend too much time looking for the perfect image, I go to the site `https://placeholder.com/`. Here, you can build a placeholder image of any size you want. To get the correct size for our application you can go directly to `http://via.placeholder.com/130x180`.

When you have the default image in place, you can start adding games the same way you added the game platforms and just repeat the process multiple times to add a few games that are set as promoted as well.

After adding the games, and going to the site again, you should see the list of games on the index page, as follows:

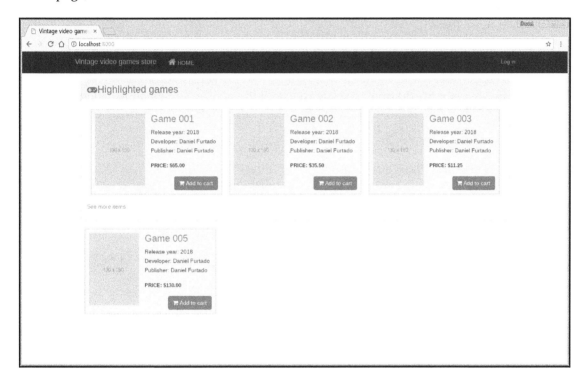

On my project, I added four promoted games. Notice that because we only show three promoted games on the first page, we render the link **See more items**.

Adding list games views

As we are not displaying all the items on the first page, we need to build pages that will display all the items if the user clicks on **See more items** link. This should be fairly simple, as we already have a partial view that lists the games for us.

Let's create two more URLs in the url.py file of the main app, and let's add these two to the urlpatterns list:

```
path(r'games-list/highlighted/', views.show_highlighted_games),
path(r'games-list/all/', views.show_all_games),
```

Perfect! Now we need to add one template to list all the games. Create a file called all_games.html at gamestore/main/templates/main with the following contents:

```
{% extends 'base.html' %}

{% block 'content' %}

 <h2>Highlighted games</h2>
 <hr/>

 {% if games %}
   {% include 'main/games-list.html' with gameslist=games
       highlight_promoted=False%}
   {% else %}
   <div class='empty-game-list'>
   <h3>There's no promoted games available at the moment</h3>
 </div>
{% endif %}

{% endblock %}
```

Add another file in the same folder called `highlighted.html`:

```
{% extends 'base.html' %}

{% block 'content' %}

<h2>All games</h2>
<hr/>

{% if games %}
  {% include 'main/games-list.html' with gameslist=games
    highlight_games=True%}
  {% else %}
  <div class='empty-game-list'>
    <h3>There's no promoted games available at the moment</h3>
  </div>
{% endif %}

{% endblock %}
```

There is nothing here that we haven't seen before. This template will receive a list of games, and it will pass it down to the `games-list.html` partial view that will do all the work of rendering the games for us. There is an `if` statement here that checks if there are games on the list. If the list is empty, it will display a message that there are no games available at the moment. Otherwise, it will render the content.

The last thing now is to add the views. Open the `views.py` file at `gamestore/main/`, and add the following two functions:

```
def show_all_games(request):
    games = Game.objects.all()

    context = {'games': games}

    return render(request, 'main/all_games.html', context)


def show_highlighted_games(request):
    games = Game.objects.get_highlighted()

    context = {'games': games}

    return render(request, 'main/highlighted.html', context)
```

These functions are very similar; one gets a list of all games and the other one gets a list of only promoted games

Let's open the application again. As we have more promoted items in the database, let's click on the link **See more items** in the **Highlighted games** section of the page. You should land on the following page:

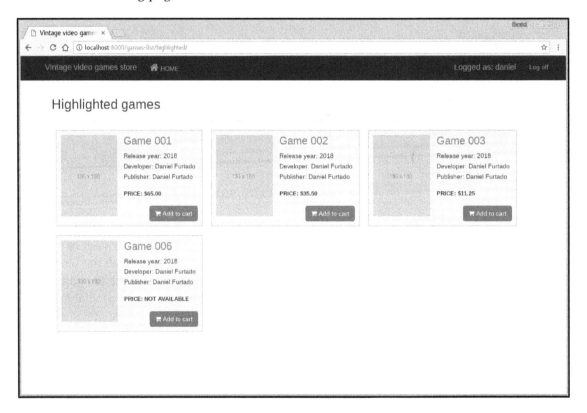

Perfect! It worked just as expected.

Next up, we are going to add functionality to the buttons so we can add those items to the cart.

Creating the shopping cart model

It seems like now we have an application up and running, we can display our games, but there's a big issue here. Can you guess what? Okay, this question wasn't so hard, I gave the answer for that in the title of the section. Anyway, our users cannot buy the games—we need to implement a shopping cart so we can start making our users happy!

Now, there are many ways you can implement a shopping cart on an application, but we are going to do it by simply saving the cart items on the database instead of doing an implementation based in the user session.

The requirements for the shopping cart are as follows:

- The users can add as many items they wish
- The users should be able to change the items in the shopping cart; for example, they should be able to change the quantity of an item
- Removal of items should be possible
- There should be an option to empty the shopping cart
- All the data should be validated
- If the user owning that shopping cart is removed, the shopping cart and its items should also be removed

With that said, open the file `models.py` in the `gamestore/main` directory, and let's add our first class:

```
class ShoppingCartManager(models.Manager):

    def get_by_id(self, id):
        return self.get(pk=id)

    def get_by_user(self, user):
        return self.get(user_id=user.id)

    def create_cart(self, user):
        new_cart = self.create(user=user)
        return new_cart
```

The same way we created a custom `Manager` for the `Game` object, we are also going to create a `Manager` for the `ShoppingCart`. We are going to add three methods. The first one is `get_by_id`, which, as the name says, retrieves a shopping cart, given an ID. The second method is `get_by_user`, which receives as a parameter an instance of `django.contrib.auth.models.User`, and it will return the cart given a user instance. The last method is `create_cart`; this method will be called when the user creates an account

Now that we have the manager with the methods that we need, let's add the
`ShoppingCart` class:

```
class ShoppingCart(models.Model):
    user = models.ForeignKey(User,
                                null=False,
                                on_delete=models.CASCADE)

    objects = ShoppingCartManager()

    def __str__(self):
        return f'{self.user.username}\'s shopping cart'
```

This class is super simple. As always, we inherit from `Model`, and we define one foreign key
for the type `User`. This foreign key is required, and if the user is deleted it will also delete
the shopping cart.

After the foreign key, we assign our custom `Manager` to the object's property, and we also
implement the special method __str__ so the shopping carts are displayed in a nicer way
in the Django admin UI.

Next, let's add a manager class for the `ShoppingCartItem` model, as follows:

```
class ShoppingCartItemManager(models.Manager):

    def get_items(self, cart):
        return self.filter(cart_id=cart.id)
```

Here, we only define one method, called `get_items`, which receives a cart object and
returns a list of items for the underlying shopping cart. After the `Manager` class, we can
create the model:

```
class ShoppingCartItem(models.Model):
    quantity = models.IntegerField(null=False)

    price_per_unit = models.DecimalField(max_digits=9,
                                            decimal_places=2,
                                            default=0)

    cart = models.ForeignKey(ShoppingCart,
                                null=False,
                                on_delete=models.CASCADE)
    game = models.ForeignKey(Game,
                                null=False,
                                on_delete=models.CASCADE)

    objects = ShoppingCartItemManager()
```

We start by defining two properties: quantity, which is an integer value, and the price per item, which is defined as a decimal value. We have `price_per_item` in this model as well, because when a user adds an item to the shopping cart and if the administrator changes the price for a product, we don't want that change in the price to be reflected on the items already added to the cart. The price should be the same price as when the user first added the product to the cart.

In case the user removes the item entirely and re-adds them, the new price should be reflected. After those two properties, we define two foreign keys, one for the type `ShoppingCart` and another one for `Game`.

Lastly, we set the `ShoppingCartItemManager` to the object's property.

We also need to import the User model:

```
from django.contrib.auth.models import User
```

Before we try to verify that everything is working, we should create and apply the migrations. On the terminal, run the following command:

python manage.py makemigrations

As we did before, we need to run the migrate command to apply the migrations to the database:

python manage.py migrate

Creating the shopping cart form

We now have the models in place. Let's add a new form that will display the cart data on a page for editing. Open the `forms.py` file at `gamestore/main/`, and at the end of the file add the following code:

```
ShoppingCartFormSet = inlineformset_factory(
    ShoppingCart,
    ShoppingCartItem,
    fields=('quantity', 'price_per_unit'),
    extra=0,
    widgets={
        'quantity': forms.TextInput({
            'class': 'form-control quantity',
        }),
        'price_per_unit': forms.HiddenInput()
    }
```

```
)
```

Here, we create an inline `formset` using the function `inlineformset_factory`. Inline `formsets` are suitable when we want to work with related objects via a foreign key. This is very convenient in the case we have here; we have a model `ShoppingCart` that relates to the `ShoppingCartItem`.

So, we pass a few arguments to the `inlineformset_factory` function. First is the parent model (`ShoppingCart`), then it's the model (`ShoppingCartItems`). Because in the shopping cart we just want to edit the quantities and also remove items from the cart, we add a tuple containing the fields from the `ShoppingCartItem` that we want to render on the page—in this case, the `quantity` and `price_per_unit`. The next argument, `extra`, specifies whether the form should render any empty extra rows on the form; in our case, we don't need that, as we don't want to add extra items in the shopping cart to the shopping cart view.

In the last argument, `widgets`, we can specify how the fields should be rendered in the form. The quantity field will be rendered as a text input, and we don't want `price_per_unit` to be visible, so we define it as a hidden input so it is sent back to the server when we submit the form to the server.

Lastly, in the same file, let's add some necessary imports:

```
from django.forms import inlineformset_factory
from .models import ShoppingCartItem
from .models import ShoppingCart
```

Open the `views.py` file, and let's add a class-based view. First, we need to add some import statements:

```
from django.views.generic.edit import UpdateView
from django.http import HttpResponseRedirect
from django.urls import reverse_lazy
from django.db.models import Sum, F, DecimalField

from .models import ShoppingCart
from .models import ShoppingCartItem
from .forms import ShoppingCartFormSet
```

Then, we can create the class, as follows:

```
class ShoppingCartEditView(UpdateView):
    model = ShoppingCart
    form_class = ShoppingCartFormSet
    template_name = 'main/cart.html'
```

```
    def get_context_data(self, **kwargs):
        context = super().get_context_data(**kwargs)

        items = ShoppingCartItem.objects.get_items(self.object)

        context['is_cart_empty'] = (items.count() == 0)

        order = items.aggregate(
            total_order=Sum(F('price_per_unit') * F('quantity'),
                            output_field=DecimalField())
        )

        context['total_order'] = order['total_order']

        return context

    def get_object(self):
        try:
            return
ShoppingCart.objects.get_by_user(self.request.user)
        except ShoppingCart.DoesNotExist:
            new_cart =
ShoppingCart.objects.create_cart(self.request.user)
            new_cart.save()
            return new_cart

    def form_valid(self, form):
        form.save()
        return HttpResponseRedirect(reverse_lazy('user-cart'))
```

This is slightly different than the view that we created so far, as this is a class-based view that inherits from an `UpdateView`. In reality, views in Django are callable objects, and when using classes instead of functions, we can take advantage of inheritance and mixins. In our case, we use `UpdateView` because it is a view to display forms that will edit an existing object.

This class view starts off by defining a few properties, such as the model, which is the model that we are going to be editing in the form. The `form_class` is the form that is going to be used for editing the data. Lastly, we have the template that will be used to render the form.

We override the `get_context_data` because we include some extra data in the form context. So, first, we call the `get_context_data` on the base class so as to build the context, then we get the list of items of the current cart so we can determine whether the cart is empty. We set this value to the context item called `is_cart_empty`, which can be accessed from the template.

After that, we want to calculate the total value of the items that are currently in the cart. To do that, we need to first calculate the total price for each item by doing (price * quantity), and then sum the results. In Django, it is possible to aggregate the values of a `QuerySet`; we have already the `QuerySet` that contains the list of items in a cart, so all we have to do is to use the `aggregate` function. In our case, we are passing two arguments to the `aggregate` function. First, we get the sum of the field `price_per_unit` multiplied by the quantity, and the results will be stored in a property called `total_order`. The second argument of the `aggregate` function defines the output data type, which we want to be a decimal value.

When we get the results of the aggregation, we create a new item in the context dictionary called `total_order` and assign the results to it. Finally, we return the context.

We also override the `get_object` method. In this method, we try to get the shopping cart for the requesting user. If the shopping cart does not exist, an exception `ShoppingCart.DoesNotExist` will be raised. In that case, we create a shopping cart for the user and return it.

Lastly, we also implement the `form_valid` method, which only saves the form and redirects the user back to the cart page.

Creating the shopping cart view

Now it is time to create the shopping cart views. This view will render the form that we just created, and the users should be able to change the quantities for every item on the cart, as well as remove items. If the shopping cart is empty, we should show a message saying that the cart is empty.

Before we add the view, let's go ahead and open the `urls.py` file in `gamestore/main/` and add the following URL:

```
path(r'cart/', views.ShoppingCartEditView.as_view(), name='user-
    cart'),
```

Here, we define a new URL, `'cart/'`, and, when accessed, it will execute the class-based view `ShoppingCartEditView`. We also define a name for the URL for simplicity.

We are going to create a new file called `cart.html` at `gamestore/main/templates/main`, with the contents as follows:

```
{% extends 'base.html' %}

{% block 'content' %}

{% load humanize %}

<div class='cart-details'>

<h3>{{ shoppingcart}}</h3>

{% if is_cart_empty %}

<h2>Your shopping cart is empty</h2>

{% else %}

<form action='' method='POST'>

  {% csrf_token %}

  {{ form.management_form }}

 <button class='btn btn-success'>
  <i class="fa fa-refresh" aria-hidden="true"></i>
     Updated cart
</button>
  <hr/>
  <table class="table table-striped">
  <thead>
    <tr>
      <th scope="col">Game</th>
      <th scope="col">Quantity</th>
      <th scope="col">Price per unit</th>
      <th scope="col">Options</th>
    </tr>
  </thead>
  <tbody>
   {% for item_form in form %}
   <tr>
     <td>{{item_form.instance.game.name}}</td>
     <td class=
```

```
           "{% if item_form.quantity.errors %}has-errors{% endif%}">
         {{item_form.quantity}}
       </td>
       <td>${{item_form.instance.price_per_unit|
              floatformat:2|intcomma}}</td>
       <td>{{item_form.DELETE}} Remove item</td>
       {% for hidden in item_form.hidden_fields %}
         {{ hidden }}
       {% endfor %}
     </tr>
     {% endfor %}
     <tbody>
    </table>
   </form>
  <hr/>
  <div class='footer'>
    <p class='total-value'>Total of your order:
       ${{total_order|floatformat:2|intcomma}}</p>
    <button class='btn btn-primary'>
       <i class="fa fa-check" aria-hidden="true"></i>
         SEND ORDER
    </button>
  </div>
    {% endif %}
  </div>
  {% endblock %}
```

The template is quite simple; we just loop through the forms and render each one of them. One thing to note here in that we are loading humanize in the beginning of the template.

 humanize is a set of template filters that we can use to format data in the template.

We use the intcomma filter from humanize to format the sum of all items in the shopping cart. The intcomma filter will convert an integer or float value to a string and add a comma every three digits.

You can try it out on the new view. However, the cart will be empty and no data will be displayed. Next, we are going to add functionality to include items in the cart.

Adding items to the cart

We are getting close to finishing up the shopping cart. Now we are going to implement a view that will include items in the cart.

The first thing we need to do is create a new URL. Open the file `url.py` in the directory `gamestore/main/`, and add this URL to the `urlpatterns` list:

```
path(r'cart/add/<int:game_id>/', views.add_to_cart),
```

Perfect. In this URL, we can pass the game ID, and it will execute a view called `add_to_cart`. Let's add this new view. Open the file `views.py` in `gamestore/main`. First, we add import statements, shown as follows:

```
from decimal import Decimal
from django.shortcuts import get_object_or_404
from django.contrib import messages
from django.contrib.auth.decorators import login_required
```

Now, we need a way to know if a specific item has been already added to the cart, so we go over to the `models.py` in `gametore/main` and add a new method to the `ShoppingCartItemManager` class:

```
def get_existing_item(self, cart, game):
    try:
        return self.get(cart_id=cart.id,
                        game_id=game.id)
    except ShoppingCartItem.DoesNotExist:
        return None
```

`get_existing_item` searches for a `ShoppingCartItem` object using as criteria the `cart id` and the `game id`. If the item is not found in the cart, it returns `None`; otherwise, it will return the cart item.

Now we add the view to the `views.py` file:

```
@login_required
def add_to_cart(request, game_id):
    game = get_object_or_404(Game, pk=game_id)
    cart = ShoppingCart.objects.get_by_user(request.user)

    existing_item =
ShoppingCartItem.objects.get_existing_item(cart,
    game)

    if existing_item is None:
```

```
            price = (Decimal(0)
                if not hasattr(game, 'pricelist')
                else game.pricelist.price_per_unit)

            new_item = ShoppingCartItem(
                game=game,
                quantity=1,
                price_per_unit=price,
                cart=cart
            )
            new_item.save()
        else:
            existing_item.quantity = F('quantity') + 1
            existing_item.save()

        messages.add_message(
                request,
                messages.INFO,
                f'The game {game.name} has been added to your cart.')

        return HttpResponseRedirect(reverse_lazy('user-cart'))
```

This function gets a request and the game ID, and we start by getting the game and the current user's shopping cart. We then pass the cart and the game to the `get_existing` function that we just created. If we don't have that specific item in the shopping cart, we create a new `ShoppingCartItem`; otherwise, we just update the quantity and save.

We also add a message to inform the user that the item has been added to the shopping cart.

Lastly, we redirect the user to the shopping cart page.

As a final touch, let's open the `site.css` file in the `gamestore/static/styles` and add the styling to our shopping cart's view:

```
.cart-details h3 {
    margin-bottom: 40px;
}

.cart-details .table tbody tr td:nth-child(2) {
    width: 10%;
}

.cart-details .table tbody tr td:nth-child(3) {
    width: 25%;
}
```

```
.cart-details .table tbody tr td:nth-child(4) {
    width: 20%;
}

.has-errors input:focus {
    border-color: red;
    box-shadow: inset 0 1px 1px rgba(0,0,0,.075), 0 0 8px
rgba(255,0,0,1);
    webkit-box-shadow: inset 0 1px 1px rgba(0,0,0,.075), 0 0 8px
rgba(255,0,0,1);
}

.has-errors input {
    color: red;
    border-color: red;
}

.cart-details .footer {
    display:flex;
    justify-content: space-between;
}

.cart-details .footer .total-value {
    font-size: 1.4em;
    font-weight: bold;
    margin-left: 10px;
}
```

Before we try this out, we need to add the link to the cart view on the top menu. Open the file base.html in gamestore/templates, locate where we do the include of the _loginpartial.html file, and include the following code right before it:

```
{% if user.is_authenticated%}
<li>
  <a href="/cart/">
    <i class="fa fa-shopping-cart"
       aria-hidden="true"></i> CART
  </a>
</li>
{% endif %}
```

Now we should be ready to test it out. Go to the first page, and try adding some games to the **cart**. You should be redirected to the **cart** page:

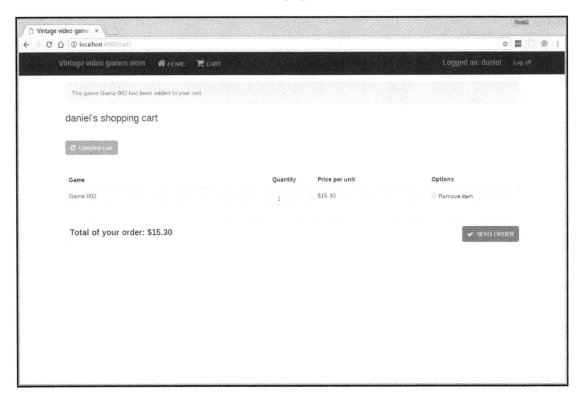

Summary

It has been a long journey, and we have covered a lot of ground in this chapter. In this chapter, you have seen how easy it is to build an application with Django. The framework really honors the phrase *Framework for perfectionists with deadlines.*

You have learned how to create a new Django project and applications, with a short walkthrough of the boilerplate code that Django generates for us when we start a new project. We learned how to create models and use migrations to apply changes to the database.

Django forms was also a subject that we covered a lot in this chapter, and you should be able to create complex forms for your projects.

As a bonus, we learned how to install and use **NodeJS Version Manager** (**NVM**) to install Node.js, so as to install project dependencies using the npm.

In Chapter 5, *Building a Web Messenger with Microservices*, we are going to extend this application and create services that will handle the store inventory.

8
Order Microservice

In this chapter, we are going to extend the web application that we implemented in Chapter 7, *Online Video Game Store with Django*. I don't know if you noticed, but there are a few important things missing in that project. The first is the ability to submit an order. As of right now, users can browse products and add items to the shopping cart; however, there's no way of sending the order and completing the purchase.

Another item that is missing is a page where the users of our application will be able to see all the orders that have been sent, as well as a history of their orders.

With that said, we are going to create a microservice called *order*, which will do everything related to orders made on the site. It will receive orders, update orders, and so on.

In this chapter, you will learn:

- The basics of how to create microservices
- How to use the Django REST Framework to create RESTful APIs
- How to consume the services and integrate them with other applications
- How to write tests
- How to deploy an application on AWS
- How to run our web application with Gunicorn behind the HTTP proxy nginx

So, let's get started!

Setting up the environment

Like all the previous chapters, we are going to start off this chapter by setting up the environment that we need to develop our services on. Let's start by creating our working directory:

```
mkdir microservices && cd microservices
```

Then, we create our virtual environment with `pipenv`:

```
pipenv --python ~/Install/Python3.6/bin/python3.6
```

> If you don't know how to use `pipenv`, in the section *Setting up the environment* in `Chapter 4`, *Exchange Rates and the Currency Conversion Tool*, there is a very good introduction about how to get started with `pipenv`.

With the virtual environment created, we need to install the project dependencies. For this project, we are going to install Django and the Django REST Framework:

```
pipenv install django djangorestframework requests python-dateutil
```

The reason that we are using Django and the Django REST Framework instead of a simpler framework like Flask is that the main idea of this project is to provide a separation of concerns, creating a microservice that will handle orders made in the online game store that we developed in the previous chapter. We don't want to only provide APIs to be consumed by the web application. It would be great to have a simple website so that we can list the orders, see the details of each order, and also perform updates such as changing the order's status.

As you saw in the previous chapter, Django already has a very powerful and flexible admin UI that we can customize to provide that kind of functionality to our users--all without spending too much time developing a web application.

After installing the dependencies, your `Pipfile` should look as follows:

```
[[source]]

verify_ssl = true
name = "pypi"
url = "https://pypi.python.org/simple"


[packages]

django = "*"
```

```
djangorestframework = "*"


[dev-packages]


[requires]

python_version = "3.6"
```

Perfect! Now, we can start a new Django project. We are going to create the project using the `django-admin` tool. Let's go ahead and create a project called `order`:

django-admin startproject order

With the project created, we are going to create a Django app. For this project, we are going to create just one app that is going to be called `main`. First, we change the directory to the service directory:

cd order

And again, we use the `django-admin` tool to create an app:

django-admin startapp main

After creating the Django app, your project structure should look similar to the following structure:

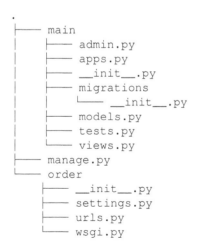

```
.
├── main
│   ├── admin.py
│   ├── apps.py
│   ├── __init__.py
│   ├── migrations
│   │   └── __init__.py
│   ├── models.py
│   ├── tests.py
│   └── views.py
├── manage.py
└── order
    ├── __init__.py
    ├── settings.py
    ├── urls.py
    └── wsgi.py
```

Next up, we are going to start creating the model for our service.

Creating the service models

In the first part of the order service, we are going to create the model that will store data about the order coming from the online video game store. Let's go ahead and open the models.py file in the main app directory and start adding the model:

```
class OrderCustomer(models.Model):
    customer_id = models.IntegerField()
    name = models.CharField(max_length=100)
    email = models.CharField(max_length=100)
```

We will create a class called OrderCustomer that inherits from Model, and define three properties; the customer_id, which will correspond to the customer ID in the online game store, the name of the customer, and lastly, the email.

Then, we will create the model that will store information about the order:

```
class Order(models.Model):

    ORDER_STATUS = (
        (1, 'Received'),
        (2, 'Processing'),
        (3, 'Payment complete'),
        (4, 'Shipping'),
        (5, 'Completed'),
        (6, 'Cancelled'),
    )

    order_customer = models.ForeignKey(
        OrderCustomer,
        on_delete=models.CASCADE
    )
    total = models.DecimalField(
        max_digits=9,
        decimal_places=2,
        default=0
    )
    created_at = models.DateTimeField(auto_now_add=True)
    last_updated = models.DateTimeField(auto_now=True)
    status = models.IntegerField(choices=ORDER_STATUS, default='1')
```

The `Order` class inherits from `Model`, and we start this class by adding a tuple containing the status that the orders in our application can have. We also define a foreign key, `order_customer`, which will create the relationship between the `OrderCustomer` and `Order`. It is then time to define other fields, starting with `total`, which is the total purchase value of that order. We then have two datetime fields; `created_at`, which is the date that the order has been submitted by the customer, and `last_update`, which is a field that is going to be used when we want to know when the order has a status update.

 When adding `auto_now_add` to a `DateTimeField`, Django uses the `django.utils.timezone.now` function, which will return the current `datetime` object with timezone information. DateField uses `datetime.date.today()`, which does not contain timezone information.

The last model that we are going to create is `OrderItems`. This will hold items belonging to an order. We will define it like this:

```
class OrderItems(models.Model):
    class Meta:
        verbose_name_plural = 'Order items'

    product_id = models.IntegerField()
    name = models.CharField(max_length=200)
    quantity = models.IntegerField()
    price_per_unit = models.DecimalField(
        max_digits=9,
        decimal_places=2,
        default=0
    )
    order = models.ForeignKey(
        Order, on_delete=models.CASCADE, related_name='items')
```

Here, we also define a `Meta` class so we can set some metadata to the model. In this case, we are setting the `verbose_name_plural` to `Order items` so that it looks correctly spelled in the Django admin UI. Then, we define `product_id`, `name`, `quantity`, and `price_per_unit`, which refer to the `Game` model in the online video game store. Lastly, we have the item quantity and the foreign key `Order`.

Now, we need to edit the `settings.py` file in `microservices/order/order` directory and add the main app to `INSTALLED_APPS`. It should look like this:

```
INSTALLED_APPS = [
    'django.contrib.admin',
    'django.contrib.auth',
    'django.contrib.contenttypes',
    'django.contrib.sessions',
    'django.contrib.messages',
    'django.contrib.staticfiles',
    'main',
]
```

The only thing left is to create and apply the database migrations. First, we run the command `makemigrations`:

```
python manage.py makemigrations
```

And `migrate` to apply the changes to the database:

```
python manage.py migrate
```

Creating the model's managers

To make our application more readable and not clutter the endpoints with a lot of business logic, we are going to create managers for our model classes. If you followed the previous chapter, you should be very familiar with this. In a nutshell, managers are an interface that provide query operations to Django models.

 By default, Django adds a manager to every model; it is stored on a property named objects. The default manager that Django adds to the models is sometimes sufficient and there's no need to create a custom manager, but it is a good practice to keep all database-related code within the model. This will make our code more consistent, readable, and easier to test and maintain.

In our case, the only model we are interested in creating is a custom model manager called Order, but before we start implementing the order manager, we need to create a few helper classes. The first class that we need to create is a class that will define custom exceptions that may occur when performing queries on our database. Of course, we could use the exceptions that are already defined in the standard library, but it is always a good practice to create exceptions that make sense within the context of your application.
The three exceptions that we are going to create are InvalidArgumentError, OrderAlreadyCompletedError, and OrderCancellationError.

The exception InvalidArgumentError will be raised when invalid arguments are passed to the functions that we are going to define in the manager, so let's go ahead and create a file called exceptions.py in the main app directory with the following contents:

```
class InvalidArgumentError(Exception):
    def __init__(self, argument_name):
        message = f'The argument {argument_name} is invalid'
        super().__init__(message)
```

Here, we define a class called InvalidArgumentError that inherits from Exception, and the only thing we do in it is override the constructor and receive an argument called argument_name. With this argument, we can specify what caused the exception to be raised.

We will also customize the exception message, and lastly, we will call the constructor on the superclass.

We are also going to create an exception that will be raised when we try to cancel an order that has the status as canceled, and also when we try to set the status of an order to completed when the order is already completed:

```
class OrderAlreadyCompletedError(Exception):
    def __init__(self, order):
        message = f'The order with ID: {order.id} is already
        completed.'
        super().__init__(message)


class OrderAlreadyCancelledError(Exception):
    def __init__(self, order):
        message = f'The order with ID: {order.id} is already
        cancelled.'
        super().__init__(message)
```

Then, we are going to add two more custom exceptions:

```
class OrderCancellationError(Exception):
    pass


class OrderNotFoundError(Exception):
    pass
```

These two classes don't do too much. They only inherit from `Exception`. We will configure and customize a message for each exception and pass it over to the super class initializer. The value of adding custom exception classes is that it will improve the readability and maintainability of our applications.

Great! There is only one more thing we need to add before starting with the manager. We will create functions in the model manager that will return data filtered by status. As you can see, in the definition of the `Order` model, we defined the status like this:

```
ORDER_STATUS = (
    (1, 'Received'),
    (2, 'Processing'),
    (3, 'Payment complete'),
    (4, 'Shipping'),
    (5, 'Completed'),
    (6, 'Cancelled'),
)
```

Which means that if we want to get all the orders with a status of `Completed`, we would need to write something similar to the following line:

```
Order.objects.filter(status=5)
```

There's only one problem with this code, can you guess what? If you guessed that *magic* number, 5, you are absolutely right! Imagine how frustrated our colleagues would be if they needed to maintain this code and see only the number 5 there and have no idea what 5 actually means. Because of this, we are going to create an enumeration that we can use to express the different statuses. Let's create a file called `status.py` in the `main` app directory and add the following enumeration:

```
from enum import Enum, auto


class Status(Enum):
    Received = auto()
    Processing = auto()
    Payment_Complete = auto()
```

```
Shipping = auto()
Completed = auto()
Cancelled = auto()
```

So, now, when we need to get all the orders with a `Completed` status, we can do:

```
Order.objects.filter(Status.Received.value)
```

Much better!

Now, let's create the model manager for it. Create a file called `managers.py` in the mail app directory, and we can start by adding a few imports:

```
from datetime import datetime
from django.db.models import Manager, Q

from .status import Status

from .exceptions import InvalidArgumentError
from .exceptions import OrderAlreadyCompletedError
from .exceptions import OrderCancellationError

from . import models
```

Then, we define the `OrderManager` class and the first method called `set_status`:

```
class OrderManager(Manager):

    def set_status(self, order, status):
        if status is None or not isinstance(status, Status):
            raise InvalidArgumentError('status')

        if order is None or not isinstance(order, models.Order):
            raise InvalidArgumentError('order')

        if order.status is Status.Completed.value:
            raise OrderAlreadyCompletedError()

        order.status = status.value
        order.save()
```

This method takes two parameters, order, and status. The `order` is an object of type `Order` and the status is an item of the `Status` enumeration that we created previously.

We start this method by validating the arguments and raising the corresponding exception. First, we validate if the fields have a value and are the correct type. If the validation fails, it will raise an `InvalidArgumentError`. Then, we check if the order that we are trying to set the status for is already completed; in this case, we cannot change it anymore, so we raise an `OrderAlreadyCompletedError`. If all the arguments are valid, we set the order's status and save.

In our application, we want to be able to cancel an order that is still not being processed; in other words, we will allow orders to be canceled only if the status is `Received`. Here is what the `cancel_order` method should look like:

```
def cancel_order(self, order):
    if order is None or not isinstance(order, models.Order):
        raise InvalidArgumentError('order')

    if order.status != Status.Received.value:
        raise OrderCancellationError()

    self.set_status(order, Status.Cancelled)
```

This method only gets the `order` argument, and first, we need to check if the order object is valid and raise an `InvalidArgumentError` if it is invalid. Then, we check if the order's status is `not Received`. In this case, we raise an `OrderCancellationError` exception. Otherwise, we go ahead and call the `set_status` method, passing `Status.Cancelled` as an argument.

We also need to get a list of all orders for a given customer:

```
def get_all_orders_by_customer(self, customer_id):
    try:
        return self.filter(
            order_customer_id=customer_id).order_by(
            'status', '-created_at')
    except ValueError:
        raise InvalidArgumentError('customer_id')
```

The `get_all_orders_by_customer` method gets the `customer_id` as an argument. Then, we use the filter function to filter orders by the `customer_id` and we also order it by status; the orders that are still being processed will be on the top of the QuerySet.

In case the `customer_id` is invalid, for example, if we pass a string instead of an integer, a `ValueError` exception will be raised. We catch this exception and raise our custom exception `InvalidArgumentError`.

The financial department of our online video game store had the requirement of getting a list of all complete and incomplete orders for a specific user, so let's go ahead and add some methods for it:

```
def get_customer_incomplete_orders(self, customer_id):
    try:
        return self.filter(
            ~Q(status=Status.Completed.value),
            order_customer_id=customer_id).order_by('status')
    except ValueError:
        raise InvalidArgumentError('customer_id')

def get_customer_completed_orders(self, customer_id):
    try:
        return self.filter(
            status=Status.Completed.value,
            order_customer_id=customer_id)
    except ValueError:
        raise InvalidArgumentError('customer_id')
```

The first method, `get_customer_incomplete_orders`, gets an argument called `customer_id`. It is like the previous method; we will catch a `ValueError` exception in case the `customer_id` is invalid, and raise an `InvalidArgumentError`. The interesting part of this method is the filter. Here, we use a `Q()` object, which encapsulates an SQL expression in the form of a `Python` object.

Here, we have `~Q(status=Status.Completed.value)`, which is the 'not' operator, which is the same as saying the status is not `Status.Complete`. We also filter `order_customer_id` to check if it's equal to the method's `customer_id` argument, and lastly, we order the QuerySet by status.

`get_customer_completed_orders` is basically the same, but this time, we filter orders that have a status equal to `Status.Completed`.

The `Q()` object allows us to write much more complex queries making use of `|` (OR) and `&` (AND) operators.

Next, every department that is responsible for taking care of the order life cycle wants an easy way to get orders at a certain stage; for example, the workers responsible for shipping the games want to get a list of all orders that have a status equal to `Payment Complete` so they can ship these orders to the customers. So, we need to add a method that will do just that:

```
def get_orders_by_status(self, status):
    if status is None or not isinstance(status, Status):
        raise InvalidArgumentError('status')

    return self.filter(status=status.value)
```

This is a very simple method; here, we get the status as an argument. We check if the status is valid; if not, we raise an `InvalidArgumentError`. Otherwise, we continue and filter the orders by status.

Another requirement from our finance department is to get a list of orders in a given date range:

```
def get_orders_by_period(self, start_date, end_date):
    if start_date is None or not isinstance(start_date, datetime):
        raise InvalidArgumentError('start_date')

    if end_date is None or not isinstance(end_date, datetime):
        raise InvalidArgumentError('end_date')

    result = self.filter(created_at__range=[start_date, end_date])
    return result
```

Here, we get two parameters, `start_date` and `end_date`. As with all the other methods, we start by checking if these arguments are valid; in this case, the arguments cannot be `None` and have to be an instance of the `Datetime` object. If any of the fields are invalid, an `InvalidArgumentError` will be raised. When the arguments are valid, we filter the orders using the `created_at` field and we also use this special syntax, `created_at__range`, which means that we are going to pass a date range and it will be used as a filter. Here, we are passing `start_date` and `end_date`.

There is just one method that might be interesting to implement and it can add value to the administrators of our application. The idea here is to add a method that, when called, automatically changes the order to the next status:

```
def set_next_status(self, order):
    if order is None or not isinstance(order, models.Order):
        raise InvalidArgumentError('order')
```

```
if order.status is Status.Completed.value:
    raise OrderAlreadyCompletedError()

order.status += 1
order.save()
```

This method gets just one argument, the order. We check if the order is valid, and if it is invalid, we raise an `InvalidArgumentError`. We also want to make sure that once the order gets to the `Completed` status, it can no longer be changed. So, we check if the order is of the status `Completed`, then we raise an `OrderAlreadyCompleted` exception. Lastly, we add 1 to the current status and save the object.

Now, we can change our `Order` model so that it makes use of the `OrderManager` that we just created. Open the model.py file in the main app directory, and at the end of the `Order` class, add the following line:

```
objects = OrderManager()
```

So, now we can access all the methods that we defined in the `OrderManager` through `Order.objects`.

Next up, we are going to add tests to our model manager methods.

Learning to test

So far in this book, we haven't covered how to create tests. Now is a good time to do that, so we are going to create tests for the methods that we created in the model manager.

Why do we need tests? The short answer to this question is that tests will allow us to know that the methods or functions are doing the right thing. The other reason (and one of the most important, in my opinion) is that tests give us more confidence when it comes to performing changes in the code.

Django has great tools out of the box for creating unit and integration tests, and combined with frameworks like Selenium, it is possible to basically test all of our application.

With that said, let's create our first tests. Django creates a file called test.py in the app directory when creating a new Django app. You can write your tests in there, or if you prefer to keep the project more organized by separating the tests into multiple files, you can remove that file and create a directory called tests and place all your tests files in there. Since we are only going to create tests for the Order model manager, we are going to keep all the tests in the tests.py file that Django created for us.

Creating the test files

Open the `test.py` file and let's start by adding a few imports:

```
from dateutil.relativedelta import relativedelta

from django.test import TestCase
from django.utils import timezone

from .models import OrderCustomer, Order
from .status import Status

from .exceptions import OrderAlreadyCompletedError
from .exceptions import OrderCancellationError
from .exceptions import InvalidArgumentError
```

Great! We start by importing the relative delta function so we can easily perform date operations, like adding days or months to a date. This will be very helpful when testing the methods that get orders for a certain period of time.

Now, we import some Django-related things. First is the `TestCase` class, which is a subclass of `unittest.TestCase`. Since we are going to write tests that will interact with the database, it is a good idea to use `django.tests.TestCase` instead of `unittest.TestCase`. Django's `TestCase` implementation will make sure that your test is running within a transaction to provide isolation. This way, we will not have unpredictable results when running the test because of data created by another test in the test suite. We also import some of the model classes that we are going to use in our test, the `Order`, the `OrderCustomer` models, and also the Status class when we are going to test the method that changes order statuses.

When writing tests for your application, we don't want to only test the *good* scenarios, we also want to test when things go wrong, and bad arguments are passed to the functions and methods that are being tested. For this reason, we are importing our custom error classes, so we can make sure that the right exception is being raised in the right situation.

Now that we have the imports in place, it is time to create the class and the method that will set up data for our tests:

```
class OrderModelTestCase(TestCase):

    @classmethod
    def setUpTestData(cls):
        cls.customer_001 = OrderCustomer.objects.create(
            customer_id=1,
            email='customer_001@test.com'
```

```
    )

    Order.objects.create(order_customer=cls.customer_001)

    Order.objects.create(order_customer=cls.customer_001,
                            status=Status.Completed.value)

    cls.customer_002 = OrderCustomer.objects.create(
        customer_id=1,
        email='customer_002@test.com'
    )

    Order.objects.create(order_customer=cls.customer_002)
```

Here, we create a class called `OrderModelTestCase`, inheriting from the `django.test.TestCase`. Then, we define the `setUpTestData` method, which will be the method that will be responsible for setting up the data that will be used by each test.

Here, we create two users; the first one has two orders and one of the orders is set to `Completed`. The second user has only one order.

Testing the cancel order function

The first method that we are going to test is the `cancel_orders` method. As the name says, it will cancel an order. There a few things we want to test in this method:

- The first test is quite straightforward; we only want to test if we can cancel an order, setting its status to `Cancelled`
- The second test is that it shouldn't be possible to cancel orders that have not been received; in other words, only the orders that have the current status set to `Received` can be canceled
- We need to test if the correct exception is raised in case we pass an invalid argument to the `cancel_order` method

With that said, let's add our tests:

```
def test_cancel_order(self):
    order = Order.objects.get(pk=1)

    self.assertIsNotNone(order)
    self.assertEqual(Status.Received.value, order.status)

    Order.objects.cancel_order(order)
```

```
        self.assertEqual(Status.Cancelled.value, order.status)

    def test_cancel_completed_order(self):
        order = Order.objects.get(pk=2)

        self.assertIsNotNone(order)
        self.assertEqual(Status.Completed.value, order.status)

        with self.assertRaises(OrderCancellationError):
            Order.objects.cancel_order(order)

    def test_cancel_order_with_invalid_argument(self):
        with self.assertRaises(InvalidArgumentError):
            Order.objects.cancel_order({'id': 1})
```

The first test, `test_cancel_order`, starts off by getting an order with ID 1. We assert that the returned value is not `None` using the `assertIsNotNone` function, and we also use the function `assertEqual` to make sure that the order has the status 'Received'.

Then, we call the `cancel_order` method from the order model manager passing the order, and lastly, we use the `assertEqual` function again to verify that the order's status is in fact changed to `Cancelled`.

The second test, `test_cancel_complated_order`, starts by getting the order with ID equal to 2; remember that we have set this order with the `Completed` status. Then, we do the same thing as the previous test; we verify that the order is not equal to `None`, and we verify that the status is set to `Complete`. Finally, we use the `assertRaises` function to test that the correct exception is raised if we try to cancel an order that is already cancelled; in this case, an exception of type `OrderCancellationError` will be raised.

Lastly, we have the `test_cancel_order_with_invalid_argument` function, which will test if the correct exception will be raised if we pass an invalid argument to the `cancel_order` function.

Testing the get all orders function

Now, we are going to add tests to the `get_all_orders_by_customer` method. For this method, we need to test:

- If the correct number of orders is returned when given a customer ID

- If the correct exception is raised when passing an invalid argument to the method

```
def test_get_all_orders_by_customer(self):
    orders =
Order.objects.get_all_orders_by_customer(customer_id=1)

    self.assertEqual(2, len(orders),
                     msg='It should have returned 2 orders.')

def test_get_all_order_by_customer_with_invalid_id(self):
    with self.assertRaises(InvalidArgumentError):
        Order.objects.get_all_orders_by_customer('o')
```

The tests for the `get_all_orders_by_customer` method are quite simple. In the first test, we fetch the orders for the customer with ID `1` and test if the returned number of items is equal to `2`.

In the second test, we assert if calling `get_all_orders_by_customer` with an invalid argument, in fact, raises an exception of type `InvalidArgumentError`. In this case, the test will successfully pass.

Getting customer's incomplete orders

The `get_customer_incomplete_orders` method returns all the orders with the statuses that are different from `Completed` given a customer ID. For this test, we need to verify that:

- The method returns the correct number of items and also if the item returned does not have a status equal to `Completed`
- We are going to test if an exception is raised when an invalid value is passed as an argument to this method

```
def test_get_customer_incomplete_orders(self):
    orders =
Order.objects.get_customer_incomplete_orders(customer_id=1)

    self.assertEqual(1, len(orders))
    self.assertEqual(Status.Received.value, orders[0].status)

def test_get_customer_incomplete_orders_with_invalid_id(self):
    with self.assertRaises(InvalidArgumentError):
        Order.objects.get_customer_incomplete_orders('o')
```

The test `test_get_customer_incomplete_orders` starts off by calling the `get_customer_incomplete_orders` function and passing as an argument a customer ID equal to 1. Then, we verify that the number of returned items is correct; in this case, there's only one incomplete order, so it should be 1. Lastly, we check if the item that was returned in fact has a status different to `Completed`.

The other test, exactly like the previous one testing that tested exceptions, just calls the method and asserts that the correct exception has been raised.

Getting customer's completed orders

Next, we are going to test `get_customer_completed_order`. This method, as the name says, returns all the orders that have a status of `Completed` for a given customer. Here, we will test the same scenarios as `get_customer_incompleted_orders`:

```
def test_get_customer_completed_orders(self):
    orders = Order.objects.get_customer_completed_orders(customer_id=1)

    self.assertEqual(1, len(orders))
    self.assertEqual(Status.Completed.value, orders[0].status)

def test_get_customer_completed_orders_with_invalid_id(self):
    with self.assertRaises(InvalidArgumentError):
        Order.objects.get_customer_completed_orders('o')
```

First, we call `get_customer_completed_orders`, passing a customer ID equal to 1, and then we verify that the number of items returned is equal to 1. To finish it up, we verify that the item that was returned has, in fact, a status set to `Completed`.

Getting orders by status

The `get_order_by_status` function returns a list of orders given a status. There are two scenarios we have to test here:

- If the method returns the correct number of orders given a specific status
- That the correct exception is raised when passing an invalid argument to the method

```
def test_get_order_by_status(self):
    order = Order.objects.get_orders_by_status(Status.Received)
```

```
        self.assertEqual(2, len(order),
                         msg=('There should be only 2 orders '
                              'with status=Received.'))

        self.assertEqual('customer_001@test.com',
                         order[0].order_customer.email)

    def test_get_order_by_status_with_invalid_status(self):
        with self.assertRaises(InvalidArgumentError):
            Order.objects.get_orders_by_status(1)
```

Simple enough. The first test we call is `get_orders_by_status`, passing as an argument `Status.Received`. Then, we verify that only two orders are returned. For the second test, for the `get_order_by_status` method, like the previous exceptions tests, run the method, passing an invalid argument and then verify that the exception of type `InvalidArgumentError` has been raised.

Getting orders by period

Now, we are going to test the `get_order_by_period` method, which returns a list of orders given an initial and an end date. For this method, we are going to perform the following tests:

- Call the method, passing as arguments, and orders created within that period should be returned
- Call the method, passing as arguments valid dates where we know that no orders were created, which should return an empty result
- Test if an exception is raised when calling the method, passing an invalid start date
- Test if an exception is raised when calling the method, passing an invalid end date

```
    def test_get_orders_by_period(self):

        date_from = timezone.now() - relativedelta(days=1)
        date_to = date_from + relativedelta(days=2)

        orders = Order.objects.get_orders_by_period(date_from, date_to)

        self.assertEqual(3, len(orders))

        date_from = timezone.now() + relativedelta(days=3)
        date_to = date_from + relativedelta(months=1)
```

```
        orders = Order.objects.get_orders_by_period(date_from, date_to)

        self.assertEqual(0, len(orders))

    def test_get_orders_by_period_with_invalid_start_date(self):
        start_date = timezone.now()

        with self.assertRaises(InvalidArgumentError):
            Order.objects.get_orders_by_period(start_date, None)

    def test_get_orders_by_period_with_invalid_end_date(self):
        end_date = timezone.now()

        with self.assertRaises(InvalidArgumentError):
            Order.objects.get_orders_by_period(None, end_date)
```

We start this method by creating `date_from`, which is the current date minus one day. Here, we use the `relativedelta` method of the `python-dateutil` package to perform date operations. Then, we define `date_to`, which is the current date plus two days.

Now that we have our period, we can pass these values as arguments to the `get_orders_by_period` method. In our case, we set up three orders, all created with the current date, so this method call should return exactly three orders.

Then, we define a different period where we know that there won't be any orders. The `date_from` function is defined with the current date plus three days, so `date_from` is the current date plus 1 month.

Calling the method again passing the new values of `date_from` and `date_to` should not return any orders.

The last two tests for `get_orders_by_period` are the same as the exception tests that we implemented previously.

Setting the order's next status

The next method from the `Order` model manager that we are going to create is the `set_next_status` method. The `set_next_status` method is just a method that can be used for convenience and it will set the next status of an order. If you remember, the `Status` enumeration that we created means that every item in the enumeration is set to `auto()`, which means that items in the enumeration will get a numeric sequential number as a value.

When we save an order in the database and set its status to, for example, Status.Processing, the value of the status field in the database will be 2.

The function simply adds 1 to the current order's status, so it goes to the next status item unless the status is Completed; that's the last status of the order's lifecycle.

Now that we have refreshed our memories about how this method works, it is time to create the tests for it, and we will have to perform the following tests:

- That the order gets the next status when set_next_status is called
- Test if an exception will be raised when calling set_next_status and passing as an argument an order with the status Completed
- Test if an exception is raised when passing an invalid order as an argument

```
def test_set_next_status(self):
    order = Order.objects.get(pk=1)

    self.assertTrue(order is not None,
                    msg='The order is None.')

    self.assertEqual(Status.Received.value, order.status,
                     msg='The status should have been
                     Status.Received.')

    Order.objects.set_next_status(order)

    self.assertEqual(Status.Processing.value, order.status,
                     msg='The status should have been
                     Status.Processing.')

def test_set_next_status_on_completed_order(self):
    order = Order.objects.get(pk=2)

    with self.assertRaises(OrderAlreadyCompletedError):
        Order.objects.set_next_status(order)

def test_set_next_status_on_invalid_order(self):
    with self.assertRaises(InvalidArgumentError):
        Order.objects.set_next_status({'order': 1})
```

The first test, `test_set_next_status`, starts by getting the order with an ID equal to 1. Then, it asserts that the order object is not equal to none, and we also assert that the value of the order's status is `Received`. Then, we call the `set_next_status` method, passing the `order` as an argument. Right after that, we assert again to make sure that the status has changed. The test will pass if the order's status is equals to 2, which is `Processing` in the `Status` enumeration.

The other two tests are very similar to the order test where we assert exceptions, but it is worth mentioning that the test `test_set_next_status_on_completed_order` asserts that if we try calling the `set_next_status` on an order that has a status equal to `Status.Completed`, then an exception of type `OrderAlreadyCompletedError` will be raised.

Setting the order's status

Finally, we are going to implement the last tests of the `Order` model manager. We are going to create tests for the `set_status` method. The `set_status` method does exactly what the name implies; it will set a status for a given order. We need to perform the following tests:

- Set a status and verify that the order's status has really changed
- Set the status in an order that is already completed; it should raise an exception of type `OrderAlreadyCompletedError`
- Set the status in an order that is already canceled; it should raise an exception of type `OrderAlreadyCancelledError`
- Call the `set_status` method using an invalid order; it should raise an exception of type `InvalidArgumentError`
- Call the `set_status` method using an invalid status; it should raise an exception of type `InvalidArgumentError`

```
def test_set_status(self):
    order = Order.objects.get(pk=1)

    Order.objects.set_status(order, Status.Processing)

    self.assertEqual(Status.Processing.value, order.status)

def test_set_status_on_completed_order(self):
    order = Order.objects.get(pk=2)

    with self.assertRaises(OrderAlreadyCompletedError):
        Order.objects.set_status(order, Status.Processing)
```

```
def test_set_status_on_cancelled_order(self):
    order = Order.objects.get(pk=1)
    Order.objects.cancel_order(order)

    with self.assertRaises(OrderAlreadyCancelledError):
        Order.objects.set_status(order, Status.Processing)

def test_set_status_with_invalid_order(self):
    with self.assertRaises(InvalidArgumentError):
        Order.objects.set_status(None, Status.Processing)

def test_set_status_with_invalid_status(self):
    order = Order.objects.get(pk=1)

    with self.assertRaises(InvalidArgumentError):
        Order.objects.set_status(order, {'status': 1})
```

We are not going to go through all the tests where we are testing exceptions, because they are similar to the tests that we implemented previously, but it is worth going through the first test. On the test `test_set_status`, it will get the order with an ID equal to 1, which as we defined in the `setUpTestData`, has a status equal to `Status.Received`. We call the `set_status` method passing the order and the new status as arguments, in this case, `Status.Processing`. After setting the new status, we just call `assertEquals` to make sure that the order's status in fact changed to `Status.Processing`.

Creating the order model serializer

We now have everything we need to start creating out API endpoints. In this section, we are going to create endpoints for every method that we implemented in the `Order` manager.

For some of these endpoints, we are going to use the Django REST Framework. The advantage of using the Django REST Framework is that the framework includes a lot of out of the box features. It has different authentication methods, a really robust serialization of objects, and my favorite is that it will give you a web interface where you can browse the API, which also contains a large collection of base classes and mixins when you need to create class-based views.

So, let's dive right into it!

The first thing that we need to do at this point is to create serializer classes for the entities of our model, the `Order`, `OrderCustomer`, and `OrderItem`.

Go ahead and create a file called `serializers.py` in the main `app` directory, and let's start by adding a few import statements:

```
import functools

from rest_framework import serializers

from .models import Order, OrderItems, OrderCustomer
```

We start by importing the `functools` module from the standard library; then, we import the serializer from the `rest_framework` module. We are going to use it to create our model serializers. Lastly, we will import the models that we are going to use to create the serializers, the `Order`, `OrderItems`, and `OrderCustomer`.

The first serializer that we are going to create is the `OrderCustomerSerializer`:

```
class OrderCustomerSerializer(serializers.ModelSerializer):
    class Meta:
        model = OrderCustomer
        fields = ('customer_id', 'email', 'name', )
```

The `OrderCustomerSerializer` inherits from `ModelSerializer` and it is quite simple; it just defines some class metadata. We will set the model, the `OrderCustomer`, and also the property fields which will contain a tuple with the fields, that we are going to serialize.

Then, we create the `OrderItemSerializer`:

```
class OrderItemSerializer(serializers.ModelSerializer):
    class Meta:
        model = OrderItems
        fields = ('name', 'price_per_unit', 'product_id',
'quantity', )
```

The `OrderItemSerializer` is pretty similar to the `OrderCustomerSerializer`. The class also inherits from `ModelSerializer` and defines a couple of metadata properties. The first one is a model, which we set to `OrderItems`, and then the fields with a tuple containing every model field that we want to serialize.

The last serializer that we are going to create is the `OrderSerializer`, so let's start by defining a class called `OrderSerializer`:

```
class OrderSerializer(serializers.ModelSerializer):
    items = OrderItemSerializer(many=True)
    order_customer = OrderCustomerSerializer()
    status = serializers.SerializerMethodField()
```

First, we define two properties. The `items` property is set to `OrderItemSerializer`, which means that it will use that serializer when we need to serialize the JSON data that we are going to send when we want to add new orders. The `items` property refers to the items (the games) that an order contains. Here, we use only one keyword argument (`many=True`). This will tell you that the serializer items will be an array.

The status field is a little bit special; if you remember the status field in the `Order` model, it is defined as a `ChoiceField`. When we save an order in the database, that field will store the value 1 if the order has a status of `Received`, 2 if the status is `Processing`, and so on. When the consumers of our API call the endpoint to get orders, they will be interested in the name of the status and not the number.

So, the solution to this problem is to define the field as `SerializeMethodField`, and then we are going to create a function called `get_status`, which will return the display name of the order's status. We are going to see what the implementation of the `get_status` method looks like in a short while.

We also define the `order_customer` property, which is set to `OrderCustomerSerializer`, and that means that the framework will use the `OrderCustomerSerializer` class when trying to deserialize the JSON object we send when trying to add a new order.

Then, we define a `Meta` class, so that we can add some metadata information to the serializer class:

```
class Meta:
    depth = 1
    model = Order
    fields = ('items', 'total', 'order_customer',
              'created_at', 'id', 'status', )
```

The first property, `depth`, specifies the depth of the relationships that should be traversed before the serialization. In this case, it is set to `1`, because when fetching an order object, we also want to have information about the customers and items. Like the other serializers, we set the model to `Order` and the fields property specifies which fields will be serialized and deserialized.

Then, we implement the `get_status` method:

```
def get_status(self, obj):
    return obj.get_status_display()
```

This is the method that will get the display value for the `ChoiceField` status. This will override the default behavior and return the result of the `get_status_display()` function instead.

The `_created_order_item` method is just a helper method which we are going to use to create and prepare the order item's objects prior to performing a bulk insert:

```
def _create_order_item(self, item, order):
    item['order'] = order
    return OrderItems(**item)
```

Here, we are going to get two arguments. The first argument will be a dictionary with the data about the `OrderItem` and an `order` argument with an object of type `Order`. First, we update the dictionary passed in the first argument, adding the `order` object, then we call the `OrderItem` constructor, passing the items as an argument in the `item` dictionary.

I am going to show you what that's used for a short while. Now that we have got to the core of this serializer, we are going to implement the `create` method, which will be a method that will be called automatically every time we call the serializer's `save` method:

```
def create(self, validated_data):
    validated_customer = validated_data.pop('order_customer')
    validated_items = validated_data.pop('items')

    customer = OrderCustomer.objects.create(**validated_customer)

    validated_data['order_customer'] = customer
    order = Order.objects.create(**validated_data)

    mapped_items = map(
        functools.partial(
        self._create_order_item, order=order), validated_items
    )
```

```
OrderItems.objects.bulk_create(mapped_items)

return order
```

So, the create method will be called automatically when calling the `save` method, and it will get the `validated_data` as an argument. The `validated_date` is a validated, de-serialized order data. It will look similar to the following data:

```
{
    "items": [
        {
            "name": "Prod 001",
            "price_per_unit": 10,
            "product_id": 1,
            "quantity": 2
        },
        {
            "name": "Prod 002",
            "price_per_unit": 12,
            "product_id": 2,
            "quantity": 2
        }
    ],
    "order_customer": {
        "customer_id": 14,
        "email": "test@test.com",
        "name": "Test User"
    },
    "order_id": 1,
    "status": 4,
    "total": "190.00"
}
```

As you can see, in this JSON, we are passing all the information at once. Here, we have the `order`, the `items` property, which is a list of order items, and the `order_customer`, which contains information about the customer who submitted the order.

Since we have to perform the creation of these objects individually, we first pop the `order_customer` and the `items` so we have three different objects. The first, `validated_customer`, will only contain data related to the person who made the order. The `validated_items` object will only contain data related to each item of the order, and finally, the `validated_data` object will only contain data related to the order itself.

After splitting the data, we can now start adding the objects. We start by creating an
`OrderCustomer`:

```
customer = OrderCustomer.objects.create(**validated_customer)
```

Then, we can create the order. The `Order` has a foreign key field called `order_customer`,
which is the customer that is connected to that particular Order. What we need to do is
create a new item in the `validated_data` dictionary with a key called `order_customer`,
and set its value to the customer that we just created:

```
validated_data['order_customer'] = customer
order = Order.objects.create(**validated_data)
```

Lastly, we are going to add `OrderItems`. Now, to add the order items, we need to do a few
things. The `validated_items` variable is a list of items that belong to the underlying
order, and we need to first set the order to each one of these items, and create an
`OrderItem` object for each one of the items on the list.
There are different ways of performing this operation. You could do it in two parts; for
example, first loop through the item's list and set the order property, then loop through the
list again and create the `OrderItem` objects. However, that wouldn't be so elegant, would
it?

A better approach here is to take advantage of the fact that Python is a multi-paradigm
programming language, and we can solve this problem in a more functional way:

```
mapped_items = map(
    functools.partial(
        self._create_order_item, order=order), validated_items
)

OrderItems.objects.bulk_create(mapped_items)
```

Here, we make use of one of the built-in function maps. The `map` function will apply a
function that I specify as the first argument to an iterable that is passed as the second
argument, which then returns an iterable with the results.
The function that we are going to pass as the first argument to map is a function
called `partial`, from the `functools` module. The `partial` function is a high-order
function, meaning that it will return another function (the one in the first argument) and
will add the argument and keyword arguments to its signature. In the preceding code, it
will return `self._create_order_item`, and the first argument will be an item of the
iterable `validated_items`. The second argument is the order that we created previously.

After that, the value of `mapped_items` should contain a list of `OrderItem` objects, and the only thing left to do is call `bulk_create`, which will insert all the items on the list for us.

Next up, we are going to create the views.

Creating the views

Before we create the views, we are going to create some helper classes and functions that will make the code in the view simpler and clean. Go ahead and create a file called `view_helper.py` in the main app directory, and as usual, let's start by including the import statements:

```
from rest_framework import generics, status
from rest_framework.response import Response

from django.http import HttpResponse

from .exceptions import InvalidArgumentError
from .exceptions import OrderAlreadyCancelledError
from .exceptions import OrderAlreadyCompletedError

from .serializers import OrderSerializer
```

Here, we import some things from the Django REST Framework, the main one being the generic, which contains definitions for the generic view classes that we are going to use to create our own custom views. The status contains all the HTTP status codes, which are very useful when sending the response back to the client. Then, we import the `Response` class, which will allow us to send content to the client that can be rendered in different content types, for example, JSON and XML.

Then, we import the `HttpResponse` from Django with its equivalent of `Response` in the rest framework.

We also import all the custom exceptions that we implemented previously, so we can handle the data properly and send useful error messages to the client when something goes wrong.

Lastly, we import the `OrderSerializer`, which we will use for serialization, deserialization, and the validation model.

The first class that we are going to create is the `OrderListAPIBaseView` class, which will serve as a base class for all the views that will return a list of content to the client:

```
class OrderListAPIBaseView(generics.ListAPIView):
    serializer_class = OrderSerializer
    lookup_field = ''

    def get_queryset(self, lookup_field_id):
        pass

    def list(self, request, *args, **kwargs):
        try:
            result =
self.get_queryset(kwargs.get(self.lookup_field, None))
        except Exception as err:
            return Response(err,
status=status.HTTP_400_BAD_REQUEST)

        serializer = OrderSerializer(result, many=True)
        return Response(serializer.data, status=status.HTTP_200_OK)
```

The `OrderListAPIBaseView` inherits from generics. `ListAPIView` provides us with get and list methods, which we can override to add functionality which meets our requirements.

The class starts by defining two properties; `serializer_class`, which is set to `OrderSerializer`, and the `lookup_field`, which in this case we set to empty string. We will override this value in the child classes. Then, we define the `get_queryset` method, and that is also going to be overridden in the child classes.

Lastly, we implement the list method, which will first run the `get_queryset` method to get the data that will be returned to the user. If an error occurs, it will return a response with status `400` (BAD REQUEST), otherwise, it will use the `OrderSerializer` to serialize the data. The `result` argument is the `QuerySet` result returned by the `get_queryset` method, and the `many` keyword argument tells the serializer that we will serialize a list of items.

When the data is serialized properly, we send a response with status `200` (OK) with the results of the query.

The idea of this base class is that all the children classes will only need to implement the `get_queryset` method, which will keep the view classes small and neat.

Now, we are going to add a function that will help us with the methods that will perform a POST request. Let's go ahead and add a function called `set_status_handler`:

```
def set_status_handler(set_status_delegate):
    try:
        set_status_delegate()
    except (
            InvalidArgumentError,
            OrderAlreadyCancelledError,
            OrderAlreadyCompletedError) as err:
        return HttpResponse(err, status=status.HTTP_400_BAD_REQUEST)

    return HttpResponse(status=status.HTTP_204_NO_CONTENT)
```

This function is very simple; it will just get a function as an argument. Run the function; if one of the exceptions occurs, it will return a 400 (BAD REQUEST) response back to the client, otherwise, it will return a 204 (NO CONTENT) response.

Adding views

Now, it is time to start adding the views! Open the `views.py` file in the main `app` directory, and let's add some import statements:

```
from django.http import HttpResponse
from django.shortcuts import get_object_or_404

from rest_framework import generics, status
from rest_framework.response import Response


from .models import Order
from .status import Status
from .view_helper import OrderListAPIBaseView
from .view_helper import set_status_handler
from .serializers import OrderSerializer
```

First, we will import the `HttpReponse` from the `django.http` module and `get_object_or_404` from the `django.shortcuts` module. The latter is just a helper function that will get an object, and in case it cannot find it, it will return a response with the status 440 (NOT FOUND).

Then, we import generics for creating generic views and statuses, and from the `rest_framework`, we import the `Response` class.

Lastly, we import some of the models, helper methods, and functions, and the serializer that we are going to be using in the views.

We should be ready to start creating the views. Let's create a view that will get all the orders for a given customer:

```
class OrdersByCustomerView(OrderListAPIBaseView):
    lookup_field = 'customer_id'

    def get_queryset(self, customer_id):
        return
Order.objects.get_all_orders_by_customer(customer_id)
```

Nice! So, we created a class that inherits from the base class (OrderListAPIBaseView), which we created in the view_helpers.py, and since we have already implemented the list method, the only method that we needed to implement here was the get_queryset. The get_queryset method gets a customer_id as an argument and simply calls the get_all_orders_by_customer that we created in the Order model manager, passing the customer_id.
We also defined the value of the lookup_field, which will be used to get the value of the keyword argument that is passed on to the kwargs of the list method on the base class.

Let's add two more views to get the incomplete and complete orders:

```
class IncompleteOrdersByCustomerView(OrderListAPIBaseView):
    lookup_field = 'customer_id'

    def get_queryset(self, customer_id):
        return Order.objects.get_customer_incomplete_orders(
            customer_id
        )


class CompletedOrdersByCustomerView(OrderListAPIBaseView):
    lookup_field = 'customer_id'

    def get_queryset(self, customer_id):
        return Order.objects.get_customer_completed_orders(
            customer_id
        )
```

Pretty much the same as the first view that we implemented, we define the lookup_field and override the get_queryset to call the appropriated method in the Order model manager.

Now, we are going to add a view that will get a list of orders when given a specific status:

```
class OrderByStatusView(OrderListAPIBaseView):
    lookup_field = 'status_id'

    def get_queryset(self, status_id):
        return Order.objects.get_orders_by_status(
            Status(status_id)
        )
```

As you can see here, we are defining the `lookup_field` as `status_id` and we override the `get_queryset` to call `get_orders_by_status`, passing the status value.

Here, we use `Status(status_id)`, so we pass the `Enum` item and not only the ID.

All the views that we implemented so far will only accept `GET` requests and it will return a list of orders. Now, we are going to implement a view that supports `POST` requests so we are able to receive new orders:

```
class CreateOrderView(generics.CreateAPIView):

    def post(self, request, *arg, **args):
        serializer = OrderSerializer(data=request.data)

        if serializer.is_valid():
            order = serializer.save()
            return Response(
                {'order_id': order.id},
                status=status.HTTP_201_CREATED)

        return Response(status=status.HTTP_400_BAD_REQUEST)
```

Now, this class differs a bit from the previous ones that we created, the base class being generics. `CreateAPIView` provides us with a `post` method, so we override that method in order to add the logic that we need. First, we get the request's data and pass it as an argument to the `OrderSerializer` class; it will deserialize the data and set it to the serializer variable. Then, we call the method `is_valid()`, which will validate the received data. If the request's data is not valid, we return a `400` response (`BAD REQUEST`), otherwise, we go ahead and call the `save()` method. This method will internally call the `create` method on the serializer, and it will create the new order along with the new order's customer and the order's items. If everything goes well, we return a `202` response (`CREATED`) together with the ID of the newly created order.

Now, we are going to create three functions that will handle the order canceling, setting the next order's status, and lastly, setting a specific order's status:

```
def cancel_order(request, order_id):
    order = get_object_or_404(Order, order_id=order_id)

    return set_status_handler(
        lambda: Order.objects.cancel_order(order)
    )


def set_next_status(request, order_id):
    order = get_object_or_404(Order, order_id=order_id)

    return set_status_handler(
        lambda: Order.objects.set_next_status(order)
    )


def set_status(request, order_id, status_id):
    order = get_object_or_404(Order, order_id=order_id)

    try:
        status = Status(status_id)
    except ValueError:
        return HttpResponse(
            'The status value is invalid.',
            status=status.HTTP_400_BAD_REQUEST)

    return set_status_handler(
        lambda: Order.objects.set_status(order, status)
    )
```

As you can see, we are not using the Django REST framework class-based views here. We are just using regular functions. The first one, the `cancel_order` function, gets two parameters—the request and the `order_id`. We start by using the shortcut function, `get_object_or_404`. The `get_object_or_404` function returns a 404 response (NOT FOUND) if it cannot find the object matching the criteria passed in the second argument. Otherwise, it will return the object.

Then, we use the helper function `set_status_handler` that we implemented in the `view_helpers.py` file. This function gets another function as an argument. So, we are passing a `lambda` function that will execute the method in the `Order` model manager that we want. In this case, when the `lambda` function is executed, it will execute the `cancel_order` method that we defined in the `Order` model manager, passing the order that we want to cancel.

The `set_next_status` function is quite similar, but instead of calling the `cancel_order` inside of the `lambda` function, we will call `set_next_status`, passing the order that we want to set to the next status.

The `set_status` function contains a bit more logic in it, but it is also quite simple. This function will get two arguments, the `order_id` and the `status_id`. First, we get the order object, then we look up the status using the `status_id`. If the status doesn't exist, a `ValueError` exception will be raised and then we return a `400` response (`BAD REQUEST`). Otherwise, we call the `set_status_handle`, passing a `lambda` function that will execute the `set_status` function passing the order and the status objects.

Setting up the service URLs

Now that we have all the views in place, it is a good time to start setting up the URLs that the users of our order service can call to fetch and modify orders. Let's go ahead and open the `urls.py` file in the main `app` directory; first, we need to import all the view classes and functions that we are going to use:

```
from .views import (
    cancel_order,
    set_next_status,
    set_status,
    OrdersByCustomerView,
    IncompleteOrdersByCustomerView,
    CompletedOrdersByCustomerView,
    OrderByStatusView,
    CreateOrderView,
)
```

Perfect! Now, we can start adding the URLs:

```
urlpatterns = [
    path(
        r'order/add/',
        CreateOrderView.as_view()
    ),
    path(
        r'customer/<int:customer_id>/orders/get/',
        OrdersByCustomerView.as_view()
    ),
    path(
        r'customer/<int:customer_id>/orders/incomplete/get/',
        IncompleteOrdersByCustomerView.as_view()
    ),
    path(
        r'customer/<int:customer_id>/orders/complete/get/',
        CompletedOrdersByCustomerView.as_view()
    ),
    path(
        r'order/<int:order_id>/cancel',
        cancel_order
    ),
    path(
        r'order/status/<int:status_id>/get/',
        OrderByStatusView.as_view()
    ),
    path(
        r'order/<int:order_id>/status/<int:status_id>/set/',
        set_status
    ),
    path(
        r'order/<int:order_id>/status/next/',
        set_next_status
    ),
]
```

To add new URLs, we need to use the `path function` to pass the first argument, the URL. The second argument is the function that will be executed when a request is sent to the URL specified by the first argument. Every URL that we create has to be added to the `urlspatterns` list. Note that Django 2 simplified how parameters were added to the URL. Previously, you would need to some using regular expressions; now, you can just follow the notation `<type:param>`.

Before we try this out, we have to open the `urls.py` file, but this time in the order directory because we need to include the URLs that we just created.

The `urls.py` file should look similar to this:

```
"""order URL Configuration

The `urlpatterns` list routes URLs to views. For more information
please see:
    https://docs.djangoproject.com/en/2.0/topics/http/urls/
Examples:
Function views
    1. Add an import: from my_app import views
    2. Add a URL to urlpatterns: path('', views.home, name='home')
Class-based views
    1. Add an import: from other_app.views import Home
    2. Add a URL to urlpatterns: path('', Home.as_view(),
name='home')
Including another URLconf
    1. Import the include() function: from django.urls import
include, path
    2. Add a URL to urlpatterns: path('blog/',
include('blog.urls'))
"""
from django.contrib import admin
from django.urls import path, include


urlpatterns = [
    path('admin/', admin.site.urls),
]
```

Now, we want all the URLs that we defined on the main app to be under `/api/`. To achieve this, the only thing we need to do is create a new route and include the URLs from the main app. Add the following code in the `urlpatterns` list:

```
path('api/', include('main.urls')),
```

And let's not forget to import the `include` function:

```
from django.urls import include
```

The order service won't be public when we deploy it to the AWS; however as an extra security measure, we are going to enable token authentication for this service.

To call the service's APIs, we will have to send an authentication token. Let's go ahead and enable it. Open the `settings.py` file in the `order` directory and add the following content:

```
REST_FRAMEWORK = {
    'DEFAULT_PERMISSION_CLASSES': (
        'rest_framework.permissions.IsAuthenticated',
    ),
    'DEFAULT_AUTHENTICATION_CLASSES': (
        'rest_framework.authentication.TokenAuthentication',
    )
}
```

You can place this right after `INSTALLED_APPS`.

The `DEFAULT_PERMISSION_CLASSES` function defines the global permission policy. Here, we set it to `rest_framework.permissions.IsAuthenticated`, which means that it will deny access to any unauthorized user.

The `DEFAULT_AUTHENTICATION_CLASSES` function specifies the global authentication schemas. In this case, we are going to use token authentication.

Then, in `INSTALLED_APPS`, we need to include the `rest_framework.authtoken`. Your `INSTALLED_APPS` should look like this:

```
INSTALLED_APPS = [
    'django.contrib.admin',
    'django.contrib.auth',
    'django.contrib.contenttypes',
    'django.contrib.sessions',
    'django.contrib.messages',
    'django.contrib.staticfiles',
    'main',
    'rest_framework',
    'rest_framework.authtoken',
]
```

Perfect! Save the file, and on the terminal, run the following command:

```
python manage.py migrate
```

The Django REST framework has out of the box views, so the users can call and acquire a token. However, for simplicity, we are going to create a user who can have access to the APIs. Then, we can manually create an authentication token that can be used to do the request to the order service APIs.

Let's go ahead and create this user. Start the service with the following command:

```
python manage.py runserver
```

And browse to `https://localhost:8000/admin`.

Under the **AUTHENTICATION AND AUTHORIZATION** tab, you will see the `Users` model. Click on **Add** and create a user with the username `api_user`. When the user is created, browse back to the admin first page and under the **AUTH TOKEN,** click on **Add**. Select the `api_user` in the drop-down menu and click **SAVE**. You should see a page like the following:

Copy the key and let's create a small script just to add an order so we can test the APIs.

Create a file called `send_order.py`; it can be placed anywhere you want as long as you have the virtual environment activated, since we are going to use the package requests to send the order to the order services. Add the following content to the `send_order.py` file:

```python
import json
import sys
import argparse
from http import HTTPStatus

import requests


def setUpData(order_id):
    data = {
        "items": [
            {
```

```
                    "name": "Prod 001",
                    "price_per_unit": 10,
                    "product_id": 1,
                    "quantity": 2
                },
                {
                    "name": "Prod 002",
                    "price_per_unit": 12,
                    "product_id": 2,
                    "quantity": 2
                }
            ],
            "order_customer": {
                "customer_id": 14,
                "email": "test@test.com",
                "name": "Test User"
            },
            "order_id": order_id,
            "status": 1,
            "total": "190.00"
        }

        return data


def send_order(data):

    response = requests.put(
        'http://127.0.0.1:8000/api/order/add/',
        data=json.dumps(data))

    if response.status_code == HTTPStatus.NO_CONTENT:
        print('Ops! Something went wrong!')
        sys.exit(1)

    print('Request was successfull')


if __name__ == '__main__':

    parser = argparse.ArgumentParser(
        description='Create a order for test')

    parser.add_argument('--orderid',
                        dest='order_id',
                        required=True,
                        help='Specify the the order id')
```

```
    args = parser.parse_args()

    data = setUpData(args.order_id)
    send_order(data)
```

Great! Now, we can start the development server:

python manage.py runserver

In another window, we will run the script that we just created:

python send_order.py --orderid 10

You can see the results as follows:

What? Something went wrong here, can you guess what it is? Note the log message that was printed in the screenshot in the terminal where I have the Django development server running:

```
[21/Jan/2018 09:30:37] "PUT /api/order/add/ HTTP/1.1" 401 58
```

Ok, it says here that the server has received a PUT request to `/api/order/add/`, and one thing to notice here is that code `401` signifies `Unauthorized`. This means that the settings that we have added in the `settings.py` file worked fine. To call the APIs, we need to be authenticated, and we are using token authentication.

To create a token for a user, we need to log in in the Django administration UI. There, we will find the **AUTH TOKEN** section as follows:

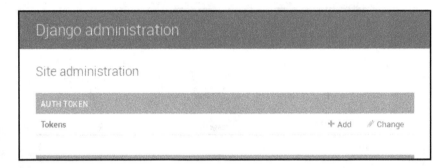

Click on that green plus sign on the right-hand side. Then, you can select the user you wish to create a token for and when you are ready, click save. After that, you will see a list of tokens that have been created:

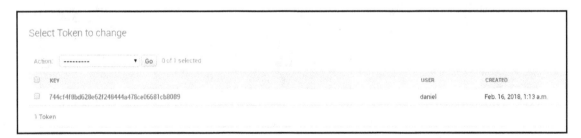

That key is the key you want to send in the request's **HEADER**.

Now that we have a token, we can modify the `send_order.py` script and add the token information to the request, so on the top of the `send_order` function, add the following code:

```
token = '744cf4f8bd628e62f248444a478ce06681cb8089'

headers = {
    'Authorization': f'Token {token}',
    'Content-type': 'application/json'
}
```

The token variable is the token that we created for the user `api_user`. To get the token, just log in to the Django admin UI and under **AUTH TOKEN,** you will see the tokens that have been created. Just remove the token that I added here and replace it with the one that was generated for the `api_user` on your application.

Then, we need to send the headers along with the request. Change the following code:

```
response = requests.put(
    'http://127.0.0.1:8000/api/order/add/',
    data=json.dumps(data))
```

Replace it with this:

```
response = requests.put(
    'http://127.0.0.1:8000/api/order/add/',
    headers=headers,
    data=json.dumps(data))
```

Now, we can go to the terminal and run our code again. You should see an output similar to the output shown in the following screenshot:

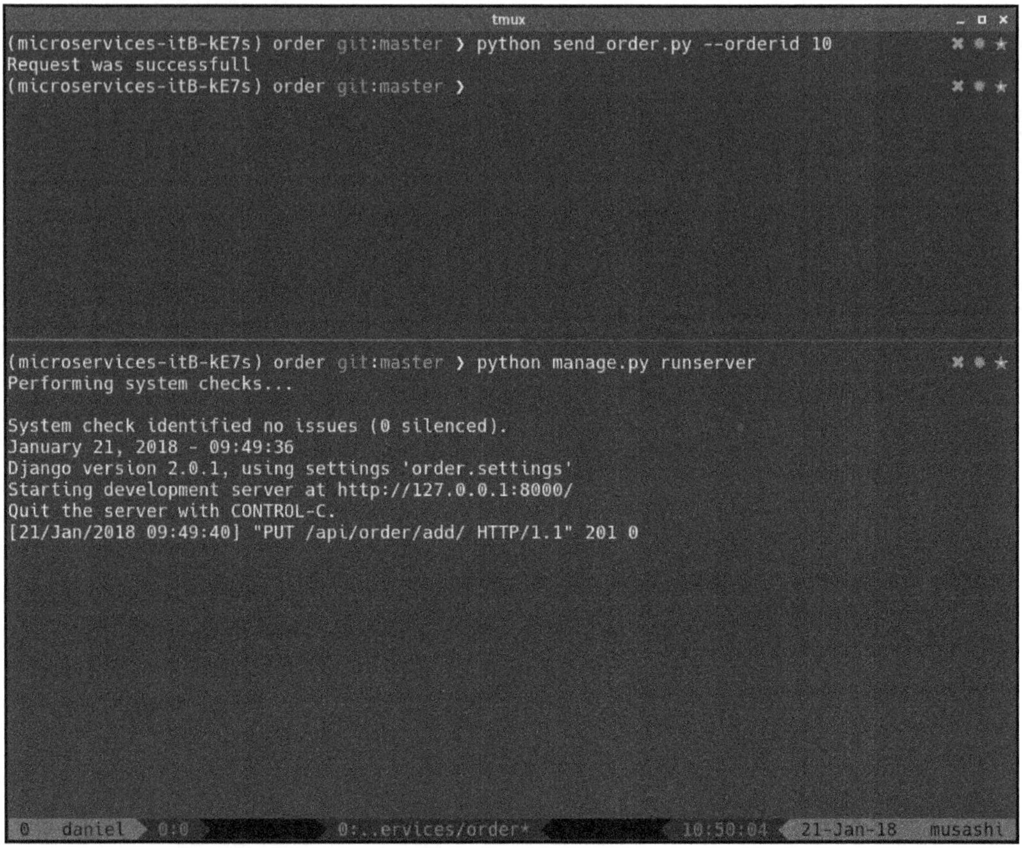

Note that now, we get the following log message:

```
[21/Jan/2018 09:49:40] "PUT /api/order/add/ HTTP/1.1" 201 0
```

This means that the authentication works properly. Go ahead and take the time to explore the Django admin UI and verify that now we have one customer and one order with a couple of items created on our database.

Let's try some of the other endpoints to see if they are working as expected. For example, we can get all the orders for that customer that we just created.

You can perform small tests to the endpoints using any tool you want. There are a few very handy browser plugins that you can install, or, if you are like me and like to do everything on the terminal, you can use cURL. Alternatively if you want to try to build something with Python, there is the `httpie` package that you can install using pip. Use the `pip install httpie --upgrade --user` command to install `httpie` on your local directory under `./local/bin`. So, don't forget to add this directory to your PATH. I like to use `httpie` instead of cURL because `httpie` shows a nice and formatted JSON output so I can get a better view of the response that I'm getting back from the endpoint.

So, let's try the first `GET` endpoint that we created:

```
http http://127.0.0.1:8000/api/customer/1/orders/get/
'Authorization: Token 744cf4f8bd628e62f248444a478ce06681cb8089'
```

And you should see the following output:

```
HTTP/1.1 200 OK
Allow: GET, HEAD, OPTIONS
Content-Length: 270
Content-Type: application/json
Date: Sun, 21 Jan 2018 10:03:00 GMT
Server: WSGIServer/0.2 CPython/3.6.2
Vary: Accept
X-Frame-Options: SAMEORIGIN

[
    {
        "items": [
            {
                "name": "Prod 001",
                "price_per_unit": 10,
                "product_id": 1,
                "quantity": 2
            },
            {
                "name": "Prod 002",
                "price_per_unit": 12,
                "product_id": 2,
                "quantity": 2
            }
        ],
        "order_customer": {
            "customer_id": 14,
            "email": "test@test.com",
```

```
                "name": "Test User"
            },
            "order_id": 10,
            "status": 1,
            "total": "190.00"
        }
    ]
```

Perfect! Just as expected. Go ahead and try the other endpoints!

Next up, we are going back to the online video game store and send the order.

Integration with the game online store

Now that we have the service up and running, we are ready to finish the online video game store project from Chapter 7, *Online Video Game Store with Django*. We are not going to perform many changes, but there are two improvements that we are going to do:

- At the moment, in the online video game store, it is not possible to submit orders. The users of our site can only add items to the cart, visualize, and edit the cart's items. We are going to finish that implementation and create a view so that we can submit the order.
- We are going to implement one more view where we can see the order history.

So, let's get right to it!

The first change that we are going to do is add the authentication token for the api_user that we created in the service orders. We also want to add the base URL to the order service, so it will be easier for us to build up the URLs that we need to perform the requests. Open the settings.py file in the gamestore directory and add these two constant variables:

```
ORDER_SERVICE_AUTHTOKEN =
'744cf4f8bd628e62f248444a478ce06681cb8089'
ORDER_SERVICE_BASEURL = 'http://127.0.0.1:8001'
```

It does not matter where you place this code, but maybe it's a good idea to just place it at the end of the file.

The next change that we are going to do is add a `namedtuple` called `OrderItem`, just to help us prepare the order's data so it is compatible with the format that the order service is expecting. Open the `models.py` file in the `gamestore/main` directory and add `import`:

```
from collections import namedtuple
```

Another change to the models file is that we are going to add a new method in the `ShoppingCartManager` class called `empty`, so that when it's called, it will remove all the cart's items. Inside of the `ShoppingCartManager` class, add the following method:

```
def empty(self, cart):
    cart_items = ShoppingCartItem.objects.filter(
        cart__id=cart.id
    )

    for item in cart_items:
        item.delete()
```

At the end of the file, let's create the `namedtuple`:

```
OrderItem = namedtuple('OrderItem',
                       'name price_per_unit product_id quantity')
```

Next up, we are going to change the `cart.html` template. Locate the `send order` button:

```
<button class='btn btn-primary'>
  <i class="fa fa-check" aria-hidden="true"></i>
   SEND ORDER
</button>
```

Replace it with the following:

```
<form action="/cart/send">
  {% csrf_token %}
  <button class='btn btn-primary'>
    <i class="fa fa-check" aria-hidden="true"></i>
     SEND ORDER
  </button>
</form>
```

Nice! We just created a form around the button and added the Cross-Site Request Forgery token within the form, so that when we click the button, it will send a request to `cart/send`.

Let's add the new URLs. Open the `urls.py` file in the main `app` directory, and let's add two new URLs:

```
path(r'cart/send', views.send_cart),
path(r'my-orders/', views.my_orders),
```

You can place these two URL definitions right after the definition of the `/cart/` URL.

Open the `views.py` file and add some new imports:

```
import json
import requests
from http import HTTPStatus
from django.core.serializers.json import DjangoJSONEncoder
from gamestore import settings
```

Then, we add a function that will help us with the serialization of the order data to be sent to the order service:

```python
def _prepare_order_data(cart):

    cart_items = ShoppingCartItem.objects.values_list(
        'game__name',
        'price_per_unit',
        'game__id',
        'quantity').filter(cart__id=cart.id)

    order = cart_items.aggregate(
        total_order=Sum(F('price_per_unit') * F('quantity'),
output_field=DecimalField(decimal_places=2))
        )

    order_items = [OrderItem(*x)._asdict() for x in cart_items]

    order_customer = {
        'customer_id': cart.user.id,
        'email': cart.user.email,
        'name': f'{cart.user.first_name} {cart.user.last_name}'
    }

    order_dict = {
        'items': order_items,
        'order_customer': order_customer,
        'total': order['total_order']
    }

    return json.dumps(order_dict, cls=DjangoJSONEncoder)
```

Now, we have two more views to add, the first being the `send_order`:

```
@login_required
def send_cart(request):
    cart = ShoppingCart.objects.get(user_id=request.user.id)

    data = _prepare_order_data(cart)

    headers = {
        'Authorization': f'Token
{settings.ORDER_SERVICE_AUTHTOKEN}',
        'Content-type': 'application/json'
    }

    service_url =
f'{settings.ORDER_SERVICE_BASEURL}/api/order/add/'

    response = requests.post(
        service_url,
        headers=headers,
        data=data)

    if HTTPStatus(response.status_code) is HTTPStatus.CREATED:
        request_data = json.loads(response.text)
        ShoppingCart.objects.empty(cart)
        messages.add_message(
            request,
            messages.INFO,
            ('We received your order!'
             'ORDER ID: {}').format(request_data['order_id']))
    else:
        messages.add_message(
            request,
            messages.ERROR,
            ('Unfortunately, we could not receive your order.'
             ' Try again later.'))

    return HttpResponseRedirect(reverse_lazy('user-cart'))
```

Next is the `my_orders` view, which will be the new view that returns the order history:

```
@login_required
def my_orders(request):
    headers = {
        'Authorization': f'Token
{settings.ORDER_SERVICE_AUTHTOKEN}',
        'Content-type': 'application/json'
    }
```

```
    get_order_endpoint =
f'/api/customer/{request.user.id}/orders/get/'
    service_url =
f'{settings.ORDER_SERVICE_BASEURL}{get_order_endpoint}'

    response = requests.get(
        service_url,
        headers=headers
    )

    if HTTPStatus(response.status_code) is HTTPStatus.OK:
        request_data = json.loads(response.text)
        context = {'orders': request_data}
    else:
        messages.add_message(
            request,
            messages.ERROR,
            ('Unfortunately, we could not retrieve your orders.'
             ' Try again later.'))
        context = {'orders': []}

    return render(request, 'main/my-orders.html', context)
```

We need to create the `my-orders.html` file, which is going to be the template that is rendered by the `my_orders` view. Create a new file called `my-orders.html` in the `main/templates/main/` directory with the following contents:

```
{% extends 'base.html' %}

{% block 'content' %}

<h3>Order history</h3>

{% for order in orders %}

<div class="order-container">
  <div><strong>Order ID:</strong> {{order.id}}</div>
  <div><strong>Create date:</strong> {{ order.created_at }}</div>
  <div><strong>Status:</strong> <span class="label label-
success">{{order.status}}</span></div>
  <div class="table-container">
    <table class="table table-striped">
      <thead>
        <tr>
          <th>Product name</th>
          <th>Quantity</th>
          <th>Price per unit</th>
```

```
        </tr>
      </thead>
      <tbody>
        {% for item in order.items %}
        <tr>
          <td>{{item.name}}</td><td>{{item.quantity}}</td>
          <td>${{item.price_per_unit}}</td>
        </tr>
        {% endfor %}
      </tbody>
    </table>
  </div>
  <div><strong>Total amount:</strong>{{order.total}}</div>
  <hr/>
</div>
{% endfor %}
{% endblock %}
```

This template is very basic; it is just looping through the orders and then looping the items and building a HTML table with the item's information.

We need to do some changes in `site.css`, where we have the custom styling of the online video game store. Open the `site.css` file in the `static/styles` folder and let's do some modifications. First, locate this code, which is shown as follows:

```
.nav.navbar-nav .fa-home,
.nav.navbar-nav .fa-shopping-cart {
    font-size: 1.5em;
}
```

Replace it with the following:

```
.nav.navbar-nav .fa-home,
.nav.navbar-nav .fa-shopping-cart,
.nav.navbar-nav .fa-truck {
    font-size: 1.5em;
}
```

At the end of this file, we can add stylings that are specific to the order history page:

```
.order-container {
    border: 1px solid #000;
    margin: 20px;
    padding: 10px;
}
```

Now, we are going to add one more menu option that will be a link to the new my orders page. Open the base.html file in the templates directory in the applications root directory, and locate the menu option CART:

```
<li>
  <a href="/cart/">
    <i class="fa fa-shopping-cart" aria-hidden="true"></i> CART
  </a>
</li>
```

Right after the closing </li> tag, add the following code:

```
<li>
  <a href="/my-orders/">
    <i class="fa fa-truck" aria-hidden="true"></i> ORDERS
  </a>
</li>
```

Finally, the last change that we are going to do is improve the layout of error messages that we show in the UI. Locate this code at the end of the base.html file:

```
{% if messages %}
  {% for message in messages %}
    {{message}}
    </div>
  {% endfor %}
{% endif %}
```

Replace it with the following code:

```
{% if messages %}
  {% for message in messages %}
    {% if message.tags == 'error' %}
      <div class="alert alert-danger" role="alert">
    {% else %}
      <div class="alert alert-info" role="alert">
    {% endif %}
    {{message}}
    </div>
  {% endfor %}
{% endif %}
```

Testing the integration

We have everything in place. Now, we need to start both the website and the services so we can verify if everything is working properly.

One thing to keep in mind is that for testing, we will need to run the Django application in different ports. We can run the website (game online store) using the default port 800, and for the order services, we can use port 8001.

Open two terminals; in one terminal, we are going to start the online video game store:

```
python manage.py runserver
```

And, on the second terminal, we are going to start the order service:

```
python manage.py runserver 127.0.0.1:8001
```

Great! Open the browser and head to `http://localhost:8000` and log in with our credentials. After logging in, you will notice that a few things are different. Now, there is a new option in the top menu called ORDERS. It should be empty, so go ahead and add a few items to the cart. When you are done, go to the cart view and click on the send order button.

If everything went right, you should see a notification at the top of the page, as follows:

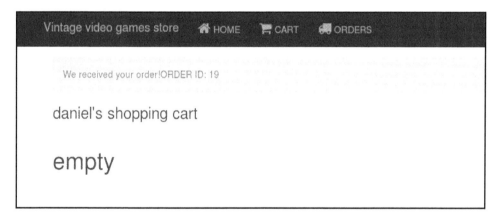

Perfect! It worked just as expected. Notice that after sending the order to the order service, the shopping cart got emptied as well.

Now, click on the ORDERS option on the top menu, and you should see the order that we just submitted:

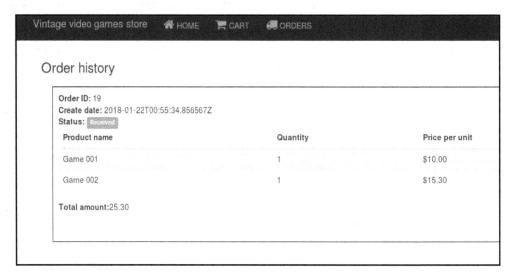

Deploying to AWS

Now, it is time to show the world the work that we have been doing so far.

We are going to deploy the gamestore Django application and also the order service to EC2 instances in Amazon Web services.

 This section is not about configuring Virtual Private Cloud, Security groups, Routing tables, and EC2 instances. Packt has plenty of excellent books and videos available that talk about this topic.

Instead, we will assume that you already have your environment set up, and focus on:

- Deploying the application
- Installing all necessary dependencies
- Installing and using gunicorn
- Installing and configuring nginx

My AWS setup is quite simple, but it definitely works for more complex setups. Right now, I have one VPC with one subnet and two EC2 instances on it (`gamestore` and order-service). See the following screenshot:

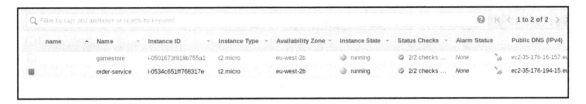

We can start with the `gamestore` application; connect via ssh to the EC2 instance that you wish to deploy the game online application on. Remember that to `ssh` in one of those instances, you will need to have the `.pem` file:

```
ssh -i gamestore-keys.pem ec2-user@35.176.16.157
```

We will start by updating any package that we have installed on that machine; it is not required, but it is a good practice since some of the packages may have security fixes and performance improvements that you probably want to have on your installs. Amazon Linux uses the `yum` package manager, so we run the following command:

```
sudo yum update
```

Just answer yes `y` to any package that needs an update.

These EC2 instances do not have Python installed by default, so we need to install it as well:

```
sudo yum install python36.x86_64 python36-pip.noarch python36-
setuptools.noarch
```

We also need to install `nginx`:

```
sudo yum install nginx
```

Then, we install our project dependencies:

```
sudo pip-3.6 install django requests pillow gunicorn
```

Perfect! Now, we can copy our application, exit this instance, and from our local machine, run the following command:

```
scp -R -i gamestore-keys.pem ./gamestore ec2-user@35.176.16.157:~/gamestore
```

This command will recursively copy all the files from the gamestore directory on our local machine over to our home directory in the EC2 instance.

Modifying the settings.py file

There is one thing we have to change here. In the settings.py file, there is a list called ALLOWED_HOSTS, which was empty when we created the Django project. We will need to add the IP address of the EC2 that we are deploying the application to; in my case, it would be:

```
ALLOWED_HOSTS=["35.176.16.157"]
```

We also need to change the ORDER_SERVICE_BASEURL that we defined at the end of the file. It needs to be the address of the instance that we are going to deploy to the order service. In my case, the IP is 35.176.194.15, so my variable will look like this:

```
ORDER_SERVICE_BASEURL = "http://35.176.194.15"
```

We are going to create a folder to keep the application since it is not a good idea to keep the application running in the ec2-user folder. So, we are going to create a new folder in the root directory called app and copy the gamestore directory over to the newly created directory:

```
sudo mkdir /app && sudo cp -R ./gamestore /app/
```

We need also to set the current permissions on that directory. When nginx is installed, it also creates a nginx user and a group. So, let's change the ownership of the entire folder:

```
cd / && sudo chown -R nginx:nginx ./gamestore
```

Finally, we are going to set up nginx, edit the /etc/nginx/nginx.conf file, and under service, add the following configuration:

```
location / {
  proxy_pass http://127.0.0.1:8000;
  proxy_set_header Host $host;
  proxy_set_header X-Forwarded-For $proxy_add_x_forwarded_for;
}

location /static {
  root /app/gamestore;
}
```

We need to restart the `nginx` service so that the service reflects the changes that we just made:

```
sudo service nginx restart
```

Finally, we go over to the `application` folder:

```
cd /app/gamestore
```

Start the application with `gunicorn`. We are going to start the application as an `nginx` user:

```
sudo gunicorn -u nginx gamestore.wsgi
```

Now, we can browse to the site. You don't need to specify port `8000` since `nginx` will route the requests coming from port `80` to `127.0.0.1:8000`.

Deploying the order service

Deploying the order service is pretty much the same as the `gamestore` project, the only difference is that we are going to install different Python dependencies and deploy the application in a different directory. So, let's get started.

You can pretty much repeat all the steps up until installing the `nginx` step. Also, make sure that you are using the elastic IP address of the other EC2 instance from now on.

After you install `nginx`, we can install the order service dependencies:

```
sudo pip-3.6 install django djangorestframework requests
```

We can now copy the project file. Go to the directory where you have the service's directory, and run this command:

```
scp -R -i order-service-keys.pem ./order ec2-user@35.176.194.15:~/gamestore
```

Like `gamestore`, we also need to edit the `settings.py` file and add our EC2 instance elastic IP:

```
ALLOWED_HOSTS=["35.176.194.15"]
```

We will also create a folder in the `root` directory so the project is not laying around in the `ec2-user` home directory:

```
sudo mkdir /srv && sudo cp -R ./order /srv/
```

Let's change the owner of the entire directory as well:

```
cd / && sudo chown -R nginx:nginx ./order
```

Let's edit the `/etc/nginx/nginx.conf` file, and, under `service`, add the following configuration:

```
location / {
    proxy_pass http://127.0.0.1:8000;
    proxy_set_header Host $host;
    proxy_set_header X-Forwarded-For $proxy_add_x_forwarded_for;
}
```

This time, we don't need to configure the static folder since the order services don't have anything like images, templates, JS, or CSS files.

Restart the `nginx` service:

```
sudo service nginx restart
```

Go over to the service's directory:

```
cd /srv/order
```

And start the application with `gunicorn`. We are going to start the application as an `nginx` user:

```
sudo gunicorn -u nginx order.wsgi
```

Finally, we can browse to the address where the `gamestore` is deployed, and you should see the site up and running.

Browsing to the site, you will see the first page. All the products are loading, and the login and logout sections are also working properly. Here's a screenshot of my system:

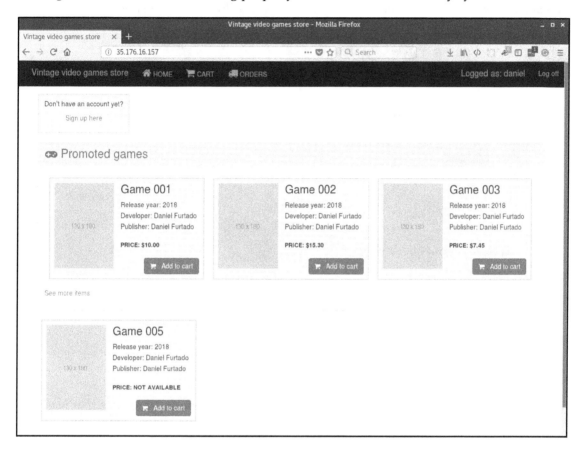

If you browse to a view that makes use of the order service, for example, the orders section, you can verify that everything is working, and if you have placed any orders on the site, you should see the orders listed here, as shown in the following screenshot:

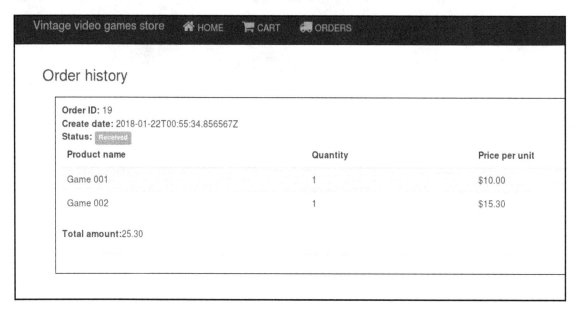

Summary

We have covered a lot of topics in this chapter; we have built the order service that was responsible for receiving orders from the web application that we developed in the previous chapter. The order service also provides other features, such as the ability to update the status of orders and provide order information using different criteria.

This microservice was an extension of the web application that we developed in the previous chapter, and in the following chapter, we are going to extend it even further by adding serverless functions to notify the users of our application when an order is successfully received and also when the order's status has changed to shipped.

9
Notification Serverless Application

In this chapter, we are going to explore AWS Lambda Functions and AWS API Gateway. AWS Lambda enables us to create serverless functions. *Serverless* doesn't mean that it is without a server; in reality, it means that these functions don't require the DevOps overhead that you would have if you were running the application on, for example, an EC2 instance.

Serverless architecture is not the silver bullet or the solution to all the problems, but there are many advantages, such as pricing, the fact that almost no DevOps is required, and support for different programming languages.

In the case of Python, tools like Zappa and the microframework for AWS Chalice, which is also developed by Amazon, make creating and deploying serverless functions incredibly easy.

In this chapter you will learn how to:

- Create a service using Flask framework
- Install and configure the AWS CLI
- Use the CLI to create S3 buckets and upload files
- Install and configure Zappa
- Deploy an application using Zappa

So without further ado, let's dive right into it!

Setting up the environment

Let's start by creating the folder in which we will place the application files. First, create a directory called `notifier` and go into that directory so we can create the virtual environment:

```
mkdir notifier && cd notifier
```

We create the virtual environment using `pipenv`:

```
pipenv --python ~/Installs/Python3.6/bin/python3.6
```

Remember that if Python 3 is in our `path`, you can simply call:

```
pipenv --three
```

To build this service we are going to use the micro web framework Flask, so let's install that:

```
pipenv install flask
```

We are also going to install the requests package, which will be used when sending requests to the order service:

```
pipenv install requests
```

That should be everything we need for now. Next, we are going to see how we can use AWS Simple Email Service to send emails from our applications.

Setting up the Amazon Web Services CLI

We also need to install the AWS command-line interface, which will save us a lot of time when deploying serverless functions and also when creating S3 buckets.

The installation is quite simple, as it can be installed via pip, and the AWS CLI has support for Python 2 and Python 3 and runs on different operating systems, such as Linux, macOS, and Windows.

Open a terminal and type the command:

```
pip install awscli --upgrade --user
```

The upgrade option will tell pip to update all the requirements that are already installed, and the `--user` option means that pip will install the AWS CLI in our local directory, so it won't touch any library that is installed globally on our system. On Linux systems, when installing a Python package using the `--user` option, the package will be installed in the directory `.local/bin`, so make sure that you have that in your `path`.

Just to verify that the installation worked properly, type the following command:

```
aws --version
```

You should see an output similar to this:

```
aws-cli/1.14.30 Python/3.6.2 Linux/4.9.0-3-amd64 botocore/1.8.34
```

Here you can see the AWS CLI version, as well as the operating system version, Python version, and which version of `botocore` is currently in use. `botocore` is the core library used by the AWS CLI. Also, boto is an SDK for Python, which allows developers to write software to work with Amazon services like EC2 and S3.

Now we need to configure the CLI, and we will need to have some information at hand. First, we need the `aws_access_key_id` and the `aws_secret_access_key`, as well as your preferred region and output. The most common value, the output option, is JSON.

To create the access keys, click on the drop-down menu with your username on the top right hand of the AWS console page, and select **My Security Credentials.** You will land on this page:

Your Security Credentials

Use this page to manage the credentials for your AWS account. To manage credentials for AWS Identity and Access Management (IAM) users, use the IAM Console.

To learn more about the types of AWS credentials and how they're used, see AWS Security Credentials in AWS General Reference.

+ Password

+ Multi-factor authentication (MFA)

+ Access keys (access key ID and secret access key)

+ CloudFront key pairs

+ X.509 certificate

+ Account identifiers

Here you can configure different account security settings, such as changing the password or enabling multi-factor authentication, but the one you should choose now is **Access keys (access key ID and secret access key)**. Then click on **Create New Access Key**, and a dialog will be opened with your keys. You will also be given the option to download the keys. I suggest you download them and keep them in a safe place.

Go here `https://docs.aws.amazon.com/general/latest/gr/rande.html` to see the AWS regions and endpoints.

Now we can `configure` the CLI. In the command line, type:

```
aws configure
```

You will be asked to provide the access key, the secret access key, the region, and the default output format.

Configuring a Simple Email Service

Amazon already has a service called Simple Email Service that we can use in order to send email through our application. We will be running the service in sandbox mode, which means that we will also be able to send emails to verified email addresses. This can be changed if you plan to use the service in production, but for the purposes of this book, it will suffice to just have it running in sandbox mode.

 If you plan to have this application running in production and wish to move out of the Amazon SES sandbox, you can easily open a support case for increasing the email limit. To send the request, you can go to the SES home page, and on the left-hand menu, under the section *Email Sending*, you will find the link `Dedicated IPs`. There, you will find more information and also a link where you can apply to increase your email limit.

To get it working, we will need to have two email accounts that we can use. In my case, I have my own domain. I have also created two email accounts—`donotreply@dfurtado.com`, which will be the email that I will use to send emails, and `pythonblueprints@dfurtado.com`, which is the email that will receive the email. A user in an online (video) game store application will use this email address and we will place a few orders so we can test the notification later on.

Registering the emails

So let's start adding the emails. We are going to register `donotreply@dfurtado.com` first. Log in to the AWS console and search for **Simple Email Service** in the search bar. On the left side, you will see a few options. Under **Identity Management,** click on **Email Addresses**. You will see a screen like this:

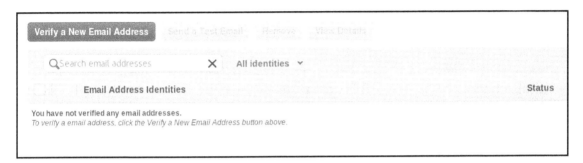

As you can see, the list is empty, so let's go ahead and add two emails. Click on **Verify a New Email Address** and a dialog will appear where you can enter an email address. Just enter the email that you wish to use and click on **Verify This Email Address** button. By doing this a verification email will be sent to the email address that you specified, and therein you will find a link for the verification.

Repeat the same steps for the second email, the one that will receive the messages.

Now, go over to the left side menu again and click on **SMTP Settings** under **Email Sending**.

There you will see all the configurations necessary to send emails, and you will also have to create SMTP credentials. So click on the button **Create My SMTP Credentials**, and a new page will be opened where you can input the IAM username that you wish. In my case, I'm adding `python-blueprints`. After you have done that, click the button **Create**. After the credentials have been created, you will be presented with a page where you can see the SMTP username and password. You will have the option to download these credentials if you like.

Creating an S3 bucket

In order to send a template email to the users, we need to copy our templates to an S3 bucket. We can easily do that through the web, or you can use the AWS CLI that we just installed. The command to create the S3 bucket in the `es-west-2` region is something like:

```
aws s3api create-bucket \
--bucket python-blueprints \
--region eu-west-2 \
--create-bucket-configuration LocationConstraint=eu-west-2
```

Here we use the command `s3api`, which will provide us with different sub-commands to interact with the AWS S3 service. We call the sub-command `create-bucket`, which, as the name suggests, will create a new S3 bucket. To this sub-command, we specify three arguments. First, `--bucket`, which specifies the S3 bucket's name, then `--region`, to specify which region the bucket will be created - in this case, we are going to create the bucket in the `eu-west-2`. Lastly, locations outside the region `us-east-1` request the setting `LocationConstraint` so the bucket can be created in the region that we wish.

Implementing the notification service

Now that we have everything set up, and the files that we are going to use as a template to send emails to the customers of the online (video) game store are in place in the python-blueprints S3 bucket, it is time to start implementing the notification service.

Let's go ahead and create a file called `app.py` in the `notifier` directory, and to start with, let's add some imports:

```python
import smtplib
from http import HTTPStatus
from smtplib import SMTPAuthenticationError, SMTPRecipientsRefused

from email.mime.text import MIMEText
from email.mime.multipart import MIMEMultipart

import boto3
from botocore.exceptions import ClientError

from flask import Flask
from flask import request, Response

from jinja2 import Template
import json
```

First, we import the JSON module so we can serialize and deserialize data. We import
`HTTPStatus` from the HTTP module so we can use the HTTP status constants when
sending responses back from the service's endpoints.

Then we import the modules that we will need to send emails. We start by importing the
`smtplib` and also some exceptions that we want to handle.

We also import `MIMEText`, which will be used to create a `MIME` object out of the email
content, and the `MIMEMultipart` that will be used to create the message that we are going
to send.

Next, we import the `boto3` package so we can work with the *AWS* services. There are some
exceptions that we will be handling; in this case, both exceptions are related to the *S3*
buckets.

Next are some Flask related imports, and last but not least, we import the `Jinja2` package
to template our emails.

Continuing working on the `app.py` file, let's define the constant that will hold the name or
the *S3* bucket that we created:

```
S3_BUCKET_NAME = 'python-blueprints'
```

Then we create the Flask app:

```
app = Flask(__name__)
```

We are also going to add a custom exception called `S3Error`:

```
class S3Error(Exception):
    pass
```

Then we are going to define two helper functions. The first one is to send emails:

```
def _send_message(message):

    smtp = smtplib.SMTP_SSL('email-smtp.eu-west-1.amazonaws.com',
    465)

    try:
        smtp.login(
            user='DJ*******DER*****RGTQ',
            password='Ajf0u*****44N6**ciTY4*****CeQ*****4V')
    except SMTPAuthenticationError:
        return Response('Authentication failed',
                        status=HTTPStatus.UNAUTHORIZED)
```

```
try:
    smtp.sendmail(message['From'], message['To'],
     message.as_string())
except SMTPRecipientsRefused as e:
    return Response(f'Recipient refused {e}',
                    status=HTTPStatus.INTERNAL_SERVER_ERROR)
finally:
    smtp.quit()

return Response('Email sent', status=HTTPStatus.OK)
```

Here, we define the function _send_message, which gets just one argument, message. We start this function by creating an object that will encapsulate an SMTP connection. We use SMTP_SSL because the AWS Simple Email Service required TLS. The first argument is the SMTP host, which we created at the AWS Simple Email Service, and the second argument is the port, which will be set as 456 when SMTP connections over SSL are required.

Then we call the login method, passing the username and the password, which can also be found in the AWS Simple Email Service. In cases where an SMTPAuthenticationError exception is thrown we send an UNAUTHORIZED response back to the client.

If logging into the SMTP server is successful, we call the sendmail method, passing the email that is sending the message, the destination recipient, and the message. We handle the situation where some of the recipients reject our message, in that we return an INTERNAL SERVER ERROR response, and then we just quit the connection.

Lastly, we return the OK response stating that the message has been sent successfully.

Now, we create a helper function to load the template file from the S3 bucket and return a rendered template for us:

```
def _prepare_template(template_name, context_data):

    s3_client = boto3.client('s3')

    try:
        file = s3_client.get_object(Bucket=S3_BUCKET_NAME,
        Key=template_name)
    except ClientError as ex:
        error = ex.response.get('Error')
        error_code = error.get('Code')

        if error_code == 'NoSuchBucket':
            raise S3Error(
```

```
            f'The bucket {S3_BUCKET_NAME} does not exist') from ex
        elif error_code == 'NoSuchKey':
            raise S3Error((f'Could not find the file "
                {template_name}" '
                f'in the S3 bucket {S3_BUCKET_NAME}')) from ex
        else:
            raise ex

    content = file['Body'].read().decode('utf-8')
    template = Template(content)

    return template.render(context_data)
```

Here we define the function `_prepare_template` and we take two arguments; `template_name`, which is the file name that we stored in the S3 bucket, and `context_data`, which is a dictionary containing the data that we are going to render in the template.

First, we create an S3 client, then we use the `get_object` method to pass the bucket name and the `Key`. We set the bucket keyword argument to `S3_BUCKET_NAME`, which we defined at the top of this file with the value of `python-blueprints`. The `Key` keyword argument is the name of the file; we set it to the value that we specified in the argument `template_name`.

Next, we access the key `Body` in the object returned from the S3 bucket, and call the method `read`. This will return a string with the file contents. Then, we create a Jinja2 Template object passing the contents of the template's file, and finally, we call the render method passing the `context_data`.

Now, let's implement the endpoint that will be called to send a confirmation email to the customer whose order we receive:

```
@app.route("/notify/order-received/", methods=['POST'])
def notify_order_received():
    data = json.loads(request.data)

    order_items = data.get('items')

    customer = data.get('order_customer')
    customer_email = customer.get('email')
    customer_name = customer.get('name')

    order_id = data.get('id')
    total_purchased = data.get('total')
```

```
message = MIMEMultipart('alternative')

context = {
    'order_items': order_items,
    'customer_name': customer_name,
    'order_id': order_id,
    'total_purchased': total_purchased
}

try:
    email_content = _prepare_template(
        'order_received_template.html',
        context
    )
except S3Error as ex:
    return Response(str(ex),
    status=HTTPStatus.INTERNAL_SERVER_ERROR)

message.attach(MIMEText(email_content, 'html'))

message['Subject'] = f'ORDER: #{order_id} - Thanks for your
order!'
message['From'] = 'donotreply@dfurtado.com'
message['To'] = customer_email

return _send_message(message)
```

So here, define a function called `notify_order_received`, which we decorate with the `@app.route` to define the route and the methods that are allowed when calling this endpoint. The route is defined as `/notify/order-received/` and the `methods` keyword argument takes a list with the allowed HTTP methods. In this case, we want to allow only POST requests.

We start this function by getting all the data that has been passed in the request. In Flask applications this data can be accessed on `request.data`; we use the `json.loads` method to pass `request.data` as an argument, so it will deserialize the JSON objects into a Python object. Then we get the items, which are a list with all the items included in the order, and we get the value of the attribute `order_customer` so we can get the customer's email and the customer's name.

After that, we get the order ID, which can be accessed via the property `id`, and lastly, we get the total purchase value that is in the property `total` of the data that has been sent to this endpoint.

Then we create an instance of MIMEMultiPart that passes as an argument alternative, which means that we will create a message with the MIME type set to multipart/alternative. After that, we configure a context that will be passed to the email template, and we use the _prepare_template function to pass the template that we want to render and the context with the data that will be displayed in the email. The value of the rendered template will be stored in the variable email_content.

Lastly, we do the final setup for our email message; we attach the rendered template to the message, we set subject, sender, and destinations, and we call the _send_message function to send the message.

Next, we are going to add the endpoint that will notify the users when their order has changed status to Shipping:

```
@app.route("/notify/order-shipped/", methods=['POST'])
def notify_order_shipped():
    data = json.loads(request.data)

    customer = data.get('order_customer')

    customer_email = customer.get('email')
    customer_name = customer.get('name')

    order_id = data.get('id')

    message = MIMEMultipart('alternative')

    try:
        email_content = _prepare_template(
            'order_shipped_template.html',
            {'customer_name': customer_name}
        )
    except S3Error as ex:
        return Response(ex,
status=HTTPStatus.INTERNAL_SERVER_ERROR)

    message.attach(MIMEText(email_content, 'html'))

    message['Subject'] = f'Order ID #{order_id} has been shipped'
    message['From'] = 'donotreply@dfurtado.com'
    message['To'] = customer_email

    return _send_message(message)
```

Here we define a function called `notify_order_shipped` and decorate it with the `@app.route` decorator, passing two arguments and the route, which is set to `/notify/order-shipped/`, and define that the method that is going to be accepted in this endpoint is the `POST` method.

We start by getting the data that has been passed in the request - basically the same as the previous function, the `notify_order_received`. We also create an instance of `MIMEMultipart`, setting the `MIME` type to multipart/alternative. Next, we use the `_prepare_template` function to load the template and render using the context that we are passing in the second argument; in this case, we are passing only the customer's name.

Then we attach the template to the message and do the final set up, setting the subject, the send, and the destination. Finally, we call `_send_message` to send the message.

Next, we are going to create two email templates, one that we are going to use when sending an order confirmation notification to the user and the other for when an order has been shipped.

Email templates

Now we are going to create the templates that are going to be used when sending the notification emails to the online (video) game store's customers.

In the application's `root` directory, create a directory called `templates` and create a file called `order_received_template.html`, with the contents shown as follows:

```html
<html>
  <head>
  </head>
  <body>
    <h1>Hi, {{customer_name}}!</h1>
    <h3>Thank you so much for your order</h3>
    <p>
      <h3>Order id: {{order_id}}</h3>
    </p>
    <table border="1">
      <thead>
        <tr>
          <th align="left" width="40%">Item</th>
          <th align="left" width="20%">Quantity</th>
          <th align="left" width="20%">Price per unit</th>
        </tr>
      </thead>
```

```
       <tbody>
         {% for item in order_items %}
         <tr>
           <td>{{item.name}}</td>
           <td>{{item.quantity}}</td>
           <td>${{item.price_per_unit}}</td>
         </tr>
         {% endfor %}
       </tbody>
     </table>
     <div style="margin-top:20px;">
       <strong>Total: ${{total_purchased}}</strong>
     </div>
   </body>
 </html>
```

Now, let's create another template in the same directory called
`order_shipped_template.html`, with the contents shown as follows:

```
 <html>
   <head>
   </head>
   <body>
     <h1>Hi, {{customer_name}}!</h1>
     <h3>We just want to let you know that your order is on its way!
     </h3>
   </body>
 </html>
```

If you have read `Chapter 7`, *Online Video Game Store with Django,* you should be familiar
with this syntax. The Jinja 2 syntax has a lot of similarities when compared to the Django
template language.

Now we can copy the template to the S3 bucket that we created previously. Open a terminal
and run the following command:

```
aws s3 cp ./templates s3://python-blueprints --recursive
```

Perfect! Next, we are going to deploy our project.

Deploying the application with Zappa

Now we have got to a very interesting section of the chapter. We are going to deploy the Flask app that we created using a tool called **Zappa** (`https://github.com/Miserlou/Zappa`). Zappa is a tool developed in Python (by **Rich Jones**, the principal author of Zappa) that makes it very easy to build and deploy serverless Python applications.

The installation is pretty straightforward. Within the virtual environment that we have been using to develop this project, you can just run the `pipenv` command:

```
pipenv install zappa
```

After the installation, you can start the configuration. You just need to make sure that you have a valid AWS account and the AWS credentials file is in place. If you followed this chapter from the beginning and installed and configured the AWS CLI you should be all set.

To configure Zappa for our project you can run:

```
zappa init
```

You will see the ASCII Zappa logo (very beautiful BTW), and it will start asking some questions. The first one is:

```
Your Zappa configuration can support multiple production stages, like
'dev', 'staging', and 'production'.
What do you want to call this environment (default 'dev'):
```

You can just hit *Enter* to default to dev. Next, Zappa will ask the name of an AWS S3 bucket:

```
Your Zappa deployments will need to be uploaded to a private S3 bucket.
If you don't have a bucket yet, we'll create one for you too.
What do you want call your bucket? (default 'zappa-uc40h2hnc'):
```

Here you can either specify an existent or create a new one. Then, Zappa will try to detect the application that we are trying to deploy:

```
It looks like this is a Flask application.
What's the modular path to your app's function?
This will likely be something like 'your_module.app'.
We discovered: notify-service.app
Where is your app's function? (default 'notify-service.app'):
```

As you can see, Zappa automatically found the Flask app defined in the `notify-service.py` file. You can just hit *Enter* to set the default value.

Next, Zappa will ask if you would like to deploy the application globally; we can keep the default and answer n. Since we are deploying this application in a development environment, we don't really need to deploy it globally. When your application goes into production you can evaluate if you need to deploy it globally.

Lastly, the complete configuration will be displayed, and here you have to change the review and make any modifications if needed. You don't need to be too worried about saving the configuration or not because the Zappa settings file is just a text file with the settings in JSON format. You can just edit the file at any time and change it manually.

If everything went well, you should see a file called `zappa_settings.json` on the root's directory of your application, with the contents similar to the content shown as follows:

```
{
    "dev": {
        "app_function": "notify-service.app",
        "aws_region": "eu-west-2",
        "project_name": "notifier",
        "runtime": "python3.6",
        "s3_bucket": "zappa-43ivixfl0"
    }
}
```

Here you can see the `dev` environment settings. The `app_function` specifies the Flask app that I created on the `notify-service.py` file, the `aws_region` specifies in which region the application will be deployed - in my case since I'm in Sweden, I chose `eu-west-2` (London) which is the closest region to me. The `project_name` will get by default the name of the directory where you run the command `zappa init`.

Then we have the runtime, which refers to the Python version that you are running with the application. Since the virtual environment that we created for this project used Python 3, the value for this property should be a version of Python 3 - in my case, I have installed 3.6.2. Lastly, we have the name of the AWS S3 bucket that Zappa will use to upload the project files.

Now, let's deploy the application that we just created! On the terminal, simply run the following command:

```
zappa deploy dev
```

Zappa will perform lots of tasks for you, and at the end it will display the URL where the application has been deployed. In my case I've got:

```
https://rpa5v43ey1.execute-api.eu-west-2.amazonaws.com/dev
```

Yours will look slightly different. So, we have defined two endpoints in our Flask application, `/notify/order-received` and `/notify/order-shipped`. These endpoints can be called with the following URLs:

```
https://rpa5v43ey1.execute-api.eu-west-2.amazonaws.com/dev/notify/order-rec
eived
```

```
https://rpa5v43ey1.execute-api.eu-west-2.amazonaws.com/dev/notify/order-shi
pped
```

If you want to see more information about the deployment, you can use the Zappa command: `zappa status`.

In the next section, we are going to learn how to restrict access to these endpoints and create an access key that can be used to make the API calls.

Restricting access to the API's endpoints

Our Flask application has been deployed, and at this point anyone can make a request to the endpoints that have been configured on the AWS API Gateway. What we want to do is restrict the access only to requests that contain an access key.

To do that, log into our account on AWS console and on the **Services** menu search for and select **Amazon API Gateway**. Under the API on the left side menu, you will see the **notifier-dev**:

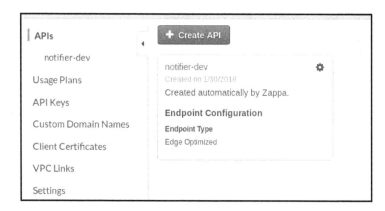

Great! Here we are going to define a usage plan. Click on **Usage Plans** and then click on the **Create** button, and you will see a form for creating a new usage plan. Enter the name `up-blueprints`, uncheck the checkboxes for **Enable throttling and Enable Quota**, and click the **Next** button.

The next step is to associate an API stage. So far we have only dev, so let's add the **stage dev**; click on **Add API Stage** button, and on the drop-down list select the **notifier-dev** and the **stage dev**. Make sure to click on the check button, the same row as the drop-down menus, otherwise, the **Next** button won't be enabled.

After clicking **Next** you will have to add an API key to the **Usage Plan** that we just created. Here you will have two options; add a new one or pick an existing one:

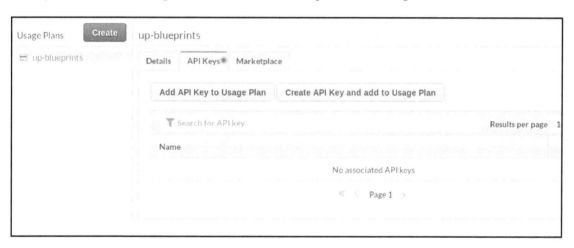

Let's add a new one. Click on the button labeled **Create API Key and add to Usage Plan**. The API Key creation dialog will be shown, so just enter the name `notifiers-devs` and click save.

Great! Now if you select API Keys on the left side menu, you should see the newly created API Key on the list. If you selected it, you will be able to see all the details regarding the key:

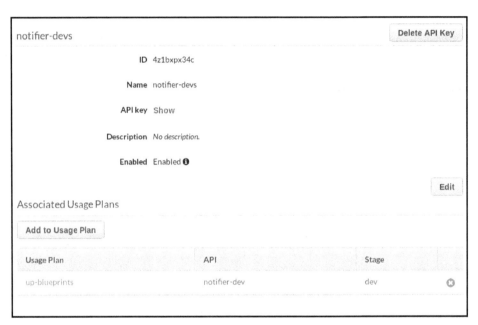

Now, on the left side menu, select **APIs -> notifier-dev -> Resources,** and on the tab **Resources**, select the root route /. On the right side panel, you can see the / **Methods**:

Note that **ANY** says Authorization **None** and that API Key is set to **Not required**. Let's change that so the API Key is required. On the **Resources** panel, click on **ANY**, you should see now a panel similar to the screenshot shown as follows:

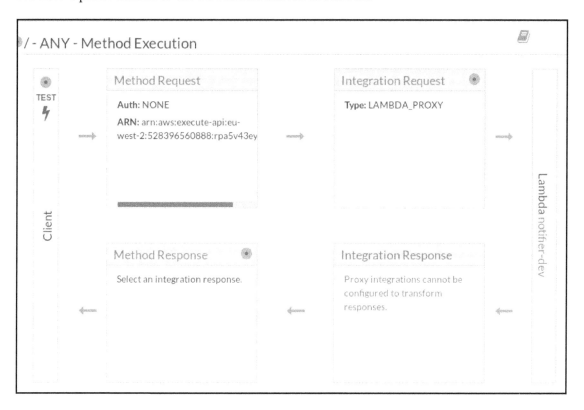

Click on **Method Request**:

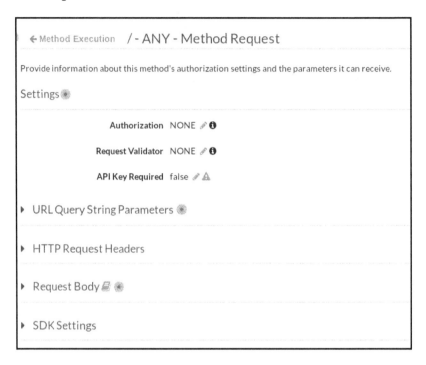

Click on the pen icon next to API Key Required and, on the drop-down menu, select the value **true**.

Great! Now, the API calls to the **stage dev** should be restricted to requests with the API key **notifier-dev** in the request's Header.

Lastly, head over to API Keys and click on notifier-keys. On the right side panel, in the API Key, click on the link **show**, and the API key will be displayed for you. Copy that key, because we are going to use it in the next section.

Modifying the order service

Now that we have the notifier application deployed, we have to modify our previous project, the order microservice, to make use of the notifier application and send notifications when a new order arrives and when the status of the order changes to shipped.

The first thing we have to do is to include the notifier service API key and its base URL in the settings.py file in the directory, called order on the order's root directory, and include the following content at the end of the file:

```
NOTIFIER_BASEURL =
'https://rpa5v43ey1.execute-api.eu-west-2.amazonaws.com/dev'

NOTIFIER_API_KEY = 'WQk********P7JR2******kI1K****r'
```

Replace these values with the corresponding values on your environment. If you don't have the value for the NOTIFIER_BASEURL, you can obtain it running the following command:

```
zappa status
```

The value you want is the API Gateway URL.

Now, we are going to create two files. The first one it is a file called notification_type.py in the order/main directory. In this file, we will define an enumeration with the notification types that we want to make available in our service:

```
from enum import Enum, auto


class NotificationType(Enum):
    ORDER_RECEIVED = auto()
    ORDER_SHIPPED = auto()
```

Next, we are going to create a file with a helper function that will make the calls to the notification service. Create a file called notifier.py in the order/main/ directory with the contents shown as follows:

```
import requests
import json

from order import settings

from .notification_type import import NotificationType


def notify(order, notification_type):
    endpoint = ('notify/order-received/'
                if notification_type is
NotificationType.ORDER_RECEIVED
                else 'notify/order-shipped/')

    header = {
        'X-API-Key': settings.NOTIFIER_API_KEY
```

```
}

response = requests.post(
    f'{settings.NOTIFIER_BASEURL}/{endpoint}',
    json.dumps(order.data),
    headers=header
)

return response
```

From the top, we included some import statements; we are importing requests to perform the request to the notifier service, so we import the module json, so we can serialize the data to be sent to the notifier service. Then we import the settings so we can get hold of the constants that we defined with the base URL to the notifier service and the API key. Lastly, we import the notification type enumeration.

The function notify that we defined here takes two arguments, the order and the notification type, which are the values defined in the enumeration NotificationType.

We start by deciding which endpoint we are going to use, depending on the notification's type. Then we add an entry X-API-KEY to the request's HEADER with the API key.

After that, we make a POST request that passes a few arguments. The first argument is the endpoint's URL, the second is the data that we are going to send to the notifier service (we use the json.dumps function so the data is sent in JSON format), and the third argument is the dictionary with the header data.

Lastly, when we get the response back we just return it.

Now we need to modify the view that is responsible for handling a POST request to create a new order, so that it calls the notify function when an order is created in the database. Let's go ahead and open the file view.py in the order/main directory and add two import statements:

```
from .notifier import notify
from .notification_type import NotificationType
```

The two lines can be added before the first class in the file.

Perfect, now we need to change the method post in the CreateOrderView class. Before the first return statement in that method, where we return a 201 (CREATED) response, include the code shown as follows:

```
notify(OrderSerializer(order),
       NotificationType.ORDER_RECEIVED)
```

So here we call the notify function, passing the serialized order using the `OrderSerializer` on the first argument, and the notification type - in this case, we want to send an `ORDER_RECEIVED` notification.

We will allow the user of the order service application to update the order using the Django Admin. There, they will be able to, for example, update an order's status, so we need to implement some code that will handle data changes made by users using the Django Admin.

To do this, we need to create a `ModelAdmin` class inside of the `admin.py` file in the `order/main` directory. First, we add some import statements:

```
from .notifier import notify
from .notification_type import NotificationType
from .serializers import OrderSerializer
from .status import Status
```

Then we add the following class:

```
class OrderAdmin(admin.ModelAdmin):

    def save_model(self, request, obj, form, change):
        order_current_status = Status(obj.status)
        status_changed = 'status' in form.changed_data

        if (status_changed and order_current_status is
            Status.Shipping):
             notify(OrderSerializer(obj),
             NotificationType.ORDER_SHIPPED)

        super(OrderAdmin, self).save_model(request, obj, form,
        change)
```

Here, we create a class called `OrderAdmin` that inherits from the `admin.ModelAdmin`, and we override the method `save_model` so we have the chance to perform some actions before the data is saved. First, we get the order current status, then we check if the field `status` is between the list of fields that have been changed.

The if statement checks if the status field has changed, and if the current status of the order equals to `Status.Shipping` then we call the notify function, passing the serialized order object and the notification type `NotificationType.ORDER_SHIPPED`.

Lastly, we call the `save_model` method on the super class to save the object.

The last piece of this puzzle is to replace this:

```
admin.site.register(Order)
```

Instead, put this:

```
admin.site.register(Order, OrderAdmin)
```

This will register the admin model `OrderAdmin` for the `Order` model. Now, when the user saves the order in the Django admin UI, it will call the `save_model` in the `OrderAdmin` class.

Testing all the pieces together

Now that we have the notifier application deployed and we have also made all the necessary modifications to the order service, it is time to test if all the applications are working together.

Open a terminal, change to the directory where you have implemented the online (video) game store, and execute the following command to start up the Django development server:

```
python manage.py runserver
```

This command will start the Django development server running on the default port `8000`.

Now let's start the order microservice. Open another terminal window, change to the directory where you implemented the order microserver, and run the following command:

```
python manage.py runserver 127.0.0.1:8001
```

Now we can browse to `http://127.0.0.1:8000`, log in to the application and add some items to the cart:

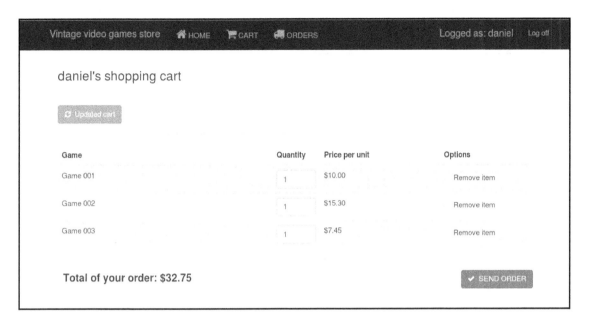

As you can see, I added three items and the total amount of this order is **$32.75**. Click on the button **SEND ORDER**, and you should get a notification on the page that the order has been sent.

Great! Working as expected so far. Now we check the user's email, to verify if the notification service actually sent the order confirmation email.

Fair enough, the user just got the email:

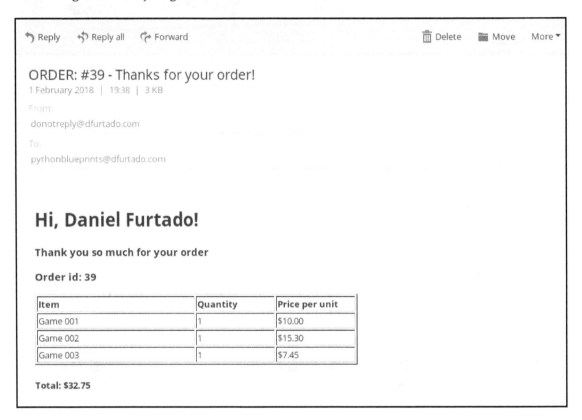

Note that the sender and the destination recipients are the emails that I registered in the AWS Simple Email Service.

So now let's log in to the order service's Django admin and change the status for the same order to verify that the confirmation email that the order has been shipped will be sent to the user. Remember that the email will only be sent if the order has changed its status field to shipped.

Browse to `http://localhost:8001/admin/` and log in with the administrator credentials. You will see a page with the menu shown as follows:

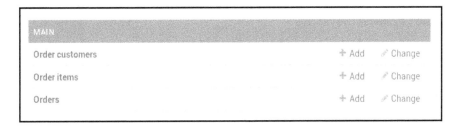

Click on **Orders** and then select the order that we just submitted:

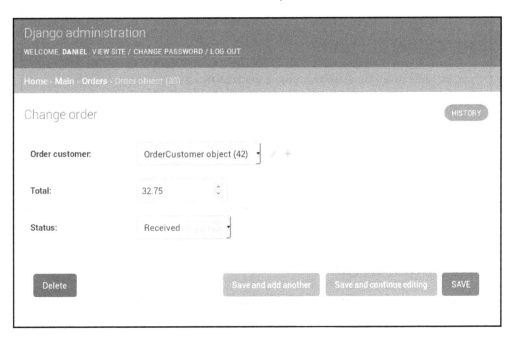

On the drop-down menu **Status**, change the value to **Shipping** and click the button **SAVE**.

Now, if we verify the order customer's email again we should have got another email confirming that the order has been shipped:

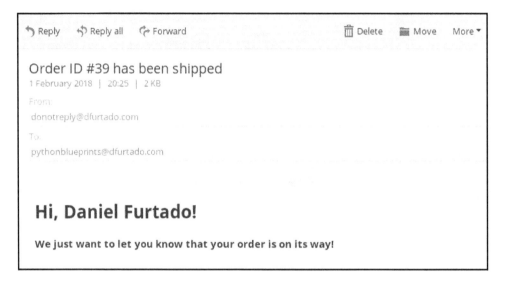

Summary

In this chapter, you have learned a bit more about serverless functions architecture, how to build a notification service using the web framework Flask, and how to deploy the final application to AWS Lambda using the great project Zappa.

Then, you learned how to install, configure, and use the AWS CLI tool, and used it to upload files to an AWS S3 bucket.

We also learned how to integrate the web application that we developed in `Chapter 7`, *Online Video Game Store with Django*, and the order microservice that we developed in `Chapter 8`, *Order Microservice*, with the serverless notification application.

Other Books You May Enjoy

If you enjoyed this book, you may be interested in these other books by Packt:

Python Microservices Development
Tarek Ziadé

ISBN: 978-1-78588-111-4

- Explore what microservices are and how to design them
- Use Python 3, Flask, Tox, and other tools to build your services using best practices
- Learn how to use a TDD approach
- Discover how to document your microservices
- Configure and package your code in the best way
- Interact with other services
- Secure, monitor, and scale your services
- Deploy your services in Docker containers, CoreOS, and Amazon Web Services

Cloud Native Python
Manish Sethi

ISBN: 978-1-78712-931-3

- Get to know "the way of the cloud", including why developing good cloud software is fundamentally about mindset and discipline
- Know what microservices are and how to design them
- Create reactive applications in the cloud with third-party messaging providers
- Build massive-scale, user-friendly GUIs with React and Flux
- Secure cloud-based web applications: the do's, don'ts, and options
- Plan cloud apps that support continuous delivery and deployment

Leave a review - let other readers know what you think

Please share your thoughts on this book with others by leaving a review on the site that you bought it from. If you purchased the book from Amazon, please leave us an honest review on this book's Amazon page. This is vital so that other potential readers can see and use your unbiased opinion to make purchasing decisions, we can understand what our customers think about our products, and our authors can see your feedback on the title that they have worked with Packt to create. It will only take a few minutes of your time, but is valuable to other potential customers, our authors, and Packt. Thank you!

Index

www.ingramcontent.com/pod-product-compliance
Lightning Source LLC
Chambersburg PA
CBHW060645060326
40690CB00020B/4528